Language A

CONCEPT-BASED LEARNING

Teaching for Success   Kathleen Clare Waller

HODDER
EDUCATION
AN HACHETTE UK COMPANY

I would like to thank all the people who have helped shape my philosophy in approaching the teaching of language and literature. The ideas, creativity and passion of my colleagues at Lexington High School (Massachusetts), the Lycée International (Paris), the American School of Milan, Renaissance College Hong Kong and Vienna International School have been valuable in my own growth as a learner and in the effect on my students' learning. Additionally, mentors and classmates at Bowdoin College, Boston College and The University of Hong Kong have been inspirational and added to my conceptual understanding of the world.

Thank you, also, to workshop leaders, conference collaborators, yoga teachers, fellow writers and artists, friends and, especially, my family far and wide who are supportive and inspirational. I dedicate this book to my husband – who always believes in me and put me in touch with the amazing team at Hodder to make this happen – and my son – who gave me a new perspective on learning and the benefit of maternity leave in which to write.

Kathleen C. Waller

Orders: please contact Bookpoint Ltd, 130 Park Drive, Milton Park, Abingdon, Oxon OX14 4SE. Telephone: +44 (0)1235 827827. Fax: +44 (0)1235 400401. Email education@bookpoint.co.uk Lines are open from 9 a.m. to 5 p.m., Monday to Saturday, with a 24-hour message answering service. You can also order through our website: www.hoddereducation.com

ISBN: 9781510463233

© Kathleen Clare Waller 2019

First published in 2019 by

Hodder Education,
An Hachette UK Company
Carmelite House
50 Victoria Embankment
London EC4Y 0DZ

www.hoddereducation.com

Impression number   10 9 8 7 6 5 4 3 2 1
Year   2023 2022 2021 2020 2019

Cover photo © sveta - stock.adobe.com

Typeset by Integra Software Services Pvt. Ltd., Pondicherry, India.

Printed in Spain

A catalogue record for this title is available from the British Library.

Contents

Concept-based learning (CBL) in language A

Concept-based learning (CBL)

What is the point of a language A class, or language and literature, language arts, English or whatever name you call it? What is really at the heart of what we teach? Although we sometimes rightly focus on essay writing, canonical novels or grammar, the purpose goes beyond the skill or the ability to create discourse *within* an academic realm. We are looking at languages of human communication over time and discovering how to use them as tools to share in our human experience, to appreciate the beauty around us and to engage in debates about ideas. Language A courses should accomplish two main tasks: to appreciate literature as an art form and to help students find their voice.

The Indian-born British novelist Salman Rushdie once explained the vast reaches of our discipline: 'Literature is the one place in any society where, within the secrecy of our own heads, we can hear *voices talking about everything in every possible way*' (1990). Literature is our place to explore ourselves and the world around us, so there is no reason why it cannot be meaningful to anyone.

Language A courses have been historicized and constrained for ages. Not long ago, we began to hear minor voices and new perspectives while seeing new types of texts in our classrooms. Recently in the International Baccalaureate Diploma Programme (IB DP), our curriculum has truly been let free. The IB is joining the movement toward concepts.

'Not concepts', you might be thinking. 'Wishy-washy, floaty ideas that do not really accomplish any kind of rigour or knowledge in your English A, Japanese A or Spanish A course. We already have so much added to our plate – text types and genres, works in translation and time periods – how can we ever teach something meaningful anymore?'

But this is precisely what conceptual learning *can* be with the right type of structure to back it up. In its reliance on content and skills, it creates a meaningful learning experience for your students that more readily moves beyond the classroom walls. The term was coined by H. Lynn Erickson in her book *Concept-based Curriculum and Instruction for the Thinking Classroom* (2006), where she passionately and strategically lays out a way to use this method to achieve 'big ideas' and 'synergistic thinking'.

More on that later, but for now, we can understand Erickson's model as one that brings together skills and content as building blocks toward understanding ourselves and the people and world around us. To achieve these deep, purposeful ideas, both the skills and content must be mastered. To develop a point about new definitions of gender in the world, a language A student needs analytical skills to provide textual examples, language skills to express the idea and organizational skills to complete the essay or speech to present his or her ideas. Further, the student needs the content: texts with rich details, examples from different philosophical perspectives and writers from different cultural backgrounds. The skills we teach should help students find content even beyond that which we provide in the classroom or as extension resources. The texts we analyse and discuss should help students improve their language and literacy skills. Thus, a reciprocal arrangement between skills and content should be a constant in our CBL classrooms.

Skill blocks build the walls, and content bricks create an arch; together they bring us stability toward timeless conceptual understanding. (Split, Croatia)

The IB has used CBL in the Primary Years Programme (PYP) and Middle Years Programme (MYP) for years. Because the nature of these curricula is not prescriptive, there has always been the danger that CBL could indeed be dumbed down, creating ineffective, lazy approaches to teaching. But the schools who have researched and developed strategies, engaged in workshops with Erickson and layered in specific skills and content that students need to learn, have created successful programmes. Concepts can elevate the motivation in your classroom and the ideas and skills – the full knowledge base – your students take with them when they graduate. It takes planning and consideration to create and be challenged, to design something that helps students get to the next level. The autonomy of the curriculum can be a challenge, but a welcome one.

Another negative preconception of CBL classrooms is that the expertise of subject area is taken away from teachers. Again, the reality is the opposite. For a deep and purposeful understanding of literature and language, and their use in our lives, we need highly-trained teachers with strong academic grounding in these areas with a desire to continue expanding their knowledge base. But we also need teachers who can put the knowledge into play, who can engage students with it dynamically, giving it meaning. With the more creative shape our courses are moving into, you have more agency and autonomy in designing what you need to reach your students.

You might be reading this book from a variety of perspectives. Maybe you are an experienced IB DP language A teacher looking for new ways to organize your course. Maybe you are new to concept-based learning and have no idea why IB has decided to go in this direction. Maybe you have read the new guide and are stuck on where to begin changing your course. Maybe you are new to teaching either the language and literature or the literature course, or perhaps you are completely new to IB DP! You know how to teach, but there seem to be so many things you need to do well with this DP course. You want to be creative, but you want to prepare students effectively for the exams.

This book is designed to help any of you navigate the new IB DP language A courses. The learning outcomes and assessments have been streamlined for the language and literature and literature courses, to understand both and allow you dexterity in your teaching and the courses you can offer. This book is an interpreter of the IB guide: a primer on creating your course, organizing your syllabus and approaching the preparation of students for assessment. But more than that, this book hopes to help you make your course come to life.

This book may also offer a resource for those working in isolation in a small DP programme, helping students with self-taught language A courses or working in a language that is infrequently taught. While the examples here are from English-focused curricula, they include texts in other languages and activities and timelines that would be useful for any language, as well as valuing a multilingual approach in your classroom. The course guides are exactly the same for any language and the new IB online text list streamlines the old multiple prescribed list of authors (PLA) and single prescribed literature in translation (PLT) into a single source. We are often working from the same texts in different languages. Leading several workshops for my current school's Mother Tongue programme (language A teachers in a variety of languages – Chinese, Italian, Arabic, French, Greek, etc) opened my eyes to the way we can all collaborate. There may be slight, though important, differences in ways of approaching reading and writing, with some variance in what examiners will be looking for in written papers, especially with regards to writing style. However, my hope is that this book unites us in creating a global multilingual dialogue of teaching the IB DP language A course and shall offer several avenues where this dialogue may be realized.

DP language A now

Although some may fear a constraint in CBL, the IB DP language A courses conversely now have more freedom: more choice in the texts you teach and fewer assessments to take up your teaching time. What will you do with the extra time? You have a lot of choice, and for this reason, it is even more important to have a structured idea of where you will go with your students, although it is also important to maintain adaptability and flexibility within this structure.

Some teachers have experimented with a conceptual and inquiry-based approach to teaching these courses in the past, but it has not been a requirement until the 2019 guide for the 2021 exams. The IB now provides a loose framework that must be adhered to in this vein, but I offer further consideration to develop these aspects in your classroom in a meaningful way. Chapter 3 goes into more detail here, especially for those who have not used CBL as part of the MYP or the American Common Core. However, even those who have done so may need guidance in applying it to the DP. I propose sample syllabi, unit structures and lesson plans to help you use CBL effectively and dynamically and go beyond the seven major concepts required of IB, in both language A courses.

The course now also aims to include more international-mindedness, reflected in greater use of works in translation with flexibility in how you use them. You can take this as far as you would like. Along the way, I propose areas for this development, but I hope that the dialogue includes *you* in the future – that we visit each other's schools, engage in dialogue online or at workshops and learn ways to include different languages and cultures in our classrooms. In this book, we investigate the use of texts from many countries and in many languages, and we also take a careful look at developing perspectives from around the world. Additionally, we begin to understand that there are different cultural methods in using language to produce texts at a word, sentence and holistic level; a Turkish or Japanese examiner will view a Paper 1 commentary slightly differently from a French one, and this is not wrong. Although we cannot investigate each language and cultural method of text production here, I offer further resources and ways to ensure you are giving the students the right advice in your language A course.

Global issues are also a part of the new course, required as a component of investigation in assessment. However, rather than have categories (like MYP), the course allows students and teachers to investigate *any* global issue, although the IB suggests categories to guide you. The conceptual focus areas that I break the course units into in Chapter 3 allow for an easy entry into these issues. They are the big ideas that come from using skills and content. A global issue can be related to individuals, societies, humanity, nature, the universe … essentially, they are the conceptual understandings made into a tight phrase that can be explored, in this case, through literature and related language A course content. Examples include:

- one's ability to love
- the effect and legitimacy of civil disobedience in political change
- the meaning of life
- the purpose of nature in our lives
- what the possible existence of parallel universes means for an individual.

They can be 'hot topics', those that are currently in the media and on Twitter feeds, or they can be timeless debates and questions.

The global issue by nature is one that will have connections to other subjects and especially the theory of knowledge (TOK) course, which aims to bring together different subjects of the DP. Students explicitly select and explore a global issue as part of one of the assessments in DP language A. You will additionally investigate many global issues in class, giving your students motivation to become stronger in their use of skills and content in language A. Global issues make the course meaningful: they go beyond the classroom, linking what students are learning in the media, everyday observations and future endeavours to the texts they are studying.

Further, the course now aims to include more explicit reference to the IB core: the extended essay (EE), theory of knowledge (TOK) and creativity, activity, service (CAS). These connections are rather fluid in the language A course by nature of similar assessment to the core components. Core connections are integrated throughout this book and can be used as points for unit design and lesson ideas in your classroom. Many of you may also currently be, or aspire toward being, EE supervisors and TOK teachers, while nearly all of you will supervise a CAS activity or project. I highly recommend all three. They are fun ways to get to know your students more, work with new ideas and expand your understanding of the purpose of the IB Diploma. If your school treats these core elements as 'add-ons' or 'extra points', please try them out yourself! Find ways to make them meaningful and engaging. They can be the best part of a student's academic experience if done properly and creatively. Although CAS is not assessed for point value, the new global issues focus helps students consider the impact of their activities in relation to what they have learned in the classroom.

Finally, the approaches to teaching and learning (ATT and ATL) required explicitly in the MYP are becoming a part of the DP, though the connection has been documented as far back as 2014. The IB website keeps a document published from a conference in that year by Jenny Gillett that concisely and clearly explains the way ATT and ATL are designed to improve students' conceptual learning and allow for real-world transference. ATT are comprised of teaching methods that use inquiry, CBL, local and global contexts, collaboration, differentiation and being informed by assessment data or feedback. ATL are divided into five learning skills categories, all with further breakdown for MYP units that you can access on the IB website: social, thinking, research, communication and self-management. All of these ATT and ATL areas are interwoven throughout this book when appropriately connected to the learning.

These learning skills and pedagogical practices are, no doubt, methods you are using already. However, you may be teaching them implicitly or assuming students have certain skills that they need to develop further. Short, focused, explicit instruction can help students understand how to use these skills. Further, if the load of developing the skills is divided among subject areas, they become easier to teach and more transferable. For example, if you know the Individuals and societies teachers have been working with Socratic seminars to develop critical thinking and oral expression, you can simply reference it and dive right into the activity. If a science teacher has taken students through developing research strategies online on Evernote or Diigo, for example, you can have students use the same online account with a new topic/folder to keep track of an inquiry for a topic in your classroom. These skills will help students go deeper in their IB DP curriculum as a whole and give them valuable skills to use at university or in jobs in the future. They are half the building blocks in the Erickson model of CBL and, therefore, much more than an add-on tick box for your unit planning.

■ Embedding best practice

INTERNATIONAL MINDEDNESS

Look for these purple boxes for connections to multicultural and multinational perspectives and using multilingualism in your classroom. These boxes will also focus on explicitly international topics like translation.

GLOBAL ISSUES

These green boxes will contain explicit connections to global issues, which will be embedded in nearly everything you do in the course. Here, you will find ways to make the global issues more explicit in your classroom with ideas for your students to take action.

CORE CONNECTIONS

A yellow box will contain a core connection. Here, there will be ideas to explicitly link your course material to the EE, TOK or CAS, ideally making both areas more meaningful.

■ ATT & ATL

■ Blue boxes will expand on ATT or ATL skills, though they will also be embedded through course and lesson design. ATT you see here might be labelled as inquiry, differentiation or extension. ATL will be linked to the MYP keywords to define the area of learning skills.

◼ A quick look at DP language A

The following visual is a way to imagine the IB DP language A course, bearing in mind all the key components we have just gone through. By the end of reading this text, you will have a deeper understanding of each key area in the diagram as well as tools to help your students access these parts.

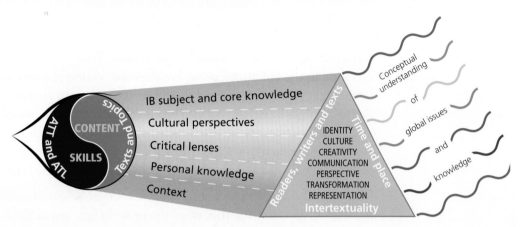

How the elements of a language A course interact

The drawing represents a student's iris divided into 'skills' and 'content' – the two building blocks needed for conceptual understanding – as a yin-yang shape. Each requires the other to look outward. The vision toward the world is one shaped in a triangular prism by the three language A areas of exploration that the course is broken into, while the scope is additionally influenced by critical lenses, IB subject and core knowledge, cultural perspectives, personal knowledge and context. All of these areas lead outward to deeper and better understandings of global issues (anything about the world around us) as well as knowledge in general. This knowledge might be about ourselves, a group of people, a particular place, or humanity as a whole. In this way, students have the tools to be their own philosophers and advocates. They should be able to read texts with much greater purpose after leaving your classroom.

Comparing the two language A courses

This book addresses teaching both the literature and the language and literature courses. The shared dialogue is made possible by the streamlining of the courses, allowing more opportunity for teachers to move between them. It should facilitate a revival of the literature course that some students (and teachers) see as outdated or more difficult in comparison. To understand how we can move ahead in this collaborative fashion between the courses, we need to understand briefly where they came from and why some people may have biases one way or the other.

There used to be an A2 and an A1 course. A2 was for students studying in a language A that was not their mother tongue but with enough command to place them out of the language B course. Both A1 and A2 had Standard Level (SL) and Higher Level (HL) options available, so rather than a level of course, the designation was about a level of language skills. A2 had literary elements, but also focused on more everyday texts and conversation strategies. In 2011, A2 became language and literature and A1 became literature, again both with SL and HL options. Language and literature was now meant to be at the same level of language skill as the other, but either the background of the courses or part-way focus on shorter mass media texts may have been a self-fulfilling prophecy. Most teachers and examiners (and students) will tell you that they saw a higher level of work and language skills in the literature courses.

In the 2019 DP guide, we keep the two names from 2011 with the SL and HL level options in each, but much has been streamlined. The learning outcomes are exactly the same, as are the assessments (except for literary forms and text type, which we will look at later). The three big areas of exploration, their adjoining questions and seven key concepts are also the same for both courses. Therefore, some of the issue of hierarchizing the courses *should* be taken away. True, you have to study more works of literature in the literature course, but the other course requires a greater array of non-literary text types. You can and should go as deeply into purpose, critical theory and textual analysis in either course. The choices now *should* be simply about content focus areas, enabling teachers to teach more freely between the courses and students to be given more freedom in their course selection. The same is true for the literature and performance course, but we will not be investigating it in this book.

Why and how do students choose different courses? When advising students, I usually ask them to go with what they enjoy the most. In fact, any of the four language A courses in this book can prepare students for subjects (majors in the US) in English literature or other related fields. Of course, students planning on this focus would be better served through the HL course, which allows them to read more widely and get more feedback on their writing. However, aspiring journalists need not feel that they 'should' take the language and literature course if they are drawn to a deeper study of literature; several successful journalists I know closely consider their study of literature to be what made them better writers. Others prefer the very focused approach to professional text types. For example, some in PR and advertising say that from an early stage, their focus on visual and subversive content, as well as structural layout, has given them an edge in what they do and in acquiring the necessary internships to secure a job after tertiary education.

Further consideration depends on requirements of the universities, or other programmes, that students plan to apply to after high school. In the US, grades, teacher references and college essays rule applications. Therefore, an aspiring journalist may have the freedom to pursue whatever interests him or her at the time, often not deciding and declaring until the end of the sophomore year at university. In the UK and most European systems, your subject is declared by the autumn of senior year in high school, and is somewhat dependent on the IB DP course choices (or A levels, etc) you made back when you were as young as 15! There are ways to make changes later, but it can become costly and difficult. Some Asian university systems have a hybrid between the two, with a sort of foundation year that offers freer movement between majors or subjects. Another option is to wait and take a gap year, which gives the student more time to decide.

The point here is that to help students choose the right language A course, you might have to understand their university options. If you are at an international school, it is likely students are looking at different countries, not just different types of universities. Do they want to go to the US, and can their parents afford for them to do so? Do they want to apply to several countries? Will they have 'predicted grades' (on IB DP assessment) they need to achieve to get an offer? This is also a job for your DP coordinator and school counsellor to help with, so you may want to ask them questions if you do not understand. Sometimes just knowing what questions to ask the students will help them to be more introspective about their choices.

The reality is that you will probably get some overall 'weak' students in your HL language A classes, especially in the language and literature course. This is because some of the students simply cannot handle the mathematics skills required for HL mathematics or science. The language and literature course has fewer 'long texts' than the literature and is viewed as more practical (though I always ask students to consider that they will need to know many text types in the language and literature course that are unrequired in literature). In any case, some language A teachers feel used or offended that weaker students are funnelled into their HL courses. As long as no one is judging your performance based on your course average, please see this as an opportunity! The student will have more hours with you during the week, you can provide more feedback on their written and oral work and you can more effectively guide them through reading strategies. This advance in literacy might help them in all their areas of study.

Additionally, I often find that many of the 'weak' students have different kinds of perspectives and understandings of the world that can help the entire class. If they are listened to and given positive feedback on their ideas, they will be able to assert their opinions and work with the class toward greater conceptual understanding of global issues. Literature is, after all, a reflection of the human condition. This condition includes all academic levels of achievement. Some famous authors were terrible at their language A classes in high school – Benjamin Zephaniah is a famous example. Illiterate and dyslexic, he finally found his voice in prison and went on to become a novelist, poet and writer for *The Guardian* ('Young and dyslexic? You've got it going on', 2015). Often, it is the weak students who need you as their teacher the most. These relationships can be the most rewarding, but we also need to be realistic with students from the start about their grades. For example, over-predicting a grade when a student applies to universities in the UK can leave them without options for university. It is a fine balance, but one that is not difficult if honest communication is maintained between student and teacher.

Likewise, an SL class can often have the 'best' students at your school. I found this to be true at the school I was working at in Hong Kong, where many students were pressed into business and science focuses and left English to SL. The SL classes had students who were excellent writers and critical thinkers, many working toward, and earning a grade of, 7.

Overall, the class is what you make of it with your students. As a careful conductor, your classroom will come alive, creating a language you all share, and your students will teach you things you could never imagine.

What can students get out of these courses?

The structures of the IB DP language A course are now minimal, but the learning outcomes are vast. You have the power to make the learning experience for your students come alive: giving students tools to use to enrich their lives; helping students achieve literacy skills and grades to get into the right programme after high school. In each chapter, you will learn practical ways to achieve these goals and ideas to move forward in your own direction, all within the parameters of the IB requirements. The content of each chapter is outlined below.

◾ Organizing your language A Diploma course

The first way to make sure students achieve the learning outcomes set by IB is through the design of your course syllabus. The design has a lot of choice. Chapter 2, Organizing your language A Diploma course, aims to make those choices more structured, so that you can carefully consider what will help your students to end up with the course aims below. You may notice how these aims link to concept-based learning as well as the IB learner profile and core. If you are new to these areas, you should understand the connection by the end of the book. The outcomes are the same for both courses, SL and HL, and are set by the IB.

◾ Course aims

The aims of the course are as follows:

1 Engage with a range of texts, in a variety of media and forms, from different periods, styles and cultures.

2 Develop skills in listening, speaking, reading, writing, viewing, presenting and performing.

3 Develop skills in interpretation, analysis and evaluation.

4 Develop sensitivity to the formal and aesthetic qualities of texts and an appreciation of how they contribute to diverse responses and open up multiple meanings.

5 Develop an understanding of relationships between texts and a variety of perspectives, cultural contexts and local and global issues, and an appreciation of how they contribute to diverse responses and open up multiple meanings.

6 Develop an understanding of the relationships between studies in language and literature and other disciplines.

7 Communicate and collaborate in a confident and creative way.

8 Foster a lifelong appreciation and enjoyment of language and literature.

You will notice that some of the above aims are clearly skills focused (2, 3, 4, 7), some are content dedicated (1, 8) and others are about transference and real-world connections (5, 6 and 8 again). In this way, you can understand how they would fit into the illustrated model of the course (page 7), one that plays on the interconnection of all these areas toward a conceptual understanding. Often as subject-specific teachers, we have a default to focus on the content more than anything else. The IB is moving us in a different direction. While we should not abandon our deep understandings and passions for our subject, we need to realize two shifts in mindset: they can only be useful through the application of essential skills, and our content is not contained in a fixed vessel – language and literature are living and breathing forms of artistry and communication.

◾ Developing a concept-based learning course

In Chapter 3, we begin by taking a closer look at developing a concept-based learning course. Concepts are big ideas that bring together content and skills for deeper understanding. They should answer the question: 'So what?' In other words, what is the greater purpose in learning the components of the language A course? How does it relate to other subject areas? Concepts can make the course content come alive, creating motivation in your classroom. Students want to learn more about the world, humanity, society and themselves. They are naturally curious. These concepts allow for deep discussion and understanding that is designed by you but is largely student driven. Beyond

IB designated concepts, we understand how to create units linked to conceptual focus areas, texts and assessments and how to make CBL lessons. Sample syllabi and plenty of text suggestions are given in this chapter.

■ Using critical theory

In Chapter 4, you will learn ways to help your students understand texts from different perspectives, which in turn leads to a deeper understanding of concepts and global issues. Ultimately, the chapter presents skills of analysis. Teachers have long been experimenting with the use of theory in the classroom; some do so explicitly and some implicitly, drawing from theory to shape a lesson. This chapter allows students to use the tools themselves; it gives them power in understanding the world in different ways and it challenges them to see new things and to read extension texts of university-level study. Further, it does not suppose one should read from a particular view and instead allows students to access several views to make comparisons and merge findings toward their own creative reading of the text.

■ Developing student writing and speaking

In Chapter 5, we look at developing student writing and speaking through a conceptual framework. While writing and language skills are components of all coursework for the DP, the language A course has an especially careful and explicit connection, allowing opportunities for students to find their voices. Rather than the burden of writing, this chapter helps you to change the attitudes of your students to see writing and speaking as powerful tools. They are also, of course, necessary components of assessment in these courses, so students may be dually motivated. The chapter looks at foundational structures and guidelines to use as springboards, allowing students to follow with their own creativity, but always with the focus that good ideas only come through to the audience when they are clearly articulated.

■ Approaching assessments

Chapter 6 focuses on approaching assessments. It provides ways to shape your units and lessons toward success in the IB assessments as well as formative work to help students get there. There are examples of how to guide students through the process of the assessments as well as some exemplar material, though more of this is available in other books in this series. The focus is mainly on practical ways to help students develop lines of inquiry and an understanding of global issues which are needed for the assessments. Essentially, we look at how the conceptual method leads to better student work, which should be rewarded in their marks. It also includes an explanation of the examination process to help you understand it, so you may also relay this information to your students or perhaps choose to become an examiner yourself.

■ Assessment objectives

Like the course aims, the IB has set identical assessment objectives for both courses:

1 Know, understand and interpret:

- a range of texts, works and/or performances and their meanings and implications
- contexts in which texts are written and/or received
- elements of literary, stylistic, rhetorical, visual and/or performance craft
- features of particular text types and literary forms.

2 Analyse and evaluate:

- the ways in which the use of language creates meaning
- the use and effect of literary, stylistic, rhetorical, visual or theatrical techniques
- relationships among different texts
- ways in which texts may offer perspectives on human concerns.

3 Communicate:

- ideas in clear, logical and persuasive ways
- in a range of styles, registers and for a variety of purposes and situations.

◼ Beyond the classroom

Finally, the conclusion in Chapter 7 brings us outward again from the course, helping you and your students find meaning in what you have accomplished over two years, besides exams and grades for university. The course can be as powerful as you make it, or as straightforward and boring as you allow. However, if you correctly move toward inquiry and global issues, you are already going in the right direction. The final chapter offers further considerations for your classroom, such as incorporating multilingualism, engaging in the mind–body connection and empowering students through action.

◼ Everything and nothing?

You will create a classroom of many texts and languages, but not one that feels overwhelming. Impossible, some will say. We are not just the four classical genres anymore (fiction, non-fiction, drama and poetry). Now we are much more: linguistics, advertising, podcasts, spoken word poetry, journalism, television, film, graphic novels, adaptations, social media, hypertexts, multimedia, critical theory, epistolary texts … the list goes on. With the added focus on inquiry and conceptual learning that might take you and your students to related historical and philosophical or religious texts, you may feel like you have suddenly been left in the middle of the Pacific Ocean.

The answer overall is that we cannot help students understand and master all these areas, but we can give them tools that are transferable, and we can get them excited about investigating further, either at university or on their own. If we approach these texts and topics as opportunities rather than burdens, we can make a meaningful, selective curriculum throughout the secondary school experience. We can help students then read widely to understand and appreciate the world and themselves, and we can help them find their written and spoken voice to express these ideas outward. Everyone wants her or his course to be dynamic, but sometimes we let time or lack of understanding rule our domains. I hope this book gives you practical advice you can use right away to make your classroom engaging, enjoyable and meaningful for both you and your students.

Organizing your language A Diploma course

Using the DP guide and My IB

The DP language A guide is your first reference point for the course you are teaching. Some of you will already be familiar with it in detail. Others may have skimmed through it, felt a bit overwhelmed, and then simply asked their department heads or colleagues for advice rather than going back to the guide. It is not an enjoyable read, but it is necessary. It presents all the requirements of the course in detail, while this book and workshops you may have been to present ways of working with that structure to create something in your classroom.

Here is my advice: *read the guide!* Read it thoroughly with highlights and notes, questions and folded pages. Keep it on your digital desktop or print it and keep it within reach on your desk. Read the section of the guide you are working with each time you teach the course. So often, we forget or assume, we mix up this course with the last one, SL with HL, or language and literature with literature. The latter was truer with the previous course, where slight differences in the timing of the individual oral commentary, for example, meant you might have allowed a couple of minutes of extra time to students and created automatic point deductions. These were honest mistakes but ones that could be avoided by re-reading the guide.

Now because of more freedom in the syllabus, there is less room for these mistakes, but the guide is still a useful framework and tool. It may also remind you of what you *can* do. For example, a colleague may claim that the learning portfolio must be on a digital platform. This is not true (and I explain later why giving choice and perhaps a mixed platform could be better for your students). The guide allows for any kind of portfolio, but we start to see things as truth when enough teachers are doing them. Alternatively, your school may determine department policy within the course: when you complete certain assessments, how you do the portfolio, which assessments count for the course grade, etc. These can be useful stratagems based on your cohort of students, the structures of the school and perceived fairness from students and parents. However, you should know where there might be flexibility that can be changed in the future.

◼ My IB

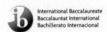

The My IB homepage

You can always find the latest version of the guide on My IB, an interactive website for IB teachers. You would find this in the Programme Resource Centre → DP Resources → Studies in language and literature. Sometimes amendments are made based on unintentional confusion or ambiguities in the original guide. The text and author lists to choose from can also be found here as well as further teacher support materials, including exemplars, discussion boards and teaching tools. Especially because things change, and also to empower all teachers to take ownership of their work, every IB educator should check in as frequently as time allows and share information with colleagues.

Before you can access any of this, you need to obtain a login. You can do this by registering and requesting acceptance, which will in turn go to your DP coordinator. (There are also sections for MYP and PYP on the same website, so you can register once for all and simply click on the areas of the school that you may need to access.) Once you have approval, you can create a profile, as detailed as you like.

The forum (Programme Communities → Discussions → Diploma Programme → DP Studies in language and literature) is an interesting place to get ideas and answers. Some teachers are frequently on the site and ready to provide their answers. Remember, however, that these responses will not be official from IB. Rather, think of them as idea generators and ways of bouncing ideas off other colleagues. You might ask if someone has had success teaching a particular text for Paper 2 and what strategies they have used. You might also ask what pairs well with a certain text. You might ask how other schools are addressing the learner portfolio. People will respond, but like any blog with comments, just be careful whom you trust. If you work at a small school, or perhaps if you are the only language A teacher at your school, you may find this forum especially useful. A lot of the coffee talk about ideas that we have in our shared offices or at the start of happy hours in the staff room can take place online. The forum is not exceptionally organized, but it is better than the one on the old site. So, if you gave up a few years ago, please go back and have a look!

Beyond the forums, if you really need an answer to a question about the course or a particular student, use the IB Answers feature through the home page. You may have a question about details involving a transfer student or a student's learning disabilities (though this may also be handled by your coordinator). Often with language A, the questions are about texts. For example, a Swedish A teacher I work with was unsure if she could use a very short play called *Idlaflickorna* (*Association Idla*, though not available in English) by Kristina Lugn. Even though she is on the PLA, the pagination limits are somewhat vague in text selection. We wanted to make sure the students would not lose points when their work was assessed, so I helped her use IB Answers for the first time. Eventually we got a satisfactory answer and she was pleased to be able to teach this gem of a text. (She kept the email just in case she was questioned in the future. On rare occasion, you may receive conflicting information, even at this level, so it is useful to hold on to your evidence!) Sometimes if the same questions come up, they are published on the site for all to access.

Additionally, you can get more information on My IB about the IB core: extended essay (EE), theory of knowledge (TOK) and creativity, activity, service (CAS). The first two components combined make up three points of the IB's potential 45 marks, while CAS is a pass/fail portfolio. The EE can be completed in any subject or world studies, which many language A teachers end up supervising. The 4000-word research paper allows students to follow a line of inquiry that interests them. TOK is usually a taught course that looks at epistemology through all subjects (or areas of knowledge – AOK) and through the ways of knowing (WOK). Additional components that include perspectives, ethical lenses and knowledge questions have valuable connections to your language A classroom. Add these two elements of the core to your profile even if you do not supervise or teach them. You will see connections throughout this book in yellow to help you get started, and you can seek further information on My IB for anything you want more detail on. I recommend you at least get a rough idea on each of them if you do not already, or if your school will not be providing a training session.

Finally, you can learn more about professional development (PD) opportunities through the IB site. The searchable list of workshops is valuable and varied and is available to see without login. Additionally, the forums provide a reference point for educators to share their own PD, or to guide others toward conferences and workshops like Learning 2.0, ECIS (Educational Collaborative for International Schools), InThinking, etc.

■ Other resources

In addition to the IB resources listed in the previous section, I offer further resources throughout the book. These include resources both related to content development and understanding, as well as digital tools to help with ATT and ATL skills.

This book is accompanied by four companion texts from Hodder Education for students and teachers: *English Literature for the IB Diploma; Literary Analysis for English Literature for the IB Diploma: Skills for Success; English Language and Literature for the IB Diploma; Textual Analysis for English Language and Literature for the IB Diploma: Skills for Success*. This is a coursebook and skills development book for both literature and language and literature courses. Further content resources and curricula links are woven throughout all books.

Finally, I invite you to virtually connect with me in a network of idea-sharing aiming for a future of better educational models through the conceptual framework. You can find ideas and ways to connect on my website, Conceptual Literature: **www.conceptualliterature. com**. Further annotated resources are available on the website.

Even with My IB and other resources to help you with ideas and further PD, I advise at this point you start by only reading the IB guide. Anything else will be ideas of interpretation. You do not want to funnel yourself early on into a singular mindset. Instead, read the guide and keep it somewhere handy, *then* read on in this book. Rather than prescribing what you should do, I shall offer ways of opening up the course to possibilities. Rather than worrying about the stresses of assessment, we shall work toward an attitude that assessment is a meaningful part of the students' experience, one that research has proven helps students use stress in a positive way (Damour, 2018).

First, however, we start by organizing the information you need to get started with your syllabus. You and your students will want to know in August or September where you are going over the next two years. What is the purpose of your journey? Although you can take pit stops and re-route the direction, everyone wants to know the destination. However, the full impression of the language A course, just like an excursion, can last well beyond that initial end goal.

Texts and parts

Let us begin by making sense of all the requirements and what we should consider as we make our text selections. But first, what is a text? Or rather, what has a text become?

Language A has become an overwhelming web of texts, languages, art and cultures, where texts can be anything readable: books, songs, emails, social media, brochures, films, paintings and even complexities like cities and living beings. The course now seems to encompass everything: how we read and write the whole world, how we communicate ideas in any subject area and how we integrate the various arts in dialogue toward appreciation of aesthetic beauty and understanding big ideas. There is the danger that the English (or Russian, Chinese, French ...) classroom is everything and nothing, but the potential that it is a powerful space of discovery and joy.

The curricula we are investigating here and from which we are creating our own syllabi have many of the possibilities above, but also give us parameters, luckily those that are not overly formulaic, with a lot of choice for you and your students. I like to think of the DP courses as tasters; you will never teach all of 'modern Japanese literature', 'the evolution of journalism' or 'postmodern graphic novels' in two years when you have different texts, times, places and more to consider in your syllabus. However, you can help students along a path of discovery and give them transferable skills to help them in future endeavours in the world of language and literature, whether in an academic setting or on their own, as they read a novel or the news on their commute. Ultimately, if we come back to the idea of a conceptual understanding dependent on skills and content, we can see all these as building blocks rather than linear checklists. The toolboxes will grow throughout the student's lifetime.

■ What is a text?

The IB uses two very specific designations for texts, which will be essential as you decide on your syllabus. They put texts into categories of 'literary' and 'non-literary' before further narrowing them into forms and text types. Although the etymology of *literature* tells us that the word delineates to the written word, IB and others have given it a connotation of art. Literature is language used as art and for IB, this is comprised of the four classical forms: fiction (including graphic novels), non-fiction, drama and poetry. They can still cover quite a lot of ground. If, for example, you enjoy an essayist who also writes journalistic pieces, you can use their work in the non-fiction designation. David Foster Wallace, also on the IB list of authors, is a great example for his diverse essays and journalistic pieces and one that I shall show you as part of a sample syllabus. He writes about tennis and beauty in his *New York Times* article 'Roger Federer as Religious Experience' (2006); he dives into the complexities of grammar and language with humour and wit in 'Authority and American Usage' (2001); he takes us to fascinating observations on culture and why Americans might not get Kafka's humour in 'Some Remarks on Kafka's Funniness' (1998); I could go on and on. You could use Wallace as some of your media non-literary texts in language and literature or as literary essays in the literature course.

You will see that IB tries to distinguish these 'literary texts' as 'works' of literature. Text came into vogue with post-structuralism and postmodernism, allowing the reader to (re-) interpret the work as a text. In other words, it gives the reader and contemporary context agency rather than suppose a pre-determined intention and fixed meaning (in a work). Roland Barthes wrote 'From Work to Text' in 1971 to explain this transition. Additionally, Barthes argues that a text allows us to work beyond hierarchies established with 'works' of literature: 'the Text does not stop at (good) Literature; it cannot be contained in a hierarchy, even in a simple division of genres. What constitutes the Text is, on the contrary (or precisely), its subversive force in respect of the old classifications.' However, there is 'a determination of the work by the world' (Ibid.), a fixed meaning. In this way, a canonical text might be a 'work', but we can still establish new truths from the classic by reading with intertextuality, for example. Essentially, IB is probably just trying to help us distinguish what is read in each course, but I think it's important we bear in mind the meaning of this language in the greater discourse of language and literature worldwide. IB is in no way asking us to only study literary works as those fixed in meaning by a hierarchized history.

The literature course requires 13 literary texts in all 4 major genres for HL, and 8 within at least 3 genres for SL, while the language and literature course requires 6 literary texts in 3 genres for HL, and 4 within at least 2 genres for SL. You will see a chart on page 26 to keep track of all these numbers. There will be some differences in several language A courses based on cultural methods of approaching literature. For example, for the Spanish course, rather than prose fiction as we have in English, the approach is emphasized over the articulation. Narration is a genre and includes both narrative verse and narrative prose. For German, 'prose other than fiction' is specifically autobiographical prose. For this reason, depending on your language of instruction, you may have to slightly adjust the tables I present to help you navigate your literary text choices. A few minutes of defining and clarifying will give you a table you can use repeatedly in reference.

> ## CORE CONNECTIONS
>
> ### TOK – AOK – The arts
>
> We can draw on literature's position in the greater dialogue of art. During the study of the area of knowledge called the arts, many TOK courses will investigate the question: what constitutes art? They may further break this down into what TOK calls 'knowledge questions that ask' for example, how art is a method of sharing knowledge, or to what extent art reflects truth or the knowledge, of a culture.
>
> To investigate the aesthetic and the purpose of art in literature, or more simply literature as art, I recommend looking at the foreword to Oscar Wilde's *The Picture of Dorian Gray* with your students. Wilde concludes in his preface that 'All art is quite useless', explaining instead that the aesthetic and beauty rather than function are most important. But then, the foreword is also a piece of art. Should we believe him? Does it matter if we do? We will come back to this excerpt in the next chapter as we investigate the conceptual focus: Beauty. In Wilde's novel, a painter character and supernatural painting are central to the story, thereby including further questions about the role of other art forms in society. The characters have debates about the arts and the reader has to determine which perspective is valid.
>
> If you study the whole text, you can go into another text type by looking at the transcripts from Wilde's trial (*Irish Peacock and Scarlet Marquess: The Real Trial of Oscar Wilde*, compiled by Merlyn Holland, Wilde's grandson, in 2003), in which he was essentially accused of sodomy, and which used excerpts from his fictional book as evidence. His responses and those of the lawyers create a rich dialogue of debate around what literary art is and how it can or cannot be used as truth. Perhaps extend this to the beginning of Virginia Woolf's 'A Room of One's Own', which states: 'There is more truth in fiction than in fact.' Allow students to respond in journals or create a debate with students on each side. Overall, engaging in this topic of literature as art makes students more aware of the purpose of such texts and helps them understand why politicians like Barack Obama might declare: 'When I think about my role as citizen … the most important stuff I've learned I think I've learned from novels' (Robinson, 2015), even though they are responsible for the improvement of the real world.

■ Non-literary texts

On the other side for IB are the non-literary texts. These are texts that do not necessarily have artistic value and are used more for communication between people, or for the delivery of the news, as well as propaganda and advertising. It is a more comprehensive category and looks at text types instead of genres. These include diary entries, feature articles, editorials, pamphlets, websites, television show transcripts, radio shows, Twitter feeds, blogs and many more. There is no exhaustive list from IB, though there are suggestions on page 21 of the guide, so be creative and also look at those texts from the exemplar course material.

The literature course does not require any non-literary texts on the syllabus, but I recommend you still include some (as noted on my sample unit plans) as extension or guided inquiry to give students a wider knowledge base. The language and literature course requires at least six non-literary text types throughout the course, the IB proposes some of these text types on pages 21–22 of the guide. This is probably too few for your students to be adequately prepared for the unseen written commentary (Paper 1), but this may be because the types are open to interpretation. If you consider 'newspaper writing' a text type, for example, you will actually have to go into several text types in print and then online to make it a meaningful analysis with a clear understanding of the differences. A lot of what you can cover here will come down to time and your students' needs. There will always be more you could have covered, and this idea is going to be something you have to let go of. Often doing something better with a lot of care and mindfulness has a greater effect on your students than covering a lot of ground quickly. You may have to adjust your pace to their needs on a daily, weekly or yearly basis. Some things will have to be covered, but I would not recommend you stay within the safety zone of 'what's likely to be on the test'.

■ Do not fear new textualities!

Russian travel bloggers Murad and Natalia Osmann share their views of the world they encounter on #FOLLOWMETO Travel

The world of blogs, hashtags, social media and online commenting are all important areas to explore in the classroom. This is where students are doing much of their reading and analysing of language and the world. We need to help them navigate with skills that can transfer to forms of text we have yet to encounter. Do not be afraid of what are sometimes called 'new textualities' but are often far from new. 'New' textualities also include experimental literary platforms like hypertext fictions, multimedia poetry and web-based interactive stories. If you are somebody who thinks teaching 21st century texts are too new, please consider that we are now a couple of decades in!

I recommend also trying out web-based applications that allow you to access different texts. For example, although Twitter can be overpowering if you receive notifications and check your feed several times a day, learning what it is like to search by hashtag and create content yourself will help you to more fully understand this firstly journalistic tool. Snapchat is another one to try, even if you have negative preconceptions of this medium. We conducted a self-evaluation of social media in one of my classes, where students described the Snapchat experience as 'more like real life' and 'not as scary as texts that can be read over and over again'. Have you ever looked at a text message multiple times, trying to decode the tone or the choice of language? Their idea that disappearing messages were like 'old school telephone calls' had me intrigued, so I tried out the app to see how it felt to be free of over-analysis. Keep asking your students what they are reading online and what tools they are using to communicate – they know what is new! They know what is being consumed. Whether you like the content or not, part of our job is to help them navigate and decode. Keep exploring, and perhaps creating, too.

You can look at other types of texts as extension in your classroom. Of course, multimedia texts are continuously evolving, which may make for good discussion if difficult to pin down. Similarly, films can be used as part of the course, perhaps as adaptation or inquiry material, but are not part of assessment. Or perhaps you have a lot of visual art or design students and would like to make connections to a painting or the shape of a chair to understand a culture's outlook on the world. Even more creatively, you can look at abstract texts, like the city, or groups of people, that can be 'read'. We shall investigate this possibility in the next section. I find that often going beyond the curriculum and challenging students to think beyond the parameters of the course helps students not only with motivation and interest but also with their grades. Although these texts are unlikely to be a part of assessments, they can give students a deeper conceptual understanding and can help them to discover a deeper sense of purpose in the core texts. This purpose makes up the spine of their assessments.

■ The three areas of exploration and the seven concepts

You will now have to put your chosen core texts into one of the three areas of exploration:

- Readers, writers and texts
- Time and space
- Intertextuality: connecting texts.

These are required for this course, along with the additional seven concepts, but also allow for a lot of creativity in interpretation and direction. They are areas you probably already used in the old DP course, or whatever kind of senior language and literature course you have previously taught. The structure of the areas does help to make the syllabus more meaningful and manageable, though when you first see it, you might think there is way too much ground to cover. Again, these are possibilities, and you are providing a more focused area of understanding that can lead to future endeavours from your students.

The concepts provided should be discussed with each text, according to the guide. The concepts are:

- Identity
- Culture
- Creativity
- Communication
- Perspective
- Transformation
- Representation.

I recommend explicitly linking two or three of the concepts to each unit of your course, though you will naturally bring all of them into discussion. The IB guide is vague as to how to use these concepts, giving you flexibility but perhaps also causing frustration.

To give the conceptual approach more meaning, I like to use my own focus areas, which you will see on the charts that follow and in bold text in the accompanying explanations. These focus areas are indeed concepts as well, but narrower ones. In the next chapter we shall look at how to use both in a more purposeful and engaging course. In that chapter, I will also unpack the conceptual questions, looking at both angles you might take with your students, as well as lessons and texts that work well with them. The accompanying coursebooks in this series provide further breakdown of each question, with a chapter focused on each one in the areas of exploration.

You can teach the three areas at any point over the two years of DP, but here I discuss why you might consider a particular order, and I expand on this in the sample syllabi explanations. In fact, the order I recommend is the order listed by IB in the guide, so they probably also had this in mind. Let us now take an initial look at these areas and the seven concepts.

■ Readers, writers and texts

Readers, writers, and texts: This area introduces students to the nature of language and literature and its study. The investigation undertaken involves close attention to the details of texts in a variety of types and literary forms, so that students learn about the choices made by creators and the ways in which meaning is communicated through words, images, and sound. At the same time, study will focus on the role receivers play in generating meaning, as students move from personal response to understanding and interpretation influenced by the classroom community. (IB, 2019)

IB poses the following inquiry questions:

1 Why and how do we study language and literature?

2 How are we affected by texts in various ways?

3 In what ways is meaning constructed, negotiated, expressed and interpreted?

4 How does language use vary among text types and among literary forms?

5 How does the structure or style of a text affect meaning?

6 How do texts offer insights and challenges?

The above questions seem to be a natural way to introduce your course. There is a lot of room for personal responses from your students, introductions to various text types or genres and beginning methods of analysis that will be needed throughout the course. (If you are comparing to the old DP courses, this part most resembles Part 4 (free choice and the individual oral presentation) combined with Part 2 (close study leading to the individual oral commentary) in the literature course and pieces of the first two parts as well as all of Part 4 in the language and literature course.)

This section will naturally begin preparing your students for the Paper 1 commentary due to the prevalence of analysis skills. Experienced DP teachers know it is always a good idea to start early with Paper 1 preparation! It is an assessment that can be easily neglected until the end because it is not really a part of the syllabus. If you start early with this type of close analysis, but by working with texts you are studying as a class, the commentary work will likely come more naturally by the end of the course. Even better, you can start this during MYP, or in collaboration with MYP teachers, if you are working at a continuous through school. For example, your Year 10 and 11 curricula can have a heavy focus on Paper 1- and Paper 2-style writing, supported by graphic organizers, classroom notes, commentary wheels and other tools you can also use with DP students.

I recommend using only the minimum of required core texts with this first area of exploration and using it more as an establishing section. You might use slightly more accessible texts here, depending on your cohort, or texts that allow you to have many teachable moments, covering a lot of ground in genre study that you will cycle back to and develop later. For example, Mary Shelley's *Frankenstein* (1823) would give you a start with a classical text and genre, but one with connections to scientific discovery, ambition and the need for companionship, among other things. There are many TOK connections in the pursuit of knowledge from Victor Frankenstein, as well as linguistic discovery from the Monster. Further, Shelley uses a classic frame narration that includes the epistolary form as well as many allusions, especially to John Milton's *Paradise Lost* (1667). Bring the novel outward to film adaptation, its impact on pop culture and where it sits in the dialogue of genetic engineering, and you have a wonderful mini-unit to start you off. You could easily use this text to answer any of the questions above. Other classical texts that come to mind that could accomplish a similar task: *A Tale of Two Cities* (1859), *Crime and Punishment* (1866), *The Catcher in the Rye* (1951), *Chronicle of a Death*

Foretold (1981) ... anything you think your students would respond well to, with a varied number of themes and stylistic features that can be addressed.

Then, if you are teaching the literature course, teach one (SL) or two (HL) more core texts that continue a focus area. Maybe you are looking at perspectives more closely? In *Frankenstein*, we directly hear from Watson, Frankenstein and the Monster in a classic frame narration structure. William Faulkner's *As I Lay Dying* (1930) is a beautiful, sad and funny story told from different family and community members' perspectives following a woman's death. We even get the perspective of the deceased woman – a provocative idea for that time! Or, you could focus on ambition and continue with William Shakespeare's *Macbeth* (1606), the ultimate portrayal of human ambition gone wrong, or Niccolo Machiavelli's *The Prince* (1513). We shall look more closely at thematic focus ideas in the next chapter.

If you are teaching the language and literature course, you could move from *Frankenstein* to scientific articles about genetic mutation in different sections of newspapers (features, editorials, even film reviews) then perhaps toward a dialogue on artificial intelligence and what that has to do with Shelley's questions about the definition of being human. Numerous films and television shows can be used to bring reluctant speakers in your classroom into the dialogue. Then you can move toward online blogs and multimedia platforms that deal with the topic.

In this first section of the course, use a variety of forms, text types or narrative structures to start a dialogue of how these affect readers. These become the skill blocks toward conceptual understanding that can be used in formations with other content knowledge as well. Use an array of literary and non-literary texts for language and literature, or works originally in different languages for literature, to aptly prepare students for the individual orals. Finally, use focus areas your students can easily connect to.

I shall go into more detail about how to use this strategy and what texts you might choose in Chapter 3, where we will connect text choices to unit planning, conceptual questions and assessment.

■ Time and space

Time and space: This area of exploration focuses on the idea that language is a social capacity and as such is intertwined with community, culture and history. It explores the variety of cultural contexts in which texts are produced and read across time and space as well as the ways texts themselves reflect or refract the world at large. (IB, 2019)

Here are the related questions IB poses:

1 How important is cultural context to the production and reception of a text?

2 How do we approach texts from different times and cultures to our own?

3 To what extent do texts offer insight into another culture?

4 How does the meaning and impact of a text change over time?

5 How do texts reflect, represent or form a part of cultural practices?

6 How does language represent social distinctions and identities?

The questions above about **time and space** may conjure memories of the contextual elements required in literature's old Part 1, which required an inquiring look at the works in translation, and language and literature's Part 3, which also asked for an understanding of context. The latter course's first two parts also looked at culture and context in relation to language use and text type, purpose and audience.

This part will naturally lead into your students' work on the individual oral and HL essay, both of which follow a line of inquiry developed by the student. They will build on closer analysis of style and structure in the first part toward a deeper understanding of purpose that is dependent on context.

Literature teachers may still want to use many of their works in translation for this part of the course. Understanding the cultural context of a translated work makes sense. To engage with Yukio Mishima's *The Sailor Who Fell from Grace with the Sea* (1963), you need to understand the Bushido Code, Japan's relationship with Western Culture and Japanese society post-second world war. To study Albert Camus' *The Stranger* (or *The Outsider* (1942), depending on translated title), one could look at existentialism, Algeria's history with France and possibly post-colonial theory. But then, you could take this approach for anything. Other texts that deal explicitly with a time period or which are allegorical may also be good choices. Cold War literature by Mary McCarthy or Paul Auster represent ways that political threats impact personal psyches, and in turn become metaphors for the greater world. An allegory like Arthur Miller's *The Crucible* (1953) or Haruki Murakami's *Kafka on the Shore* (2002) represent opportunities for layered looks at history, the addition of paired texts and connections to what they have to do with today. I take a closer look at these two texts in Chapter 4; they may be two of the best you can include on your syllabus.

Language and literature teachers may similarly want to include their works in translation in this section for similar reasons. However, you may also want to select a thematic focus area, like censorship, which allows you to look at a variety of text types in different cultures relevant to that topic. For literary texts, you might select something like Dai Sijie's *Balzac and the Little Chinese Seamstress* (2000), a novel (and later film by the author as filmmaker) that takes us to the Chinese Cultural Revolution, or Azar Nafisi's *Reading Lolita in Tehran* (2003), a memoir of Iran's revolution. Next, use different text types with similar context (or a different one) to look at propaganda, media censorship or advertising campaigns. Then, you could further pair it with another literary text with a more abstract setting that addresses how texts engage with a global issue and how different societies might receive the topic. Alan Moore's graphic novel *V for Vendetta* (1989) or Aldous Huxley's novel *Brave New World* (1932) would work well. The discussion can move outward toward censorship today: where is it happening and how? Should anything be censored? How can we draw on history and historical texts to determine what, if anything, should be censored? How are texts censored on the internet? Students might generate further extension texts in this way, bringing in more types of media, blogs and even songs. In this way, you are creating a syllabus that does not end with your teaching but extends into the students' daily consumption: news reading, web browsing or required reading in other subjects.

■ Intertextuality: connecting texts

Intertextuality: This area of exploration focuses on the concerns of intertextuality, or the connections between and among media, text and audience involving diverse traditions and ideas. It focuses on the comparative study of texts so that students may gain deeper appreciation of both unique characteristics of individual texts and complex systems of connection. (IB, 2019)

Again, IB follows with six conceptual questions:

1 How do texts adhere to and deviate from conventions associated with literary forms or text types?

2 How do conventions and systems of reference evolve over time?

3 In what ways can diverse texts share points of similarity?

4 How valid is the notion of a classic text?

5   How can texts offer multiple perspectives of a single issue, topic or theme?

6   In what ways can comparison and interpretation be transformative?

This section of the course is about a dialogue of literature and texts over time. The nature of the questions posed are comparative and build on topics from the previous two parts, which is why I suggest coming to this section last. The comparative nature means these texts should be used to prepare for Paper 2. In the old course, students had between two and four texts to prepare for the Paper 2, depending on the course and level. Now the idea that you can use any text is completely freeing but can be overwhelming. How can students successfully prepare for an exam on so many texts, including those studied more than a year ago? The answer is to not necessarily prepare them all. Focus on this part of the course in preparation and possibly focus on up to only four literary texts, even if you choose to use more in this section.

As I approach this section, I draw heavily on intertextual theory, which we will look at more closely in the critical theory chapter (Chapter 4) in terms of its practical application. Julia Kristeva must be given credit as the creator of the term 'intertextuality'. The Bulgarian academic became a part of the French post-structuralist movement and has written extensively on this topic since the 1980s. Even if you do not assign or require any of her work, you can make it available to students in extension. Kristeva and others discuss the term in many articles, but I prefer to share '"Nous Deux" or a (Hi)story of Intertextuality' (Kristeva, 2002) due to its parallel look at gender and culture (as intertexts) and her extended use of a doughnut hole metaphor. They are topics that interest students in a relatable and useful way, while the doughnut is a fun, memorable symbol.

For her, the intertext is the desire for what is missing; it is an absence. The doughnut hole is the intertext: '... that American pastry which has a hole in the middle (corresponding here to the loss of meaning) [Michael Riffaterre] envisions interpretation as a craving for the small cake, a craving satisfied only when consuming what is around the empty hole, the "naught"' (Kristeva's paraphrase from Riffaterre's *Semiotics of Poetry*, page 12, 1978). The key is that something new is made in looking at texts together; big ideas are formed. **Intertextuality** should be more than a timeline of literature. I shall expand on this in the next chapter, but for this reason, on the accompanying planning charts, we represent this area of exploration with a doughnut hole, with the negative space the space of thought creation.

All texts stand within the dialogue of literature, but some more explicitly help students understand that dialogue. In this way, the canon of literature, or the classics, is likewise not dead. The IB guide also explicitly asks teachers to include classical and contemporary texts, though you might extend this to also mean non-canonical historical texts and contemporary classics. I later recommend using several of Italo Calvino's *Why Read the Classics?* (1986) essays to provoke a dialogue about precisely that question. You might choose here to look at texts that respond to those you have used in other parts of the course. Allusions and allegories from the **time and space** area of exploration can be enhanced.

Modern texts that respond to classics can be paired to find the intertext. Take the reworking of the sonnet form by a poet like Robert Frost and investigate why he uses a similar form to Shakespeare but reshapes it, in 'Design', for example. Kate Tempest, in a mixture of modern and postmodern style, delivers a spoken word poem/song on the myth of 'Icarus', which could be a topic to look at from different angles. Many poets rework classical themes or structures, or even respond directly to classical tales, which would make for a nice place to study poetry. Add to this that the Paper 1 commentary is upcoming and it is a nice time to do some close analysis of shorter texts.

You might create a whole selection around a dynamic text you enjoy. Murakami's *Kafka on the Shore* is one of those rich in possibility. With constant allusions to other literature and music, it contains many passages to investigate some of the above questions. The

Japanese novel is a retelling of Sophocles' *Oedipus Rex* (430 BC) but with a different outcome. As the title suggests, it also engages heavily with the works of Franz Kafka as well as other literary and musical allusions. Why not use these texts as well? Or consider different Japanese responses to second world war trauma. You could choose to start with the Murakami novel then select the texts you will read intertextually in collaboration with your students. There are many ways this web can spin!

There are so many other ways to approach this area of exploration. You can look at a comparison of different plays and their use of the tragic genre. You can investigate the evolution of journalism, from classical to New Journalism, coined in the 1960s by Tom Wolfe, and finally to the changes that have taken place in online journalism, including multimedia texts. It really is endless!

Although themes and connections are likely to emerge naturally from any texts you choose to teach, a carefully designed focus gives a course that covers a lot of ground, in terms of time periods, cultures, genres and more. Focus areas will especially help in this section as you move towards the Paper 2 comparative essay preparation. Above all, focus areas provide a sense of cohesiveness and purpose, one that can endure and extend beyond the classroom experience.

■ The seven concepts

These seven concepts designated by the IB are keywords we tend to use in our classrooms in a variety of ways already, and contain rich connections to the IB core as well as ATL skills. You can find a paragraph explanation for each of them in the guide, but the IB also states that they are open to your interpretation. As we look at the development of syllabi and units, you will see that I offer suggestions of explicit structural connections to each of the concepts, but as long as you use the terms in discussion and formative assessments, your students will have the tools they need to look at the course material in these ways. I include a few questions to get you started, in which you will already see crossover among the concepts. You might want to use these as carousel questions or journal prompts within your course.

Identity	■ What does it mean to be human and how do we see this in the text?
	■ How is the writer's identity represented in the text?
	■ How does the reader's identity affect the way one reads a text?
	■ How can we communicate individual perspectives?
	■ How does the text convey a cultural identity?
Culture	■ How does a text relate to its context?
	■ In what way is the text part of a dialogue of literature of a particular culture?
	■ Do texts create cultural identities or do the identities shape the texts?
	■ How do texts demonstrate a transformation of culture over time?
Creativity	■ How does imagination affect the creation and reception of a text?
	■ What is the purpose of creativity in society?
	■ How does creative thought shape identity?
	■ How original is the text and how might a response or pastiche also be considered creative?
Communication	■ How is a 'relationship ... established between a writer and a reader by means of a text' (IB guide)?
	■ What is the purpose of media communication in society?
	■ How can we correctly interpret the intended message of a text?
	■ What does communication have to do with the human identity?
Perspective	■ What insight does the perspective of the text offer?
	■ How do changes of perspective within a text or between different texts allow us to better understand a theme?
	■ How is cultural perspective communicated in a text?
	■ How does social media (or other text types) allow us to view multiple perspectives on a theme?
	■ To what extent do texts limit perspectives?

Transformation	■ How does the dialogue of literature demonstrate changes in ideas or text types over time? ■ How does adaptation demonstrate and interact with ideas from the original text? ■ What does a text type's evolution have to do with purpose and context? ■ How can a text or texts transform a reader's perspective?
Representation	■ To what extent do fictional texts represent reality? ■ To what extent do non-fiction texts have a duty to represent truth? ■ What philosophical perspectives are included in texts to understand the author's interpretation of reality? ■ What do art and aesthetics have to do with reality and truth?

■ Pulling it together

To some extent, you will use all of the IB areas of exploration and concepts throughout your course. You are meant to devote an equal amount of time to the three areas and the seven concepts. However, this need not be reflected in your course design, as you shall see. Instead, spontaneous discussions, student-led explorations and reflective comparisons will help you to devote time to all these aspects throughout the DP.

You might even choose to mix up the parts explicitly rather than keep a linear evolution. You could choose to focus on different conceptual questions spread through the course, but this might become unnecessarily complicated since nothing keeps you from touching on areas addressed in the other parts. This is another reason why I suggest the focus areas: the focus may be a more specific concept, thematic in nature, or it may have a more structural or contextual focus, even a literary or artistic movement.

Familiarize your students with all three parts of the course and the related questions early on. They may begin to make connections in discussion, journal responses and other formative work before you even explicitly teach the part of the syllabus you have designed to correspond to the designated questions. The effect of cycling back will be that students will have an even better grasp on how to respond to all the questions by the time they arrive at Paper 1 and Paper 2. In fact, they will need what they have learned from all three areas of exploration in order to successfully complete the exams independently. I recommend that each question is addressed at least once explicitly and thoroughly, even though implicit responses will continue. Perhaps even make students responsible for creatively presenting their ideas on a particular exploratory question to the rest of the group.

■ Requirements and considerations

Before considering how assessment and more detailed timing fit into the bigger picture, let us bring together what we have learned about creating your syllabus. This simple chart will help you see the requirements for each course. For any course I teach, I use a chart like this to refer back to at any time I am considering a change. I have made near mistakes with the matrix in the past; this can cost your students a minimum of two points on an assessment they are completing. It is easy to do when you have an exciting text idea. Additionally, you risk not exposing students to the wide range of texts IB rightly asks us to deliver. Finally, in the name of fairness, students are bound to compare their syllabi with those of others (even online). We have a duty to be transparent with students about requirements and the nature of creating a syllabus. This extends to assessments as well, and I shall later help you explain the mysterious way a mark from 1–7 is finally calculated.

A couple of items on the chart that follows on page 26 have not yet been defined here and some may need brief reminders.

Literary texts are those of artistic value in one of the four classical literary forms (fiction, non-fiction, drama, poetry).

Here a text counts as:

- 1 single major work (novel, memoir, etc)
- 2 or more 'shorter texts such as novellas' (IB guide)
- 5–10 short stories
- 5–8 essays
- 10–15 letters
- 15–20 poems or an epic poem of 600+ lines.

Any anthology counted as a literary text must be from the same author. There are slight differences for several languages other than English; check the information carefully on My IB. If in doubt, write to IB Answers for approval and keep the email.

Freely chosen texts (FC) are those literary texts that you consider of value but do not need to be on the IB list.

IB list – PRL (prescribed reading list) is the list of authors from whose works you may select for your literary texts:

- **PRL-a** = those originally published in your language A
- **PRL-t** = those translated to your language A by someone other than the author.

DP language A syllabus requirements

	SL literature	HL literature	SL language and literature	HL language and literature
Number of literary texts	9	13	4	6
Freely chosen texts (FC)	2	4	2	2
Texts from PRL-a	4	5	1	2
Texts from PRL-t	3	4	1	2
Forms (poetry, fiction, non-fiction or drama)	3	4	2	3
Time periods	3	3	2	3
Places	3	4	2	3
Continents	2	2	2	2
Use of literary texts across areas of exploration	At least 2 per area of exploration	At least 3 per area of exploration	At least 1 per area of exploration	At least 2 per area of exploration
Non-literary texts	No requirement	No requirement	At least 6 text types	At least 6 text types

Non-literary texts are any other written, oral or visual texts you find merit in teaching.

Time periods have been purposefully vague in the past. Now the IB requires you use the centuries indicated on the PRL. It is always good to have a range here that includes different time periods from the 20th century. Non-literary texts should also cover a range of time periods, though it is not explicitly indicated on the syllabus.

Places refer to countries or regions of any texts on your syllabus, as indicated on the PRL. Additionally, each course requires a minimum coverage of two continents for literary texts. Again, especially with the addition of non-literary texts, it would be ideal to cover many more places, but this more lenient requirement now allows you to, for example, focus on a single country for a part of the course.

Authors may not be studied twice as core texts in either course. Additionally, students taking a second language A should not study the same author in each course. The student may write an EE on a studied author's work, but it must be a different text than was studied in the classroom.

This chart contains all textual requirements. However, I would start with some ideas of what you want to teach, based on your passions or those of your students, and go back to the chart to build from there. You could begin with a list of 20 texts you love then look at some connections between them in terms of possible focus areas. Or, circle within the list a singular text you *must* teach and build from there. Then have a chat with a colleague about your choices. They will have new ideas that you can jot down for consideration. Some texts that work for some teachers do not work for others, and that is absolutely fine. But sometimes they will have the key to your syllabus. You can also do this through the forums on My IB. Language A teachers at small schools or those who conduct the course in an uncommonly taught language can benefit especially from the online forums. I also like talking to teachers with a different language A to find out their favourite books in their language and culture for my texts in translation. If you have students completing the bilingual diploma (taking two language A courses), you may also want to coordinate who is teaching what. I was both very pleased and extremely disappointed when I found out that Kafka – one of my favourites – was a frequently used author with our German A teachers in Vienna. I was happy to build off of their knowledge of his work but took him off my syllabus when students told me how much they loved his work … because they had already studied it.

If you are beginning to feel overwhelmed, maybe start with one of my sample syllabi on the next few pages, or that of a colleague's (again, the online forum can help you here) and tweak it according to your own ideas. All of this further information will be followed by an easy checklist for you to use on your own or with a colleague, or even your students, after you have a draft syllabus.

Here are the final items to consider for text selection, which are not required but will add richness to your syllabus:

- *Sex*: You may want to consider the sex (or gender identity) of your authors or protagonists to ensure that you include a range. Sometimes with the classics, it can be easy to inadvertently leave out female voices.

- *Sexual and gender identity*: Please do not shy away from including a text that grapples with sexual or gender identity in some way, or is somehow included in the dialogue of queer literature (more on queer theory to come in Chapter 4). Virginia Woolf's *Orlando* (1928), James Baldwin's *Giovanni's Room* (1956) and Jeffrey Eugenides' *Middlesex* (2002) are all great choices. Remember that for all these categories here we are only considering the literary text selection. Each of these aspects might be addressed further in the non-literary texts. For example, you could take a look at gender identity in Thailand by starting with an academic text: Peter A. Jackson's 'An Explosion of Thai Identities: Global Queering and Re-Imagining Queer Theory' (2000) and follow with current mixed media online texts on the subject in Thailand (preferably in Thai). These could include news articles, blogs and Twitter hashtags.

- *Race and culture*: Beyond the original language of the text, which IB requires you vary, you will want to pay attention to having voices of different racial and cultural identities, including nationality, religion and subcultures. Any of these identities may again be of the authors or the subjects of the writing. Minor voices are especially important to include.

- *Length*: A lot of language A teachers choose and advise to teach shorter literary texts. I think this advice is only useful to some extent. There is less ground to cover when your texts are shorter, but they are not necessarily the correct ones for your classroom. They can unnecessarily limit you and your students with the added negative of your students reading less and feeling less courageous about tackling longer works in the future. I recommend a combination; when teaching a long text, feel free to look at some sections more as a whole and analyse short parts more in depth that are representative of other parts. Equally, do not shy away from very short but provocative texts. You have a lot of flexibility in your choices, and sometimes spending a whole week on a single poem or short story might be worth it.

- *Difficulty*: Challenge your students! Give them some texts that are easier to handle, but even if the vocabulary is 'easy' there should be some difficult ideas in there. A course without challenge is a boring course; it is one that lacks student motivation through its safety. You might decide to make your most challenging diction in the form of short texts, like poetry and short stories. Jorge Luis Borges' short stories come to mind here. Likewise, you could take something like *Monster* by Walter Dean Myers (1999), which has an easy lexical score but deals with the difficulty faced by a young man on trial for his life. Further, its mixed print media of script, diary entries and graphic novel is fantastic for analysis.

- *Accessibility*: Depending on how your school works, you might have books for students to borrow, use a supplier for a big student book order or ask students to purchase them on their own. Check if books are out of print, difficult to find or too expensive for the school or students to afford. Depending on your language of instruction, there may also be some PRL-t texts which you cannot find in your language, or only one which you do not like the translation of. Sometimes there are ways around this (used books, online texts, your own translation, etc) but you need to investigate before setting the syllabus.

Given all the above considerations, you need to finally consider: who are your students? What are their levels of reading? Their motivations for taking the course? Their personal conflicts (if you are aware of these)? What are the languages they can speak? The places they have lived? Try to find out more before you set your syllabus in stone. Perhaps you work at a small school and know your incoming DP cohort or can poll the students before the summer holiday. Otherwise, you can keep at least a few texts flexible until you meet who is in the room.

There is no formula to choosing texts based on your students. For example, recently about a quarter of my HL literature class came from Spanish-speaking South America, and they shared some of their culture with us as we read Gabriel García Márquez's *Chronicle of a Death Foretold* (1981). It was equally useful, in the same class, to tackle not one but *two* texts originally in Japanese, due to a fascination they commonly held with the culture. They were all well-travelled, but none had been to Japan. I was able to share some of my personal knowledge of the culture from my travels and we researched the rest together.

If you have a class whose language skills are especially weak, you may want to choose a few of the texts with lower lexical scores or especially good film versions (many dramas, such as Tennessee Williams' *A Streetcar Named Desire* (1947), *The Crucible* or any Shakespearean play work well here, or something like Dai Sijie's *Balzac and the Little Chinese Seamstress* and its film adaptation, since he is the auteur as well).

More than analysing your students, I encourage you to ask them what they want. I cannot emphasize how valuable this is! The IB guide also now encourages including students in at least part of your syllabus selection.

Design your syllabus with the ability to co-design certain elements and allow for student choice

I recently tried an experiment: to choose the entire syllabus with my students at the start of the year. I had narrowed down my selection to about 30 literary texts. We talked about the dialogue of literature, and I talked them through my love for and reasoning behind all of the texts. After a survey, we then made our choices. It was an exciting reveal; one they all felt ownership of. And, of course, the texts we ended up not choosing I made available for students to sign out and read on their own.

You can keep choice going throughout the two years with extension texts and the inclusion of related topics students would like to look at more closely. This is especially easy to manage in the language and literature course where, for example, you may know you want to teach the way Twitter came from journalists and how it is used to gather information from different perspectives, but you really do not mind which subject(s) and hashtags you analyse collectively. Let your students teach you, especially with new textualities of this nature. They may come across relevant ideas that would not be on your radar (this happened to me, for example, with Kylie Jenner's cultural appropriation via cornrows – a topic not normally on my Twitter feed, but such a fantastic one for classroom debate!).

Co-designing curriculum and the learning environment is proven to help students with motivation as well as to help teachers 'understand the perspectives, needs, and values of the students for whom the materials are being developed' (Gunckel and Moore, 2005, page 6). A Finnish study found that 'the learner-centred paradigm giv[es] learners an active agency in learning cross-curricular citizenship skills' (Mäkelä, 2018, page 48). So, when students and teachers design what is taught in the classroom with a looser framework from curriculum leaders (the IB and department leaders), the result is that the IB values of perspectives, international mindedness and transference skills are achieved. Allow for this to happen at different stages of the course, because students evolve in comprehending what they need and in cultivating their interests.

And finally, *you* need to like what you are teaching as well. Choosing much or all of your syllabus and selling it to students is important and can work as well as selecting it together. (They might not yet know what they will learn best from.) You need to be interested, challenged by daily classes and motivated to read deeply and widely in preparation. Part of taking care of yourself, and therefore being a better teacher, is making sure you enjoy your lessons. I shall address this more in the final chapter. If you teach what you love but equally listen to student and colleague suggestions, you cannot go wrong. Your passion for the literature will transfer to your students. Though you may start by drawing on what you loved in secondary school or at university, keep exploring to find other texts, both new and old, that you come to love.

■ SYLLABUS CHECKLIST

These are the essential questions for you to ask yourself or to use with a colleague, or even your students, once you have a draft of your course syllabus:

- Have you included the right amount of literary texts?
- Have you included the correct number from the PRL-a and checked that they are still on the PRL-a?
- Have you included the correct number from the PRL-t and checked that they are still on the PRL-t?
- Do you have enough places for the works originally in your language? What are they?
- Do you have enough time periods? What are they?
- Do you have a good balance between classical and minor voices? Can you identify these?
- Have you included at least six non-literary text types? (Language and literature only.)
- Have you considered who will be in your classroom and possibly what they would like to study?
- Have you included texts that you love?
- Are all the texts accessible to your students by the time you plan to teach them? Have you placed any orders or done the necessary preparation to ensure students will have the books they need?

If you can answer yes to all these questions, you are set to go! Again, any time you make a change to your syllabus, go back and make sure you are not taking away any of the requirements or desirable balances.

Required assessments

Before looking at samples of how we might put texts into parts of the course, we need to understand just the basics of the required assessments and how you might extend to use other assessments. I will keep this very brief here and expand in Chapter 6 of the book. Further, you can use the companion books in the series on specific assessments with your students.

Required assessment for DP language A

Assessment	Description	SL: time + per cent of mark	HL: time + per cent of mark	Marking
Learner portfolio	The learner portfolio (LP) is a digital or paper-based (or mixed) portfolio of student work, which may include journaling and formative assessment as well as other types of classwork and homework. The LP is meant to keep a record of the learning process that the student can refer back to in preparation for the individual oral and HL essay.	Ongoing in class and at home 0%	Ongoing in class and at home 0%	Unmarked by IB (though teachers may use as assessment)

Assessment	Description	SL: time + per cent of mark	HL: time + per cent of mark	Marking
Individual oral	Oral examination with the student and teacher, where the student has prepared a response to the prompt: 'Examine the ways in which the global issue of your choice is presented through the content and form of two of the texts that you have studied.' Literature: two literary texts, one in translation and one in original language A. Language and literature: one non-literary and one literary text (can be translated or originally in language A).	10 min + 5 min Q&A 30%	10 min + 5 min Q&A 20%	Internally assessed; externally moderated
HL essay	All HL students in each course will complete a thesis essay on a text studied in the course. The 1200–1500-word formal essay 'follow[s] a line of inquiry of their own choice.'	Not required	Sent to IB mid-March 20%	Coursework; externally assessed
Paper 1	Written commentary on unseen text(s). SL = write on one of two texts, with response to question; HL = two of two texts. Literature: only literary texts (any literary form). Language and literature: only non-literary texts (any text type).	1h 15 min 35%	2h 15 min 35%	Timed exam; externally assessed
Paper 2	Comparative essay on two texts studied; students select from four questions. Students choose freely from course texts studied as long as they are 'literary' and have not been used for other assessment (oral/HL essay).	1h 15 min 35%	2h 15 min 25%	Timed exam; externally assessed

Those of you with previous experience in DP but who are just starting to work with the new course will still recognize all these components to some extent. You will also see there are some components missing. The IB has taken away both courses' presentations to ensure that all IB marks are at least moderated externally. You can and should still use presentations as part of your course; you can find some ideas as I talk you through the upcoming sample course outlines more in the next chapter. All assessment is streamlined for the two courses; you will see that the only differences are whether students are using literary or non-literary texts for some components. Overall, there is a lot of student choice, with less assessment overall, allowing you to spend more time teaching valuable skills or using other creative formative assessments to help your students achieve the learning outcomes of the course.

The new internal assessment (IA) is made up only of the individual oral (IO). Although it sounds more like the individual oral commentary (IOC) of old, it is truly a combination of the old presentations and the IOC. This is because students have a chance to prepare to discuss a topic of their choice with the use of two texts they have studied. They work on this for some time with feedback from the teacher before the actual exam, with no need for a cumbersome exam preparation room as we had in the past. The IO relies heavily on the use of the learner portfolio (LP), which is completely new. It is a digital or paper-based portfolio of student work, which may include journaling and formative assessment as well as other types of classwork and homework. The LP is meant to keep a record of the learning process that the student can refer to in preparation for the IO. In this oral where the student is one-to-one with the teacher in the exam room, the student responds to the prompt: 'Examine the ways in which the global issue of your choice is presented through the content and form of two of the texts that you have studied.' In the first 10 minutes, students analyse extracts from two texts studied in response to this statement, ideally in a well-structured manner. They may use a prepared outline in a format provided by IB and note-free extracts of approximately 40 lines. Next, they engage in a Q&A with the teacher. Literature students use two literary texts: one in translation and one in the original language A. For this reason, you need to make sure to teach a couple of each before the assessment. Language and literature students use a non-literary and a literary text, without stipulation on the original language. For SL students, the component makes up 30 per cent of the IB mark, while it makes up only 20 per cent for HL students due to the addition of the HL essay.

The HL essay is the other part of coursework assessed and is only for HL students, again in both courses. Each HL language A student will complete a thesis essay on a text studied in the course. The 1200–1500-word formal essay 'follow[s] a line of inquiry of their own choice' (IB guide, 2019). This assessment is somewhat like the old HL literature written assignment. Although it draws on inquiry and context, it is not quite a research paper like the EE. The focus is still on textual analysis but one that is framed within a contextual and conceptual approach. The paper is externally assessed though it is completed with a couple of structured feedback sessions with the teacher. For those unfamiliar, this means that you may give a predicted or summative grade for your reports to the student, but the mark that will comprise 20 per cent of the final IB mark is given by an IB examiner with no knowledge of student or school identity. You and your students will not know this grade until July, following their exams (or January if they are sitting the November exams), and it makes up 20 per cent of the final mark. The essay will be due mid-March for May exam students, along with your grades for the IO, but all coursework is due at this time in all subjects. You will likely work with your department and DP coordinator to spread out IA and coursework deadlines throughout the two years so that everything is not suddenly due at once.

The other two components are exams. They are sat during exam time (May or November) and are assessed externally. They are similar to the old course exam papers with some slight changes to timing, text selection and streamlining of all four courses.

In Paper 1, all students will be greeted with two unseen texts that they must analyse in commentary style. SL students select one text to write about within the timeframe of 1 hour 15 minutes. HL students must analyse both texts (though not necessarily comparatively) with an extra hour of time, totalling 2 hours 15 minutes. For this reason, HL students need to be well versed in all genres or text types. The only difference between language and literature and literature is the use of non-literary and literary texts, respectively. Guiding questions will be included to help students access stylistic features. Language and literature will draw solely from non-literary texts in this section of any text type. These include visual texts as well and may even use colour as part of the layout for students to analyse. The literature Paper 1 was previously always comprised of one prose side (usually fiction, though infrequently memoir) and one poem side. Now, any of the four classical forms are considered fair game. Since HL students are required to study all four of these forms, they should be prepared for them through your coursework. The Paper 1 counts for 35 per cent of the final mark for all students.

Paper 2 is a sort of hybrid between the two courses' previous styles. This component is a comparative essay of two works studied. It is very straightforward but probably takes the most explicit preparation time of any of the components. Students have 1 hour 45 minutes for both SL and HL to complete the assessment. They will select a question from four general questions of a conceptual nature. The two works will be literary for both courses and can be chosen freely, as long as they have not been used for the other assessments. However, I recommend you guide your students and your review to focus on books you study in the second year of the course, or possibly those you will cycle back to in a different way in the language and literature course. You will have plenty of opportunity to use texts from the first year for the IO or HL essay, or simply for formative assessments and investigations. Paper 2 makes up 35 per cent of the final mark for SL students and 25 per cent for HL students, again due to the addition of the HL essay.

Now that we are starting to understand the syllabus and assessment requirements, we are ready to look at some sample ways to organize your course. What follows are syllabi templates and samples for each course, both SL and HL, followed by short rationales.

Syllabus planning template and samples

These sample 'cheat sheet' charts are just one way to shape your course. Remember: the three main areas of exploration can be taught in any order. Also, the focus area divisions and amount of texts per part are just my suggestions. You will see that even in a couple of my examples, I modify where the texts fit. Always go back to the chart (page 26) and the checklist questions (page 30) to make sure you have what you need! I have included basics, like time period, genre, place and sex of the author, though these are by no means all the information you should consider, as discussed earlier. It does, however, give you and your students an easy overview of your course. Keep in mind that the time period and place specifications from IB only pertain to the literary texts, but I find it useful to examine my approach as a whole, since non-literary texts in the language and literature course should make up half of the students' reading and allow a place to easily include more diversity. The more detailed unit planners that appear later in the book allow you to connect to conceptual and focus questions, critical theory, extension texts, formative assessment and core connections in a structured way.

You will find a blank syllabus template for you to use and adapt on IB Extras: **www. hoddereducation.com/ibextras**

HL literature

Sample HL literature syllabus for English A

When	Area of exploration	Concept focus	Core texts (13)	PRL-a (5) / PRL-t (4)	Place (4)	Time (3)	M/F	Form (4)	Summative assessments
Aug–Jan (Y1)	Readers, writers and texts	Beauty (Creativity, Representation)	1 Frankenstein, Mary Shelley	FC English	Eng (Eur)	19c 1823	F	Fiction	Mock P1 / LP mark
			2 The Picture of Dorian Gray, Oscar Wilde	FC English	Eng (Eur)	19c 1890	M	Fiction	
			3 The Bluest Eye, Toni Morrison	PRL-a	USA (NA)	20c 1970	F	Fiction	
Feb–Apr (Y1)		Parallel universes (Transformation, Perspective)	12 Franz Kafka's short stories	PRL-t German	Cze (Eur)	20c	M	Fiction	Mock IO / LP mark
			13 Kafka on the Shore, Haruki Murakami	PRL-t Japanese	Jap (Asi)	21c 2002	M	Fiction	
May (Y1)–Sep (Y2)	Time and space	Topographies (Representation, Creativity)	6 Essays on Elsewhere, André Aciman	FC English	Egypt (Afr)	21c 2011	M	Non-fiction	Mock P1 / IO (IA) / HL essay draft
			7 Poetry of Robert Frost	PRL-a	USA (NA)	20c	M	Poetry	
			8 Istanbul, Orhan Pamuk	PRL-t Turkish	Tur (Eur)	21c 2003	M	Non-fiction	
Oct–Dec (Y2)		Identity (Identity, Communication, Creativity)	9 Orlando, Virginia Woolf	PRL-a	Eng (Eur)	20c 1928	F	Fiction	
			10 The Unbearable Lightness of Being, Milan Kundera	PRL-t Cze/Fre	Fra (Eur)	20c 1984	M	Fiction	HL essay / Mock P2
	Intertextuality: connecting texts		11 Hamlet, William Shakespeare	PRL-a	Eng (Eur)	17c 1602	M	Drama	
Jan–Apr (Y2)		India (Culture, Identity, Perspective)	4 The God of Small Things, Arundhati Roy	PRL-a	Ind (Asi)	20c 1997	F	Fiction	Mock P2 / Mock P1
			5 The White Tiger, Aravind Adiga	FC English	Ind (Asi)	21c 2008	M	Fiction	P1/P2 exams

■ HL literature sample syllabus rationale

This syllabus is broken into five manageable focus areas and includes all the required elements of the course. You will find a healthy mix of voices and perspectives as you look at the texts. The free choice (FC) texts are well connected to the syllabus, have artistry and are considered by scholars in the dialogue of literature. Both canonical and minor voices are included to add a richness to the dialogue of literary voices for your students to respond to, including texts from four continents, as required in this course.

With the first area of exploration, I suggest beginning with only three texts and one focus area. You want to move away from reader response and formalist readings of the text soon, but also include them later in the course. However, starting with **beauty**, a focus both controversial and optimistic-sounding, should invite your students into the course. Everyone will have an opinion on this seemingly safe topic that can go into difficult territory very easily! Shelley and Wilde's novels included here are not on the PRL but are often considered canonical texts. They have many responses in adaptation, media and pop culture that will engage your students. Morrison's novel is rich but also a beautiful story for students to understand from a child's perspective. It has difficult material about abuse but allows students to talk about a difficult topic with your guidance. All three texts offer rich passages for detailed analysis that can help you to begin practicing Paper 1 style commentary work.

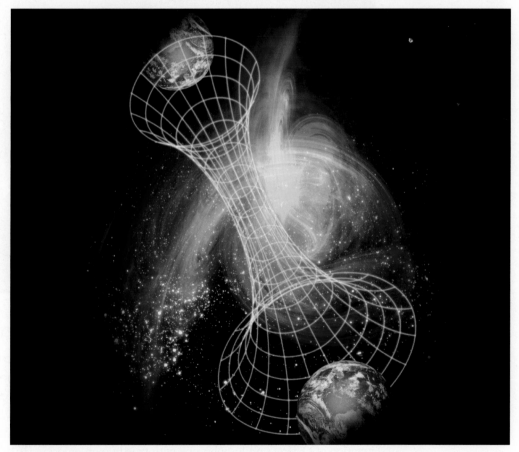

The concept of a parallel universe goes far beyond physics; as a framework to view the world, we investigate the human experience through related literature

With **time and space**, we begin with a challenging but fun focus on **parallel universes**. I placed this part here to make sure there was more diversity of PRL texts to choose from for the IO and HL essay. I have suggested challenging texts here that bring up exciting scientific debate as well as exploring the human condition on a more personal level. Kafka and Murakami create alternate realities for us to understand the world; you can take this topic in many directions. Borges' short stories would make a wonderful addition, even if you only have time for one of them as extension. **Topographies** moves to texts that truly focus on writing places. You can localize this topic with creative writing and draw on students' travel experiences or desires. In this sample, I include an American poet, Robert Frost, who engages in a continuing dialogue of transcendentalism, which you may choose to historicize with Henry David Thoreau's *Walden* or works by Ralph Waldo Emerson and Henry Wadworth Longfellow. Annie Dillard's *Pilgrim at Tinker Creek* (1974) is a direct response to their work as well as a memoir; it could easily replace Aciman as long as you have another fourth continent on your list. André Aciman's *Essays on Elsewhere* is written by a New-York based professor and novelist originally from Egypt. Aciman takes us on philosophical and sensory-based journeys through his memories. You can take a while to focus on memoir writing by pairing this with Pamuk's beautiful homage to place and family. Additionally, James Joyce's *Dubliners* (1914) works excellently as a study of one place from different perspectives. Overall from these first two concepts, your students should have a range of rich texts and topics to draw from for their IO and HL essays.

Orhan Pamuk's *Istanbul: Memories and the City* helps us think about our own relationships with home and how place has a reciprocal relationship with memory

Finally, students move into **intertextuality** with **identity**, also an IB concept. The focus can take us to both personal identities and the common human experience. *Orlando* helps us look at gender identity and history's connection with class and religious identities. Kundera's novel allows a great engagement with Nietzsche's concept of eternal return, reactions to political turmoil and sex's relationship with identity. Calvino talks about the novel as a modern iteration of Diderot's philosophy, one with true human emotion (*Why Read the Classics?* page 111). *Hamlet* is the quintessential Renaissance Man, grappling with ontological views. All three also have excellent film adaptations that may be useful in this time of the course that is prone to burnout or slumping and useful for students with other mother tongues. We then enter **India** as the intertext, the concept we add meaning to as we read around its elusive centre. You can choose any place or time of interest for this area of exploration or the previous one; we shall later investigate more closely what the difference is in teaching through the different conceptual questions. Roy and Adiga's novels are edgy in their topics that include sex, the untouchable caste and both the beauty and pains of India's complexities. *Sea of Poppies* by Amitov Ghosh (2008), would also be a great choice and one that has been included in university-level approaches toward postcolonial and Marxist theories.

All of the texts on the syllabus have a deep relationship with intertextuality, but those in this section work well for comparative papers. There are many avenues of comparison for the Paper 2, allowing you to review and compare the last five works or a couple more when preparing students for their exams. What they have learned from the other eight will help them here, but it is too much to remember the details (including quotations) to do a good job on the exam. You want to make the exams more manageable for your students, and this is one way to do it.

SL literature

■ Sample SL literature syllabus for English A

When	Area of exploration	Concept focus	Core texts (9)	PRL-a (4) PRL-t (3)	Place (3)	Time (3)	M/F	Form (3)	Summative assessments
Aug–Jan (Y1)	Readers, writers, and texts	Memory *(Identity, Representation)*	1 Mahmoud Darwish poetry (+ excerpts of his memoir, *Memory for Forgetfulness*)	PRL-t Arabic	Palest (Mid E)	20/21c	M	Poetry (Non-fiction)	Mock P1 LP mark
			2 *Chronicle of a Death Foretold*, Gabriel G. Marquez	PRL-t Spanish	Colum (SA)	20c 1981	M	Fiction	
Feb–Apr (Y1)	Time and space	Women and Work *(Identity, Perspective, Communication)*	3 *Orlando: A Biography*, Virginia Woolf	PRL-a	Eng (Eur)	20c 1928	F	Fiction	Mock IO LP mark
			4 *NW*, Zadie Smith	PRL-a	Eng (Eur)	21c 2012	F	Fiction	
May (Y1)–Sep (Y2)		Grief *(Creativity, Culture, Perspective)*	5 *Kitchen*, Banana Yoshimoto	PRL-t Japanese	Japan (Asi)	20c 1988	F	Fiction	Mock P1 Mock P2 IO (IA)
			6 *As I Lay Dying*, William Faulkner	PRL-a	USA (NA)	20c 1930	M	Fiction	
Oct–Apr (Y2)	Intertextuality: connecting texts	Madness *(Culture, Transformation, Representation)*	7 *Hamlet*, William Shakespeare	PRL-a	Eng (Eur)	17c 1602	M	Drama	
			8 *Things Fall Apart*, Chinua Achebe	FC English	Nig (Afr)	20c 1959	M	Fiction	Mock P1 Mock P2 **P1/P2 exams**
			9 *A Streetcar Named Desire*, Tennessee Williams	FC English	USA (NA)	20c 1947	M	Drama	

■ SL literature sample syllabus rationale

For the SL course, I recommend breaking into four conceptual focus areas, since you probably have less contact time with students. You can look at roughly one per semester. You could also move one of the texts from the middle area of exploration to the last.

The first focus area here, **memory**, connects students immediately with a way of knowing (WOK) in the TOK course and a couple of texts that work well for close analysis preparation. You could equally choose another poet besides or in addition to Darwish, who process memory, of themselves or a group of people, in the medium of poetry. Darwish's death a few years ago also generated a lot of beautiful secondary source writing on a great poet from Palestine. Marquez's frequently-taught novel has easy symbols and allusions with rich prose. It is short, accessible and debate generating. Memory here is tackled through the perspectives of witnesses to a crime and their recollections of what leads up to it. Though the novel is an often-seen choice for the DP courses, I recommend *not* using it later as a Paper 2 text. As an examiner, I have seen many poor interpretations of this novel that often go too far into religious ideas that wrongly simplify the text into moral binaries. However, the creative approach to multiple narrative perspectives will help prepare students for the Smith and Faulkner novels.

CORE CONNECTIONS

TOK – WOK as focus areas

Memory, like language, is another one of the ways of knowing (WOK). By using the WOK as a focus area, you automatically have a TOK connection, and one that is signposted for your students. Memory has a strong relationship with writing, most explicitly in memoirs but also as a way of writing novels, travel essays and poetry. Many texts on the PRL-a and PRL-t focus on memory, such as Orhan Pamuk's *Istanbul: Memories and the City*, often combining sensory experiences with memory. A set of essays I often use with TOK students but that you could likewise use in your classroom is called: *The Man Who Mistook His Wife for a Hat and Other Clinical Tales* (1985) by the neurologist Oliver Sacks. You might choose to use a single essay to highlight some aspect of memory for your students and simultaneously work within a different text type. Likewise, extension texts of core authors you might study can provide relevance through the genre of memoir. For example, Ernest Hemingway's memoir of Paris, *A Moveable Feast* (1964), is filled with narrative and sensory experiences that help us understand the way Hemingway saw the world.

Sense perception is yet another WOK that could be used as a focus on your syllabus. Additionally, Diane Ackerman's *A Natural History of the Senses* (1990) gives a diverse literary approach to understanding the five senses. Any WOK would make a good focus for your syllabus; they are:

- language
- memory
- sense perception
- emotion
- reason
- imagination
- faith
- intuition.

> Likewise, interaction with another area of knowledge may be an interesting way to look at one of the IB concepts. Ethics as an area of knowledge has no subject home base in the IB and should be carefully spread throughout the subjects. You will no doubt talk about ethics in your course at various times and this could be a focus of one section, or you could extend ethics to look at the law or morals (see the law and literature focus alternative on page 49).

Women and work is a great way to explore **sex and power** in society over time. Woolf's novel explores personal identity through a sex-changing time traveller. Through the changes in the character's sex and titles, but with a continuous internal identity, Woolf explores the way external factors impact an individual. You can begin by using excerpts of Woolf's 'A Room of One's Own' to discuss the female author's relationship with money and power. To what extent does she have autonomy? How do female voices change our understanding of history or humanity? These explicit questions in the essay can be used to help students understand the more difficult novel. Smith's *NW* looks instead at several female identities in north west London in relation to their urban environment. A consideration of the two together allows us to think about how much has changed. Does a poor upbringing presuppose a woman's invisibility these days or can she surpass it?

Alternatively, for explorations of the difference between **sex** and **gender** as well as sexual and gender identity, *Orlando* and *Middlesex* would also make a beautiful pairing. If you make this switch, you would just have to replace one of the other FC with a PRL text. Written nearly a century apart, the latter novel depicts a hermaphroditic teen in a bildungsroman. Woolf proves so often her timelessness with this now hot topic of media and literary dialogue, one that your students will no doubt enjoy reading about. Tilda Swinton's portrayal of Orlando in the 1992 film is beautiful and witty, too. Following this focus, you will have two PRL-t texts and two texts in English for a balanced IO preparation.

What I like about the two **grief** novels is that they are both also funny and optimistic. They have their serious and even tragic moments, but their richness is sure to get a good response from the teens in your room. *Kitchen* is a teen love story after loss, but one deep with sensory imagery and discussion of Japanese food … a great excuse to take a little trip to a Japanese restaurant with your students. *As I Lay Dying* could likewise be used for any focus area about **perspective** or narrative structures, since each chapter takes us to a different family or community member reacting to a woman's funeral, including her own voice. Faulkner is a quintessential entry to the Southern Gothic genre.

Finally, **madness** brings up so many wonderful psychological and societal questions. Beyond the ones listed here, Joseph Conrad's *Heart of Darkness* (1899), Sylvia Plath's *The Bell Jar* (1963), Charlotte Brontë's *Jane Eyre* (1847) and Ken Kesey's *One Flew Over the Cuckoo's Nest* (1962) would all be good choices. You will quickly see that there are likewise many interesting film pairings you could use, helping those who are not native speakers or who process better visually.

HL language and literature

Sample HL language and literature syllabus for English A

When	Area of exploration	Concept focus	Core texts (6) + Non-literary	PRL-a (2) PRL-t (2)	Place (3)	Time (3)	M/F	Form (3)/text type (6)	Summative assessments
Aug–Jan (Y1)	Readers, writers, and texts	Censorship (Communication, Perspective, Representation)	1 *The Thief and the Dogs*, Naguib Mahfouz	FC Arabic	Egypt (Afr)	20c 1961	M	Fiction	
			2 *Balzac and the Little Chinese Seamstress*, Dai Sijie	PRL-t French	China (Asi)	21c 2000	M	Fiction	Mock P1 LP mark
			NL propaganda, advertisements	–	–	20c	M/F	Advertising posters, pamphlets	
			NL comparing news articles through world	–	–	21c	M/F	News articles, editorials	
Feb–Apr (Y1)		Writing the city (Creativity, Culture, Transformation)	3 *City of Glass*, Paul Auster + graphic novel adaptation	FC English	USA (NA)	20–21c 1985 + 2004	M	Fiction	Mock IO LP mark
			NL Travel writing	–	–	20–21c	F/M	Essays, blogs	
	Time and space	Civil disobedience (Identity, Communication)	4 *Yesi (PK Leung) poetry*	PRL-t Cantonese	HK (Asi)	20–21c	M	Poetry	Mock P2 IO (IA) HL Essay draft
May (Y1)– Sep (Y2)			NL essays on passive resistance over time	–	–	19–21c	F/M	Persuasive essays, letters and speeches	
			NL social media campaigns	–	–	21c	F/M	Youtube.com, Twitter, Facebook	
Oct–Nov (Y2)	Intertextuality: connecting texts	Truth and lies (Perspective, Representation)	NL social media as reality; *Catfish* film	–	–	21c	F/M	Film, social media	**HL Essay**
			NL fake news/political texts	–	–	20–21c	F/M	Political editorials, websites, satire	Mock P1
Dec–Apr (Y2)		Criminals (Identity, Transformation)	5 *The Crucible*, Arthur Miller	PRL-a	USA (NA)	20c 1953	M	Drama	Mock P2 Mock P1
			6 *Northanger Abbey*, Jane Austen	PRL-a	Eng (Eur)	19c 1803	F	Fiction	**P1/P2 exams**

■ HL language and literature sample syllabus rationale

In language and literature planning, some teachers leave the non-literary texts to later decisions, even spontaneous ones. Keep a lot of flexibility with what you might bring in, although it is a mistake not to plan through the minimum of text types the IB requires. This syllabus has 16, many of which can also be broken into sub-categories. This should really be closer to your minimum to fully prepare students for Paper 1 and truly give them a range of texts they can analyse that are part of a common human experience and likely related to their university subjects or jobs.

You are also able to divide your focus areas into solely non-literary or literary texts. Combining them achieves a fuller conceptual learning experience. It is meaningful to more fully develop topics brought up in a text in a classical genre through the non-literary texts.

We start here with **censorship** by going to Egypt and China in novel form and then anywhere in the world you and your students find interesting to study. Constantly new regulations by governments or self-censorship due to political or financial allegiances and gains are impacting media, and therefore the public, around the globe. This is a great way for students to understand themselves and others as 'readers' and what that really means for all of us.

More specific than the **topographies** focus suggested for the HL literature course, here we look at **writing the city**. The focus, or even concept, of the city is one that has evolved over centuries. We can see it vividly in all art forms. Here, I suggest especially travel writing and Auster's *City of Glass*, where a pseudo-detective Cold War novel traces a protagonist's reciprocal relationship with city spaces – the labyrinth of the New York streets, his urban apartment and Central Park benches. Further, the graphic novel adaptation is good, giving you another genre to study and an entry into looking at other visual elements of texts in advertising or media. There is a rich array of other texts you can likewise use here if you want to focus here longer; these will be addressed in a unit planner and learning activities in the next chapter.

I developed work on this focus of **writing the city** with my late supervisor, Dr Esther Cheung, at The University of Hong Kong where I helped to teach a course of the same name. Hong Kong is a distinctive and rich place for students to think about as uniquely urban and all things associated with that: proximity, ghostliness, destruction/construction, noise, ironic isolation and more. A poet who captures this city well is Yesi (also known in Hong Kong as PK Leung or Leung Ping Kwan). Here, I use his poetry as a bridge text to continue the focus on **writing the city** but it also brings us to the political context of Hong Kong. I helped with a few celebrations of his work while he was battling cancer, first doing a bilingual poetry reading with the poet, then creating a dance with a PhD classmate. I mentioned earlier the importance of teaching writers you are passionate about; being passionate about Yesi's poetry and using these unique experiences make my descriptions of the man come to life for my students. Do something that you have some personal connection to if you can.

How do writers reflect and create the city? How can we analyse political signs and art? How does the setting change our reading of the language on the signs? What is the relationship between these handmade signs and posts that you might see on social media? (Admiralty, Hong Kong, 2014)

The political context of Hong Kong was one I developed in the classroom to look at the Umbrella Movement (and ongoing related protest, media and art) in the form of social media and protest campaigns as types of **civil disobedience**. You can do this also with any type of protest that has used social media as a forum. The Arab Spring is another good one and connects to the first novel by Mahfouz suggested for this course. It is a great way to teach Twitter and hashtags – both started by journalists to the surprise of most students. You could orient students in this type of political protest first through Henry David Thoreau's essay on the topic and follow up with 20th century figures of passive resistance such as Martin Luther King, Jr, Mahatma Gandhi and French students in May 1968. The point is not to pick sides here or find political solutions. Instead, use the texts to understand the movements as well as different perspectives. Many letters from prison cells – including those of King and Nelson Mandela – also exist to add another text type and perspective to the discussion, perhaps in comparison to the 'prison discourse' on Instagram or Twitter today.

The next section on **truth and lies** brings us into the current topic of fake news or the post-truth era, but one that has truly been around for a long time. You can look at all types of media here: satire, mainstream news television, political speeches, etc, which presents an easy TOK connection. The dialogue of what is truthful in newspapers also links back nicely to part of your first novel, *The Thief and the Dogs*. *Catfish* is a documentary in which the filmmaker is duped by a woman who creates several fake Facebook profiles. This allows you to look at social media's production of reality, which can be dangerous and psychologically damaging. The term 'getting catfished', or tricked by a fake online persona, is likely a familiar term for students and comes from the film. This focus creates a great life-learning discussion for students who are busily working on their social media personas.

In the final focus area, you can use a cycle-back method that may be useful to you if you spread your literary texts throughout the two years. At this time in the course, you want to prepare your students for the Paper 2 exam and will need several possible texts to prepare for comparative writing. You can go back and use any or all of the first three literary works again in relation to **criminals**, since they all quite explicitly deal with them. The first novel is from the perspective of a recently released criminal; the second deals with crimes of the Cultural Revolution; the third is a pseudo-detective novel. Use them to compare to *The Crucible* where crime is fabricated and the 'witnesses' to witchcraft become the true criminals. There is a strong bridge to the previous **truth and lies** focus, and if you have time, you can go deeper into the allegorical focus on McCarthyism and censorship (which will be its focus in the next syllabus). If you wanted to include a Shakespeare text, *Othello* would be a good bridge between the last two concept foci. Austen's gothic novel, *Northanger Abbey*, may pair nicely with Auster's in its reworking of what it means to be a detective story and what we are really learning about the characters through the crimes. Truman Capote's *In Cold Blood* (1966), a creepy non-fiction text that takes us into the psyche of killers, Fyodor Dostoyevsky's *Crime and Punishment* (1866) and Bret Easton Ellis' *American Psycho* (1991) all take us to the perspective of killers themselves to learn something about humanity and society. Austen and Ellis' novels have an interesting connection in a rejection of class, which may make a nice Paper 2 comparison as well.

Some will find it easier to include literary form comparison in preparation for the Paper 2 if their background is solely on the previous literature course, where genre was a main focus of the exam. You may find it easier to make that decision after reading Chapter 6, Approaching assessments. It is still possible to use this element of comparison as an aspect of the paper, but the focus will be conceptual. The focus areas will guide you more toward what your students need. Additionally, the way we will look at critical theory in Chapter 4 can help you to provide layers of perspectives and thesis angles for approaching comparison and responses to Paper 2 questions.

GLOBAL ISSUES

Including the political in your course

Several parts here have the possibility of including powerful political topics in your classroom. Though these can be oscillating forces, that is exactly why I encourage you to open the topics to your students. For this reason, we examine concepts and focus areas rather than themes. A theme should offer a lesson or opinion; it must include a predicate to articulate a point. If your course were organized around themes, you would be telling your students what to think or at least offering an opinion. Instead, concepts and focus areas are like pivot points for you and your students to use for reading and conversation, where they can arrive at their own conclusions. Notice that the IB uses questions to follow their three main areas of exploration rather than statements. The learning outcomes of the course are more about how the student learns and can be open to viewing the world rather than telling them (or you) how to think.

Minor political voices, topics of gender and sexual **identity** and ways of looking at violence and criminals may all be difficult and often politicized focus areas. Further, in the **civil disobedience** focus, I encourage you to tackle an issue being debated in the news while you teach. Some topics as such are never really finished and constantly evolve and recur in the media. When I was teaching in Hong Kong, the Umbrella Revolution was sprung. Some said to leave it out of the classroom, but some of my students were going to demonstrations, and my classmates and professors at the university were heavily involved. Even if we were not protesting ourselves, it affected transport to work and the outcomes threatened to impact education (especially the languages of education in Hong Kong), free media and university student and professor rights, among other things. We had many perspectives in class: rebellious, nonchalance and pro-Mainland. Students considered the economy, political ideologies, human rights and history – a poignant moment arrived when a student shared the view of her policeman father and her own fears for him. If you are considering something else, like the recent #MeToo movement, you will likewise have different opinions shaped by students' personal experiences and ideological, religious or cultural perspectives. You need to encourage these different opinions to come out in the classroom in a safe environment. It can only work effectively if mutual respect with your students and classroom essential agreements have been established.

'Hot topics' need to be carefully structured and managed. In Chapter 3, I recommend ways to guide student inquiry toward a structured debate. Students must assume roles often different than their existing opinions (or those of their parents). Your role is to allow the conversation, show students where to find information, teach them how to discern it and to ask the difficult questions. Students are likely thinking about these topics anyway; sometimes there is more harm in allowing them to hear of them in an unfiltered space or, alternatively, in a narrowly filtered funnel of information. Your students may find some of these topics difficult at first, but in the end, they will thank you for it. I have had great experiences in my own classroom discussing Black Lives Matter following Harper Lee's *To Kill a Mockingbird* (1960) and the subject of suicide after Sophocles' *Antigone* (442 BC). Both topics have prompted further engaging and lively debate around the death penalty and abortion. I present more activities you can use in this manner in the next chapter, but it is important to keep this aspect in mind as you design your course. Topics will pop up tangentially throughout the two years, no doubt, but designing some political challenges along the way will motivate your students to read the literature, even if it is difficult or 'old' or written by someone they see as different from themselves.

■ SL language and literature

■ Sample SL language and literature syllabus for English A

When	Area of exploration	Concept focus	Core texts (4) + non-literary	PRL-a (1) PRL-t (1)	Place (2)	Time (2)	M/F	Form (2)/Text type (6)	Summative assessments
Aug–Jan (Y1)	Readers, writers, and texts	Black in America (*Identity, Culture, Representation*)	1 *Huckleberry Finn*, Mark Twain	PRL-a	USA (NA)	19c 1884	M	Fiction	Mock P1 LP mark
			NL 'If Black English Isn't a Language, Then Tell Me, What Is?' James Baldwin*	–	USA (NA)	20c	M	Essay	
			NL #BlackLivesMatter movement	–	USA (NA)	21c	M/F	News articles, social media	
		Evolution of journalism (*Transformation, Communication*)	NL Print news, 'unbiased' reporting, New Journalism	–	–	20c	M/F	20c news articles, headlines, photos, captions, etc	Mock IO LP mark
			NL Web-based news: multimedia, listicles, 'Snowfall' (NY Times)	–	–	21c	M/F	Web-based news, multimedia, web genres	
May (Y1)–Sep (Y2)	Time and space	Power of the media (*Representation, Creativity, Perspective*)	2 *The Crucible*, Arthur Miller	PRL-a	USA (NA)	20c 1953	M	Drama	Mock P1 Mock P2 **IO (IA)**
			NL *Good Night, and Good Luck*, 'terrorist hunt' articles and satire	–	–	21c	M/F	Film News articles Satire	
			3 Carol Ann Duffy poetry	PRL-a	Scot (Eur)	20/21c	F	Poetry	
Oct–Apr (Y2)	Intertextuality: connecting texts	Identities (*Identity, Creativity, Culture*)	4 *Persepolis*, Marjane Satrapi	PRL-t French	Iran (Mid E)	21c 2000	F	Graphic novel/autobiography	Mock P1 Mock P2 **P1/P2 exams**
			NL Women in ads, #MeToo movement	–	–	20/21c	M/F	Advertising, social media	

* Both James Baldwin's essays and Kendrick Lamar's song lyrics can be used as PRL literary texts here if you choose to include additional essays or songs to your course. See page 56 for more explanation, this is when I go into detail on the unit.

■ SL language and literature sample syllabus rationale

In this course, you are pretty limited with how you divide up your literary texts, since you only have four and must use one for each area of exploration. You will probably want to study at least two at the end of the course and can use the cycle-back method discussed for the HL course to allow students to use any of the four texts for Paper 2.

Our first focus is **Black in America**, which can mean a lot of things, but here focuses on 'Black English', subversive texts and social media campaigns in relation to Black history and **identity** in the USA. [Note: here we capitalize 'Black' as an ethnic identity rather than racial designation, having taken the place of African-American in US discourse (see Braganza, 2016; Perlman, 2018; and Tharps, 2014). This could also be an interesting investigation and debate in class.] Alternatively, make the first part 'Englishes' or 'Chineses' or whatever your language A is, or look at a different minority group in another culture or nation. *Huckleberry Finn* is a great way to explore dialect and the political power of language. The text's subversive nature, child **perspective** and even use of the 'N-word' are important topics of conversation for your students. For this reason, it is also popular in many other languages, though one might find it difficult to translate. China particularly has a huge affinity for the text, and China likewise has an interesting relationship with a dominant Chinese language (Putongua or Mandarin) and other dialects that Beijing is trying to phase out (at least as official languages). This has been done with other languages in the past, such as Parisian French. There is ample room for debate around the pros and cons of streamlining vs. diversifying language and the value of dialect vs. a common official language. These conversations can, of course, all be connected to **culture**.

'Englishes' are an interesting topic as well. Look at Singlish in Singapore as an example of the types of English in the USA vs. England vs. Ireland vs. Australia … the list goes on before you even get to English as a second language, which has become almost something entirely different. Why has English become such a dominant second language? Why is it so important for travel and business? Why has it become the most used language of the internet? What is the point of having other languages still? What is the point of other second languages? These are great topics and ones that are likely to be central to language and literature Paper 1 exams. Additionally, they connect easily to the TOK Way of Knowing: Language.

Again, it depends on your interests, who is in your room and what is going on in the world as you design your classroom experience. Students are likely to enjoy learning about whatever the buzz on the street is.

No doubt you will teach elements of journalism, so looking at the **evolution of journalism** can be a meaningful way to understand the transitions to New Journalism in the 20th century and then to web-based journalism in the 21st. You can look at both **transformation** and **representation** concepts here. So many new specific text types have been created since web-based journalism began and each has a specific purpose and target audience. You cannot study them all, but you can do an interesting survey while investigating a topic that interests those in your class. I recommend looking at *The New York Times*' collaborative multimedia story called 'Snow Fall: The Avalanche at Tunnel Creek' about a devastating avalanche (you can visit it via the QR code).

The text is known as a game-changer for its beauty (despite the tragic nature of the text) and its many types of media all joined together: GIF, oral and video interviews, written texts, hyperlinks and scientific reports. The same newspaper has a collection through their website of other articles they have created like this that your students can explore. This publication is often noted for its excellent multimedia stories that combine thorough investigation, multiple perspectives and visual learning experience (see, Annie Schuggart's 'The best in interactive multimedia journalism 2017: pushing the limits of storytelling',

2017). It is also important to understand how web-based media changes readership and business models and how that impacts what is actually reported or what ends up in front of your eyes to be read.

Now that your students understand the development of journalism, they can look more generally at the **power of the media**, for good and for bad. Here we look at Miller's allegory in a different way than the HL course, focusing more on the McCarthy elements Miller proposed. You can look at historical media from this time and then show the phenomenal film from George Clooney: *Good Night, and Good Luck*, about the power of Ed Murrow's broadcasts in bringing down the 'witch-hunting' senator. The film also includes several speeches you can analyse. You can then find many articles from this century referring to terrorist arrests as 'witch hunts' and may even find parallels to current discourse around authoritarian governments.

Finally, in **intertextuality**, we look at **identities,** which could likewise fit nicely in the first part but more easily allows you to bring in several literary texts before the Paper 2. One way to use the feminist theory lens here with the literary texts is to also include the #MeToo movement and women in advertising, looking at social media and advertising as further text types before Paper 1. Duffy's poetry looks at society but also often comes back to personal stories and relationships. Satrapi's graphic novel is also a memoir, bringing a look at cultural identity into the mix through the author's upbringing in Iran and subsequent move to Austria. Many literary texts work well with identity. Some of my favourites are the aforementioned *Middlesex, Orlando* and *The Unbearable Lightness of Being,* as well as Zadie Smith's *White Teeth* (2000).

■ Nine more focus ideas

You might like a syllabus that has been mentioned on the previous pages but want to substitute a focus of your own or one of the ideas below. Play around! Use these as a spring board to create something else. You may have noticed there are some texts I have mentioned multiple times, and you will see some of them again in the chart below. Rather than limit you, this strategy is to show how you can develop several versatile texts to allow for movement within your syllabus and topics without completely reinventing the wheel.

Of course, the texts listed here are not nearly exhaustive. Just make sure you go back to the checklist of considerations (page 26) once you have a draft. Some of these extra ten focus ideas will be referred to and developed further in the following chapters, when I look at examples of conceptual learning and approaching assessment. You can apply them to either course. Likewise, as I expand on some of the foci we have discussed already as units of study, I offer different texts or angles to help your students access the big ideas.

Conceptual focus ideas

Area of exploration	Focus	Text ideas
Readers, writers, and texts	**The body** (or specifically sport, mind–body connection or female body as muse) (*Identity, Representation*)	**Fiction:** ■ *Island* (Huxley, 1962) ■ *The Stones of Florence* (M. McCarthy, 1959) ■ *The Sailor Who Fell from Grace with the Sea* (Mishima, 1963) **Non-fiction:** ■ *What I Talk about when I Talk about Running* (Murakami, 2007) ■ 'Roger Federer as Religious Experience' (Wallace, 2006) ■ *Eat Sweat Play: How Sport Can Change Our Lives* (Anna Kessel, 2016) ■ Advertising campaigns: Dove, women's hygiene products, sport, smoking, alcohol … ■ 'The female nude' in painting, poetry, film, etc
	Violence (*Culture, Perspective*)	**Fiction:** ■ *Blood Meridian* (C. McCarthy, 1985) ■ *The Handmaid's Tale* (Atwood, 1985) ■ *The Vegetarian* (Han Kang, 2007) **Drama:** ■ *King Lear* (Shakespeare, 1606) ■ *A Streetcar Named Desire* (Williams, 1947) ■ *Death and the Maiden* (Dorfman, 1991) ■ *Antigone* (Sophocles, 442 BC) **Non-fiction:** ■ *In Cold Blood* (Capote, 1966) ■ *Death in the Afternoon* (Hemingway, 1932) ■ *The Tokyo Gas Attack and the Japanese Psyche* (Murakami, 1997) ■ News reporting of terrorism and shootings ■ Editorials and op-ed on the death penalty
	Englishes (or your language A and its dialects) (*Culture, Communication, Representation*)	**Fiction:** ■ *Super Sad True Love Story* (Shteyngart, 2010) *Huckleberry Finn* (Twain, 1884) ■ *Native Speaker* (Chang Rae-Lee, 1995) **Non-fiction:** ■ 'Authority and American Usage' (Wallace, 2001) ■ *On Language* (Chomsky, 2003) ■ 'If Black English Isn't a Language, Then Tell Me What Is?' (Baldwin, 1979) ■ News articles and travel essays on Singlish, English words being used in other languages (including French and Cantonese)
Time and space	**War** (or **Revolution**) (*Transformation, Identity*)	**Fiction:** ■ *The Unbearable Lightness of Being* (Kundera, 1984) ■ *A Tale of Two Cities* (Dickens, 1859) ■ *The Things they Carried* (O'Brien, 1990) ■ *Catch 22* (Heller, 1961) **Non-fiction:** ■ Philosophical writing on revolutions ■ *The Motorcycle Diaries* (Guevara, 1995, and 2004 film) ■ Post-9/11 discourse (novels, news articles, immigration now, refugees and borders) **Poetry:** ■ Dunya Mikhail (Iraq), Du Fu (China), Wilfred Owen (England)

Area of exploration	Focus	Text ideas
Time and space	**Japan** (or any country) (*Culture, Perspective, Representation*)	**Novels:** ■ *The Sailor Who Fell from Grace with the Sea* (Mishima, 1963) ■ *Kafka on the Shore* (Murakami, 2002) ■ *Kitchen* (Yoshimoto, 1988) ■ *Kokoro* (Soseki, 1914) **Non-fiction:** ■ *The Tokyo Gas Attack and the Japanese Psyche* (Murakami, 1997) ■ Accompanying media related to the gas attacks ■ Essays on Japanese travel and food **Poetry:** ■ Basho, Minoru Yoshioka, Rynūchi Tamara
	Postmodernism (or any artistic movement) (*Creativity, Transformation*)	**Fiction:** ■ *White Noise* (DeLillo, 1985) ■ *Extremely Loud and Incredibly Close* (Foer, 2005) ■ *The Savage Detective* (Bolaño, 1998) ■ *A Visit from the Goon Squad* (Egan, 2010) ■ *NW* (Smith, 2012) ■ *To the Lighthouse* (Woolf, 1927) ■ *4321* (Auster, 2017) **Non-fiction:** ■ *Consider the Lobster* (Wallace, 2005) ■ *The Book of Embraces* (Eduardo Galeano, 1989) ■ *Alfred and Emily* (Lessing, 2008 – part fiction/non-fiction) **Poetry:** ■ Inua Ellams (UK/Nigeria) ■ Kate Tempest (UK) ■ Samantha Barendson (France; trilingual!) ■ Ben Okri (Nigeria)
Intertextuality: connecting texts	**Law and literature** (*Representation, Communication*)	**Fiction:** ■ 'Before the Law' and 'In the Penal Colony' (Kafka, 1915/1919) ■ *Billy Budd, Sailor*, 'Bartleby, the Scrivener' and 'Beneto Cereno' (Melville, 1924/1853/1855) ■ *Crime and Punishment* (Dostoyevsky, 1866) ■ *Chronicle of a Death Foretold* (Marquez, 1981) **Drama:** ■ *Antigone* (Sophocles, 442 BC) ■ *King Lear* (Shakespeare, 1606) ■ *Hamlet* (Shakespeare, 1601) ■ *The Crucible* (Miller, 1953) **Non-fiction:** ■ *In Cold Blood* (Capote, 1966) ■ *Irish Peacock and Scarlet Marquess: The Real Trial of Oscar Wilde* (compiled by Merlyn Holland, 2003) **Film:** ■ *Philadelphia, I Do, Here and There* **Media and social media:** ■ Black Lives Matter ■ #MeToo ■ Religious 'law' within constraints of government laws (unless theocracy) – religious texts or media coverage

Area of exploration	Focus	Text ideas
Intertextuality: connecting text	**Adaptation** (*Transformation, Creativity*)	■ Jane Austen: 1813 novel *Pride and Prejudice* (television show; films, including BBC, Bollywood's *Bride and Prejudice* and *Pride and Prejudice Zombies*) ■ Paul Auster: 1985 novel *City of Glass,* and graphic novel adaptation (Coughlin, 2006), *Smoke* – op-ed/short story by Auster (*New York Times*, 'Dec. 25, 1990: A Brooklyn Story') and film adaptation with Wayne Wang ■ Zhang Aileen (Eileen Chang): 1943 novel *Love in a Fallen City* and film adaptation (1984) by Ann Hui; 1979 novella *Lust, Caution* and film adaptation (2007) by Ang Lee ■ William Shakespeare: 1604 play *Othello,* direct film adaptations and *O* film set on high school basketball courts (many other Shakespearean examples)
	Exile (or *migration*) (*Identity, Communication, Perspective*)	**Fiction:** ■ *Balzac and the Little Chinese Seamstress* (Dai Sijie, 2000) ■ *Snow* (Pamuk, 2002) ■ *The Writer as Migrant* (Ha Jin, 2008) ■ *Broken April* (Kadare, 1978) ■ *The Unbearable Lightness of Being* (Kundera, 1984) ■ *Exit West* (Hamid, 2017) **Non-fiction:** ■ *Nothing to Envy* (Demick, 2009) ■ Media/advertising/propaganda/political speeches on the topic, specifically relating to the place you are studying in a lengthier text **Poetry:** ■ Federico Garcia Lorca, Mahmoud Darwish

Timing and unit planning

The plans we have just gone through have suggested rough timelines, but you will eventually want to break this down further for your own sanity and that of your students. Making a clear week-by-week plan, but one that is adaptable to unexpected needs, absences or desires, is essential. You can revise at the end of each semester or every couple of months based on how everything is progressing.

The pacing of the course will feel more natural after you have taught it in entirety. Until you have done so, you may want to have more frequent check-ins, going back to these plans and considering where you are at. Perhaps it is a Google doc your students can access, or it is posted monthly on a bulletin board. If you are behind, at least you know how behind you are. You can choose a shorter text, assign summer reading or speed up the tangents in your classroom. You could even have extra help sessions if you find a few students need help to catch up with a certain skill or content.

As we go through conceptually-based teaching strategies and ways to work toward the summative assessments strategically and effectively, you will gain tools to help you navigate this timing. Likewise, as you review your timing, if you are ahead, you can take more time on some of the suggested activities and creative elements of the course or include further extension texts, including films, articles or other mediums of art to round out the concepts and focus areas.

■ Can you teach the full course in one year?

Although not ideal, it is possible to teach the entire course in a year. Teachers sometimes ask me this in workshops due to limitations they are given with self-taught students or students who decide to do a second language A at a much later time (perhaps due to university choices). I have also had the experience of inheriting second year DP students from other schools who are either unprepared or have somehow forgotten everything they have accomplished in the first year.

So, can it be done? Yes, though it partially depends on decisions about course changes and IA work in your school and specifically from your DP coordinator. However, if you are forced to go this route, a few small changes can go a long way. Firstly, teach the shortest texts with the biggest value. This might seem obvious at first, but most importantly it need not dumb down the course. You can teach a set of short stories or poetry, for example, with minimal reading required. There may be loads packed into a page or two (think of a Shakespearean sonnet or a short story from Borges). There are also some excellent short dramas, for example, that can stand as a full text. If you are not sure if your text is long enough to 'count', write to IB Answers for a response in black and white.

You will not have time to analyse every page, or even every story or poem, in a tight timeline. Nor should you, however! Give your students a taste. Some will play it safe and pick more straightforward topics for their IO and HL essay, but others will dive deeper into an area you only briefly touch on. You will have the chance for checks and balances in the outlining and conferencing sessions before each of these assessments, so try not to worry about students who go too rogue. There is time to reign them in if needed. You will want students to complete these two assessments (if they are completing the HL course) by halfway through your time with them and include mock Paper 1 and Paper 2 that you have built toward in the learner portfolio work they have done. (More on this in Chapter 6.) So, if you start with your students in August for the May exams, aim for this work to all be finished by the end of November or December at the latest. Even if you have not met your student(s) before the summer, see if you are able to get their contact details to set them up with some summer reading.

All of the texts you complete by November, your students can hypothetically still use for the Paper 2 as long as they have not used them for the IO or HL essay. We will look at how to narrow preparation for this comparative essay anyway. In the meantime, remember you have flexibility. You will then complete the other texts between November and April, or ideally March with April solely for preparation and synthesis. Do not be afraid to additionally set some texts as reading on their own. Texts you think will be easier to access or are more useful for connections and practice rather than the actual Paper 2 should be the ones you devote less time to in class. Again, none of this is ideal, but it can work out. When you need to rely on students to do more of the preparation on their own, it is an even better idea to get them involved in choosing the texts or topics of study. They need to be especially motivated. And most importantly, even if you are worried, enthuse your students with confidence that all this can indeed be done!

Finally, drop some of the more creative formative assessments that I will go over later. Though these are valuable for exam marks as well as motivation and a deeper understanding beyond the classroom, you have to be more practical. Offer creative possibilities in the learner portfolio without much structure to let students play around with ideas as much as they have time for. Focus in on their specific needs and offer extra support or assign formative assessments that address these needs.

As the next chapter goes deeper into unit planning and CBL best practice, find a skeletal must-do for your course and, if time allows, add more of the rich extension and creative approaches.

Developing a concept-based learning course

What is the point of concept-based learning?

By now, if concept-based learning (CBL) is new to you, you have had a brief description of what it is and have seen the overview of requirements and suggestions about how to incorporate CBL structurally into your DP language A course and units. And if CBL is already something you have been using in other courses or grappled with for the current IB DP syllabus, you hopefully have some ideas about further possibilities of its use with your students.

However, you still might be asking yourself what CBL could add to a senior syllabus already rich with the study of language and literature. You might be wondering why the IB has added another layer of requirement to the course when language A has become so many things, included so many text types and encouraged focus on so many cultures, peoples, languages, nationalities … the list goes on.

The answer is that CBL, when used effectively, strategically organizes the many elements of your course while providing a greater sense of purpose in everything you do. Consider remarks you may have heard from students:

> All that analysis killed the book I read in English class!

> Ugh, my teacher makes reading such hard work.

> What is the point of this old stuff we read?

> My parents say science is much more useful and important than French class.

With a well-designed CBL course, however, you can avoid these comments and motivate your students to enjoy studying your course seriously, no matter what their post-secondary plans are.

This chapter aims to continue the development of your course organization and timeline by demonstrating conceptual unit planners and CBL lessons to further frame your coursework. The approaches to CBL will not be exhaustive; rather they aim to be idea sparking. You teach language and literature after all, so you are creative! Though you can take my ideas and those of CBL researchers, workshop leaders and writers, the course in your classroom is that of you and your students. Just remember to frequently go back to the guide and the streamlined charts and guidelines in this book to make sure you have not missed something your students will need to successfully complete the course without penalties.

Some people may still think concept-based learning is wishy-washy. It is easy to misunderstand it, and I had precisely this concern when I was first forced to attend a workshop on the pedagogy. We don't really need the H. Lynn Erickson-coined phrase to teach in this way, but she does do a good job of explaining what it is and its importance. I was lucky enough to see her speak in Hong Kong, but you don't need to spend thousands to travel to one of her workshops. You may want to have a look at her original book, *Concept-based Curriculum and Instruction for the Thinking Classroom* (2006), or her presentation for the IB that you can find online: 'Synergistic Thinking and Conceptual Understanding in the IB Programmes' (2011) if you have not had previous training. You may find some of her writing and that of other CBL researchers more pertinent to the primary years or younger years of secondary. Again, you may have to be creative about how to transfer the ideas to your older students. Although primary school is where the pedagogy began, concepts have even more power in the later years because of the added focus on content and a larger skills and content base overall. Lois Lanning makes CBL relevant to secondary language A explicitly in *Designing a Concept Based Curriculum for English Language Arts* (2012). She has worked directly with Erickson in transferring this framework to the US Common Core curriculum standards.

Concepts have a foundation of skills and content (Erickson has a cube visual you can search online if it helps you to see it). No one is taking away content! No one is taking away skills! You can still teach literary movements or classics as well as grammar and traditional essays. Nothing is being dumbed down. These are sometimes the complaints, and they are valid if CBL is taught in a wishy-washy way.

We do not want CBL to become an excuse to focus on unguided inquiry, a large choice of texts (where the teacher might not read them with the students) and student ideas claimed in writing without backup through analysis and deep understandings. Pedagogical pendulums are dangerous because people do sometimes use them as an excuse to do something extreme and wrong, either lazy or extremely conservative/liberal, etc. Perhaps it is guided by an economic agenda, as in some charter schools run by private companies. They use 'research' to back it up, but often this research has an extremely small cohort, or the correlational data can be alternatively explained. After all, it is often unethical to disadvantage students by isolating variables in their learning. This is why numerous studies as well as your own trial and error are needed to make a case for larger changes to pedagogy.

Concepts are meant to make the curriculum you study more meaningful, to take it beyond the text and the classroom, to make the content and skills transferable to other subjects and to 'real life', and to help students take ownership of their learning.

Concepts guide the way you design your syllabus and units for the DP language A course. This is essential. However, the possibilities extend to include explicit CBL lessons designed to enhance student learning. In this chapter, we first explore the three required IB areas of exploration and conceptual questions in practice. The sample unit planners come from the topics suggested in the sample syllabi of the last chapter. We investigate how you might approach the conceptual questions through core and extension texts. You will also see connections to critical theory and assessment on the unit planners. For now, there will only be a slight mention of a connection to these components. In Chapter 4, we shall explicitly explore these elements of the unit organizers.

The organizers also demonstrate required connections to the IB core, international mindedness, global issues and ATT and ATL. However, the connections are not exhaustive. For global issues in particular, they should also be generated by your students and take different directions than you may have planned. ATT and ATL are intrinsic in how you teach each day, so there will be much more than the focus areas you link on the planner. TOK connections are also vast, and you can find further supporting questions after each area of exploration in the IB guides.

We will then take a closer look at the explicit CBL lessons and inquiry-based learning, an important component of CBL that helps achieve a dynamic student-centred environment, one that does not sacrifice rigour.

I aim to help you relinquish control by creating an environment where you can trust your students to assist the development of a learning space. The dynamism of what CBL aims to be is dependent on mutual trust between you and your students. A space of risk and respect: a space where no day's lesson is the same, but it requires no extra preparation than normal once you understand how to organize it. In fact, the pedagogy offers ways to cut busy work, focusing instead on purposeful teaching and learning that saves both you and your students time and allows you to function at your best.

You may be familiar with the factual, conceptual and debatable questions from the MYP curriculum as well as Bloom's taxonomy that creates levels of thinking strategies. Although Lanning utilizes both types of questioning in her book on language A, she suggests it is too hierarchical. At least the revised Bloom's taxonomy she reminds us of is more active and connected to 'creating' and knowledge making, rather than a stagnant, linear approach (pages 10–12). Rather than a hierarchized line of questioning, the units here are linked to focus questions of different types and levels. If it helps you to break them up in a different way, that is fine, but IB does not require it at the DP stage.

Erickson and Lanning use several other terms to explain their line of thinking, but what I think is most relevant for us in DP language A is the idea of 'synergistic thinking', which Lanning explains as: 'the cognitive interplay between the lower and conceptual levels of thinking' and goes on to suggest is necessary 'to discern the concepts and conceptual relationships at the heart of the unit; there are no shortcuts' (page 10). In this way, we must organize our units around concepts from the start. After we look at the way to organize content and skills with your concepts, we will investigate several teaching strategies to make these relationships clearly understood in your classroom. Students gain metacognitive skills that they can transfer to other courses and their learning in the future.

With this method of planning, more time and effort goes into preparation of the unit as a whole rather than daily lesson details. These daily lessons can come from a toolkit that includes some of the lessons that follow. However, behind any of these activities that focus on concepts and inquiry is the deeper understanding that the teacher has already arrived at. Of course, your ideas may change and develop as you move through the content with your students again.

This has been a very brief overview of CBL. If you are not familiar with using this pedagogy already, I recommend looking at some of the longer resources before designing your course. Hopefully the more you read, the more it will feel a natural extension of the good teaching you have already been doing and not a burdensome gimmicky pendulum swing. Once you truly understand CBL, you might see that it attempts to bring together *different* pendulum swings (skills, facts, content) toward a more cohesive, but not overwhelming, way of looking at the curriculum as a complete, yet malleable and transferable, entity.

■ Unit planning

A unit plan gives you more than a timeline; it gives you and your students a direction. You can make these plans into hyper-docs that link out to resources students will need, or you can wait and hyperlink your journal assignments, timelines or online platforms. There will be further suggestions later. This plan should give your students a simple overview of the focus and texts in relation to the area of exploration and conceptual questions. Further, a unit plan allows you to: break up where you would like to focus on different critical theory angles, consider which extension texts will be used and what formative activities will especially help your students with their understanding, and work toward summative assessments.

You will find a blank conceptual unit planning template for you to use and adapt on IB Extras: **www.hoddereducation.com/ibextras**

You can follow this kind of unit plan with a timeline, including a reading schedule and assessment deadlines, or you can have a running weekly timeline for the entire semester/ year/course. I recommend setting weekly reading, which includes journal responses, as the only homework besides finishing up any work on assessments that cannot be completed in class, and allowing and encouraging any extension reading. Sometimes students will also work on journals in class. The more you can do during class time, the better. This is both due to time management stress and giving immediate feedback, proven to improve learning. Reading and extension should be the main focus outside of the classroom. Both will take a substantial amount of time and you can guide students more in the classroom.

Most importantly, the following is a conceptual unit plan. It is dependent on the combination of skills and content toward an understanding of a big idea and the creation of themes. If you get these skeletal components right, it will be difficult to mess up the preparation for your students. It will give you an anchor for you both to return to. The syllabus and conceptual unit plans you create (or borrow from here) will be the oil paint on your palette. This kind of paint never really dries, but can create powerful, beautiful and unique images containing messages. This is precisely what you want your students to do, and in the next chapter, we dive into how to teach them to paint with language.

Readers, writers and texts

Recall the IB articulation of this area of exploration by looking at the quote in Chapter 2 (page 20).

In the previous chapter, we talked about using this area of exploration as a more introductory and shorter one than the others. You still have your requirements about a minimum of texts in this section, but I recommend keeping yourself to one topic that will take about three to five months and includes a lot of set up of skills your students will continue to develop later on.

If you choose to use just one topic and conceptual unit here, you will need to cover all six conceptual questions. However, this should not be difficult. As you read through the description, you may alternatively choose to do a mini unit with shorter texts to start in the first one or two months. Whichever way you decide to break it up, try to finish this section by the end of January or your first semester so there is ample time to work on context, which will be needed for the IO and HL essay.

What follows here are two unit plans that each cover all six conceptual questions, one for each of the courses – **beauty** for HL literature and **Black in America** for SL language and literature. We shall move around the courses for the next two areas of exploration. They are expansions of the sample syllabi on pages 34 and 45. Rather than explain each unit fully in detail, the six questions will follow with annotation that includes reference to both sample units. Hopefully, this will be a better way for you to begin to understand the approaches to the specific questions.

CORE CONNECTIONS

TOK and EE – unpacking questions

You may also choose to get your students to unpack the conceptual questions before the course, or individually at the start of different lessons. The ability to unpack questions – to decode meaning and connotations of the language used – is an essential skill for TOK. Students will spend a lot of time with their TOK teachers determining what the TOK questions are truly asking, or what ways they can be interpreted, as well as creating and investigating knowledge questions. In the language A courses, students will additionally need to create their own research questions and lines of inquiry for the IO and HL essay, and will have to unpack conceptual essay questions for Paper 2 without the aid of the teacher or fellow students. Likewise, each student will need to create an EE research question. Making the core connections explicit may help students to more carefully understand the nuances of all the questions they must decipher and decode or create during the DP.

■ HL literature

■ Conceptual unit planning template: Readers, writers and texts

Leonardo da Vinci's *Vitruvian Man*

Area of exploration: Readers, writers and texts Conceptual focus: Beauty (Creativity, Representation)	Conceptual questions:	Summative assessments
	1 Why and how do we study language and literature?	Mock Paper 1 (passage discussed from core texts with use of graphic organizer)
	2 How are we affected by texts in various ways?	Learner portfolio mark
	3 In what ways is meaning constructed, negotiated, expressed and interpreted?	
	4 How does language use vary among text types and among literary forms?	
	5 How does the structure or style of a text affect meaning?	
	6 How do texts offer insights and challenges?	

Core texts	Extension texts	Critical theory	Formative assessments
Frankenstein, Mary Shelley	'Roger Federer as Religious Experience', David Foster Wallace	Formalist	Journal responses in learner portfolio:
The Picture of Dorian Gray, Oscar Wilde	**Excerpts:** *On Beauty*, Zadie Smith; *Their Eyes were Watching God*, Zora Neal Hurston; *Irish Peacock and Scarlet Marquess: the Real Trial of Oscar Wilde*, Merlin Holland; 'Ode on a Grecian Urn', John Keats	Deconstruction	■ creative writing
The Bluest Eye, Toni Morrison (plus her short story in *The New Yorker*: 'Sweetness', 2015)	School primer	Feminist	■ personal opinion
	Articles on genetic engineering and beauty through psychology and sociology angles		■ textual analysis
	Variety of paintings and photography		■ drawing
			■ lexicons
			Oral reader response
			Socratic seminar
			Inquiry presentations
			Create Scoop.it pages
			Oral and group commentaries (P1)
			Critical theory charts

Focus questions: What is the definition of beauty? To what extent is there a universal definition? Is beauty scientifically measurable? Is there a reciprocal relationship between physical and abstract beauty? How does society or the media change our definitions? What else might shape our personal definitions of beauty? What is the definition of ugly? What are the pros and cons of being considered beautiful in our world? How important is it? Are you born beautiful or do you become that way? How is language use and literature beautiful? Can we take bias out of our judgment of beautiful literature? Is the aesthetic the only measure of beauty?

Core connections: TOK: the study of art and its relationship with beauty; looking at other areas of knowledge – art, psychology (human sciences); EE: inquiry and connection between texts; looking at researched articles for examples of formal register	International mindedness: perspectives on and definitions of beauty throughout the world
	Global issues: finding personal beauty, changing perceptions of beauty, the value of beauty

ATT & ATL: digital curation, discussion skills

◼ SL language and literature

◼ Conceptual unit planning template: Readers, writers and texts

Musical artist, Kendrick Lamar

Area of exploration: Readers, writers and texts Conceptual focus: Black in America (*Identity, Culture, Representation*)	Conceptual questions:			Summative assessments
	1 Why and how do we study language and literature? 2 How are we affected by texts in various ways? 3 In what ways is meaning constructed, negotiated, expressed and interpreted? 4 How does language use vary among text types and among literary forms? 5 How does the structure or style of a text affect meaning? 6 How do texts offer insights and challenges?			Mock Paper 1 (passage discussed from core texts with use of graphic organizer) Learner portfolio mark
Core texts	Extension texts	Critical theory	Formative assessments	

Huckleberry Finn, Mark Twain
 	
NL 'If Black English Isn't a Language, Then Tell Me, What Is?', James Baldwin
 	
NL #BlackLivesMatter movement
	Excerpts:
	Giovanni's Room, James Baldwin; 'The Celebrated Jumping Frog of Calaveras County' (and other satirical essays), Mark Twain; *Gender Trouble*, Judith Butler (on linguistic performativity)
	
	Articles on use of 'N-word' in rap songs and examples from lyrics
	
	Subversive texts/satire – article or examples
	
	Selection of poetry and mixed genre in *Chant of Saints*, Michael Harper
	
	Kendrick Lamar lyrics and articles related to Pulitzer Prize reception
	
	'Seven Seconds in the Bronx', Malcolm Gladwell (*Blink*, 2005)
	
	'I don't want to shoot you, brother', Joe Sexton (*ProPublica, 2018*)
		Formalist
		Deconstructionist
		Postcolonial
			Journal responses in learner portfolio:
			  ◼ creative writing
			  ◼ personal opinion
			  ◼ textual analysis
			  ◼ drawing
			  ◼ lexicons
			Oral reader response
			Socratic seminar
			Inquiry presentations
			Create Scoop.it pages
			Oral and group commentaries (P1)
			Critical theory charts	

Focus questions: How do we use language to empower or to hurt? What is the purpose of dialect? Should governments maintain a standard form of a language and for what purpose? Do different racial or cultural identities have their own languages? Does social media create a new language? How do hashtags allow social movements to spread? What part does language and media have in creating an 'us versus them' dichotomy? How can it be broken down (deconstructed)? What does history have to do with language use? To what extent do texts over time create or influence cultural identity? What are the plays and power relationships of major and minor languages? Is it valid/useful/ethical for writers to write from different racial/cultural/gender/national perspectives?

Core connections: EE: the model of inquiry you use with students to discover the impact of the #BlackLivesMatter movement can be used to choose a related movement as a topic of their EE. Another political social media movement that can then analyse language and texts that in some way shape meaning for readers would be a good topic. Also: intuition as WOK in the Gladwell essay.	International mindedness: connect race discourse to South Africa or France
ATT & ATL: differentiated texts; using critical theory; presentation skills	Global issues: value of life, law/ethics/justice, power of language

■ 1 Why and how do we study language and literature?

For this first question, you might start by asking students to come up with what they have learned in language and literature in the past and what the purpose of that knowledge has been. This question could be the framing of your first lesson of the year. Use a brainstorming strategy – perhaps think-pair-share, small group mind-mapping and feedback or oral sharing with a couple of students listing ideas on the board. It should activate knowledge in the room and give you an idea of where your students are coming from.

You may already have a short answer in mind to the question but try to hold off and let the students discover it for themselves. To demonstrate further, take a short text you love that is rich in a certain message about something universal – love, kindness, beauty … hopefully something uplifting and inspirational! Maybe it is a poem or perhaps an excerpt from a memoir – Pamuk, Aciman or Dillard's, for example – or really anything you enjoy. It might be an entry into your first topic and concept or something completely separate. You could alternatively have several of these texts that go with the unit topic and ask groups to work together before a carousel sharing method. Here you are already doing work to prepare for Paper 1, but your students will not know it. Rather than giving them specific things to look for, let them start by transferring the skills they have learned before to new content.

After coming to an answer about the purpose of the text before them, you can go back to the original question. Perhaps ask some follow up questions:

> Why do people write? Why do people work on perfecting their grammar and vocabulary?

> How malleable is language and what are the benefits and drawbacks to this?

> What do we mean by literature?

> What kind of power is there in communication?

> In what ways is the use of language an art form/a method of communication/a power in society/a way to marginalize people?

> What do you hope to get from this course?

You can follow with a passionate speech of your own about the power of language and literature or use a video like John Green's 'How and why we read: Crash Course English Literature #1' (YouTube) and the follow-ups on his CrashCourse YouTube channel, or you can let the ideas and debates rest for you to come back to over the next 20 months or so together. Now let us look at what examples you might use for these units.

■ Beauty (HL literature)

To prompt the above discussion in connection to **beauty**, a few short texts would work very well. Actually, any poem or excerpt from literature you consider beautiful would work. You could even start (or end) with a visual depiction of universal beauty. Leonardo da Vinci's *Vitruvian Man* (page 56), the *Venus de Milo* (page 59) or a photograph of Gigi Hadid (left), or any supermodel your students know, would work well to prompt discussion. As you ask students to explain why or why not the images are beautiful to themselves and to humanity in general, some of the big ideas will emerge. Students will also start to use textual analytical skills unknowingly if you ask them to come up and point out aspects of the structure, details or colour of an image. Most students feel more comfortable commenting on what they see because of our image-rich culture. In this regard, students who often feel less confident with their language and literature skills will begin to find their voices in your classroom.

You could then connect the discourse to the meme from @whitneyzombie on Instagram comparing Amy Schumer to Aphrodite. It brings up other texts in this regard: Twitter,

Gigi Hadid

photography and sculpture as well as Schumer's Instagram feed, stand-up comedy and television series. Her work is often identified as a new kind of empowered feminism, though it likewise offends many people as well. The work is often politically charged, makes use of satire and plays with language, making it ripe for many areas of your syllabus.

Now to connect the question to a literary text, I recommend two short texts, whether you include them as core or extension texts in the way you design your unit. The first is the preface to *The Picture of Dorian Gray*.

Venus de Milo

■ **Extract from *The Picture of Dorian Gray* by Oscar Wilde (1890)**

The Preface

The artist is the creator of beautiful things. To reveal art and conceal the artist is art's aim. The critic is he who can translate into another manner or a new material his impression of beautiful things.

The highest, as the lowest, form of criticism is a mode of autobiography. Those who find ugly meanings in beautiful things are corrupt without being charming. This is a fault.

Those who find beautiful meanings in beautiful things are the cultivated. For these there is hope.

They are the elect to whom beautiful things mean only beauty.

There is no such thing as a moral or an immoral book. Books are well written, or badly written. That is all.

The nineteenth century dislike of realism is the rage of Caliban seeing his own face in a glass.

The nineteenth century dislike of romanticism is the rage of Caliban not seeing his own face in a glass. The moral life of man forms part of the subject-matter of the artist, but the morality of art consists in the perfect use of an imperfect medium. No artist desires to prove anything. Even things that are true can be proved. No artist has ethical sympathies. An ethical sympathy in an artist is an unpardonable mannerism of style. No artist is ever morbid. The artist can express everything.

Thought and language are to the artist instruments of an art. Vice and virtue are to the artist materials for an art. From the point of view of form, the type of all the arts is the art of the musician. From the point of view of feeling, the actor's craft is the type. All art is at once surface and symbol.

Those who go beneath the surface do so at their peril. Those who read the symbol do so at their peril. It is the spectator, and not life, that art really mirrors. Diversity of opinion about a work of art shows that the work is new, complex, and vital. When critics disagree, the artist is in accord with himself. We can forgive a man for making a useful thing as long as he does not admire it. The only excuse for making a useless thing is that one admires it intensely.

All art is quite useless.

Here, Wilde grapples with the purpose of the aesthetic in reference to literature, but also in reference to other allusions. Though Wilde concludes that 'art is useless', the statement essentially elevates art (including the novel) above 'use[fulness]'. Do we, as humans, need art? How is literature an art? To what extent do we need aesthetic beauty in our lives? Wilde's novel questions these elements of beauty in interpersonal relationships, use of language for everyday communication, painting and the form of the novel, of course. Even if you choose not to read the novel with your students, it is a valuable way to begin a talk about the purpose of language and literature through a canonical text, though one that is somewhat in the minor mode due to its labelling as a 'homosexual text', and its use of many allusions and twists of phrase allow you to begin tapping into that dialogue of literature that will be essential for the course.

I would also include Keats' 'Ode on a Grecian Urn' (1918) in your early days of this topic. Continue to push beauty to the abstract with Keats' famous conclusion: 'Beauty is truth, truth beauty,—that is all/Ye know on earth, and all ye need to know.' He is responding to a classic form of beauty in the Grecian urn, but also of course using symbolism: two valuable teaching tools. The structure of iambic pentameter with rhyme scheme in five ten-line stanzas (or *décimas*, in the Spanish tradition) in the genre of an ode is also a nice opening to talking about poetic structure.

Both of the above short texts can lead to voluntary extension from students. Perhaps they read Wilde's novel or the transcript of his trial or they read further in Keats' oeuvre. Additionally, *Bright Star* (2009) about the life of Keats and *The Trials of Oscar Wilde* (1960) are useful films for your students to see as they begin to bring different art forms in dialogue.

CORE CONNECTIONS

TOK and the truth

Anytime we look at 'truth' and what we 'know', we also consider questions in TOK about universal and personal truths … are they different from knowledge? Of course, many literary texts deal with the idea of truth and there are further connections to non-literary texts that either attempt to present the truth or manipulate it. Keats' poem may pose an opposition in some regards to Wilde's prose. What does truth as 'beauty' look like? How can we describe it? Why do we see it in a Grecian urn and how might we also see it in a person? What does this conclusion mean in our own lives? How do language and literature additionally affect the way we see, experience or understand beauty? Additionally, the *usefulness of art* is a connection to the way art knowledge can be used by an individual or society, a likely topic of any TOK class.

■ Black in America (SL language and literature)

You have many choices with this focus. I recommend using texts from both the literary and non-literary category, so students are used to making both types a part of the dialogue. With this conceptual focus specifically, you would focus on the way texts create a discourse of politics and identity. In studying the language and literature more carefully, how are we able to better understand this discourse and the way it may be empowering or harmful?

Poetry and music would go together well here. You can read media texts related to the topics of the poetry and song lyrics and connect these shorter texts to a longer one, such as *Huckleberry Finn* (suggested in this unit) or *The Bluest Eye, Invisible Man, I Know Why the Caged Bird Sings, Their Eyes were Watching God, Monster* or the contemporary *The Sellout* from Paul Beatty (Man Booker Prize winner 2016).

The following extracts, a poem by Gwendolyn Brooks and a song by Kendrick Lamar, deal with Black identity in different ways. Brooks' is more empowering, while Lamar's is more lamentful. They make an interesting pairing in that regard, separated by time and gender. Further, both have won the distinguished Pulitzer Prize: Brooks for poetry in 1950 and Lamar for music in 2018. Many of Brooks' poems and Lamar's lyrics could be used in this unit, and you could encourage students to extend their reading by seeking out another one that speaks to them individually. Lamar and Brooks are also on the PRL and can therefore be used as some of your core literary texts.

■ 'To Those of My Sisters Who Kept Their Naturals' by Gwendolyn Brooks (1980)

'To Those Of My Sisters Who Kept Their Naturals'—never to look a hot comb in the teeth

Sisters!

I love you.
Because you love you.
Because you are erect.
Because you are also bent.
In season, stern, kind.
Crisp, soft-in season.
And you withhold.
And you extend.
And you Step out.
And you go back.
And you extend again.

Your eyes, loud-soft, with crying and with smiles,
are older than a million years,
And they are young.
You reach, in season.
And All
below the rich rouch right time of your hair.

You have not bought Blondine.
You have not hailed the hot-comb recently.
You never worshipped Marilyn Monroe.
You say: Farrah's hair is hers.
You have not wanted to be white.
Nor have you testified to adoration of that state
with the advertisement of imitation
 (never successful because the hot-comb is laughing too.)

But oh the rough dark Other music!
the Real,
the Right.
The natural Respect of Self and Seal!

Sisters!

Your hair is Celebration in the world!

■ 'The Blacker the Berry' (2015) by Kendrick Lamar

Click on the QR code to read the lyrics to Lamar's song.

The full song is powerful, confronting physical stereotypes like 'nappy hair' and a 'round' nose as well as big ideas like 'hypocr[isy]' and 'institutional[ization]'. Lamar was awarded the Pulitzer prize for music in 2018 for his work specifically on his album DAMN (2017), but also for his continued philosophical work toward a better understanding of Black identity in America, bringing a knowledge of many genres together in his hip-hop. According to *The New York Times*, the Pulitzer award was unanimous, calling DAMN 'a virtuosic song collection unified by its vernacular authenticity and rhythmic dynamism that offers affecting vignettes capturing the complexity of modern African-American life' ('Kendrick Lamar wins Pulitzer in "Big Moment for Hip-Hop"', 16 April 2018).

One could simply listen to his music and enjoy it. That is already value. But then we talk about the *why* of politics and identity. Does it kill the song or make it more alive by talking about it in this way? Students are likely to dig deep as they talk about musical lyrics and may have many other references they want to bring into the conversation. When the discussion concludes, remind them that what they have done is used textual evidence to discuss a conceptual point. This is why we study language and literature.

■ 2 How are we affected by texts in various ways?

This question asks us to consider an audience or a reader. Personal reader response style discovery is an important component of student journals and discussion to make the course meaningful beyond the classroom and to allow all students to connect with the material. It encourages you to make inquiring discovery with your students, demonstrating that understanding context or the deeper meaning of language can make one respond differently to a text.

However, the question also asks us to consider an intended audience, one who may or may not be in the classroom. The 'we' in the question is *all* humanity, not just ourselves and our students. So, next you need to study who the author is trying to reach. For both literary and non-literary texts, it is important to help students understand the way that language shapes meaning for a reader, including connotations, allusions and biases. This is an especially important focus in the language and literature course, since the nature of mass media and advertising is to have an intended target audience. You can extend the connection to the reader to include more than diction to look at structure, layout and visuals that may speak to certain groups of people more than others.

Sometimes the message is one that is intended to trick certain groups of people into thinking a certain way. Other times, there is a political appeal, from the same or opposing side. Still more, there are instances of a single intended audience – in letters, for example. Conversely, a letter to a politician printed in a newspaper changes due to the public audience, so suddenly it becomes a political message for many. In the same way, social media might single out an intended audience with the @ sign – it is visible to the public or at least a larger closed group. Layered meanings develop; even a direct compliment could be more about the person who sent the message, perhaps trying to enhance their social media image. Think of all the couples and best friends who write to each other publicly on Facebook walls or Twitter feeds. What is the purpose, really? Does it matter? You do not need to have the answers! Simply pose the questions so your students are more aware. Then, study more public figures, celebrities or politicians who use social media frequently. Together, you can try to analyse and interpret the effect on the reader. You will never fully know their intentions and that is ok. Perhaps what is more important is the way it is perceived by readers.

In addition to social media, mainstream media delivers messages to the public in a variety of ways. Propaganda, sway, biases – does the news have a duty to remain unbiased? How might they include bias, either purposefully or accidentally, and how does that affect the reader? Is censorship a kind of propaganda as well?

How we are affected by texts is altered by the text type and our motivations to read that text. Sometimes the media we consume for information also affects our thinking about ideologies or politics, even though we were only trying to stay informed about the world. With literary texts, unless we are in a classroom, we are rarely bombarded and asked to read them. Because there is more of a choice and it is more of a time commitment (if a longer text), we may tend to read texts that we hope we will learn from.

■ Beauty (HL literature)

Here, I recommend continuing with Wilde to look at excerpts from his trial (ideally after students have read the novel, but not necessarily). Your students will see first-hand how literature can be perceived and used by different audiences, even in a legal setting.

■ Extract from *Irish Peacock and Scarlet Marquess: The Real Trial of Oscar Wilde*, compiled by Merlyn Holland (2003)

Carson:	No sire, I am talking common sense.
Wilde:	Do not talk like that. I say it is a question of bad and good influence: but personally, as a mere philosophical point, I don't think – I am talking of grown human beings – that one person influences another. I don't think so. I don't believe it.
Carson:	You don't think that one man could exercise any influence over another? I may take that as a general statement?
Wilde:	As a general statement. Yes. I think influence is not a power that can be exercised at will by one person over another: I think it is quite impossible psychologically.
Carson:	You don't think that flattering a young man, telling him of his beauty, making love to him in fact, would be likely to corrupt him?
Wilde:	No.
Carson:	Wasn't that the way in your own novel that Lord Henry Wotton corrupted Dorian Gray in the first instance?
Wilde:	Lord Henry Wotton – no – in the novel he doesn't corrupt him; you must remember that novels and life are different things.
Carson:	It depends upon what you call corruption.
Wilde:	Yes, and what one calls life. In my novel there is a picture of changes. You are not to ask me if I believe they really happened; they are motives in fiction.

The lawyers are attempting to prove firstly that Wilde's novel proves he is a 'pervert' in their eyes, both gay and attempting to trap and 'influence' young men. However, Wilde discusses the novel as an art form separate from himself (we shall explore this idea again in formalist theory, Chapter 4). Then, the prosecutor tries to use Wilde's letters to a young man as his means of influence through beautiful writing (see especially pages 105–107 and page 141). If the effect of writing is a trick on the reader, then we are passive and stupid. However, Wilde can help students to see that we are masters of the way we read texts. As long as we understand them, we are affected perhaps by their aesthetic beauty or their messages in ways that help us grow rather than trick us into feeling a certain way.

Further, discuss the effect of beauty on readers. You can look both at aesthetic beauty in literature and the constructs of beauty by literature. You might start with this question explicitly as you teach *The Bluest Eye*, which begins and then deconstructs and jumbles up the language from a school primer. Look at an old school primer together; you can find them on YouTube. Did the texts that young children used to read effect the way they saw beauty around them? Morrison suggests that these social constructs of beauty, specifically for race and gender, are partially held in such texts; you can extend the notion to advertising for a language and literature course.

■ Black in America (SL language and literature)

You could add *The Bluest Eye* to this unit, since it looks specifically at a little girl's self-loathing due to poverty and her Black identity. However, looking at media around #BlackLivesMatter, for which you can find many different opinions, might be a better starting point. It can orient your students in something current and consequential. There are lots of articles that examine the statement as a political view, as a human rights issue and as personal stories. The *ProPublica* article by Sexton in our unit planner provides a beautiful multimedia piece with a different perspective about the 'black and blue' discourse in America.

The effect of language, however, can also be understood by taking a careful look at the use of the 'N-word' in Twain's novel. Many places have banned the book because it includes the word. Look carefully with students at why Twain may have used it and what the impact on readers is. Also, what is the impact on different characters in the novel? It can be historicized to post-Civil War America, but it is also an ongoing debate. Together, look at contemporary texts, such as hip-hop music, that use the word. Is it used in a similar or different way? Does it matter if the writer or singer is Black or white or another race? The question here, however, is more about how it is perceived by the reader or listener. How does the word impact us? The answer will likely be different for each person, and this is precisely what Judith Butler argues in *Excitable Speech* (1997). Butler posits that offence from language is only about the affected reader rather than the writer or speaker. It is a difficult text, but you can look at parts together with your students to pique their interest and debate whether or not you agree with this view.

■ 3 In what ways is meaning constructed, negotiated, expressed and interpreted?

You might be starting to see that all these questions are interconnected, and that they are questions you will likely address and then come back to many times in your course. This question can mean many things. If meaning is to be 'discovered', a reader may be involved before the writing is done. It is unclear where this meaning is coming from, so for the purpose of the course, I recommend you go back to language. Look at the ways layers of meaning are added to language through connotation, context, structure, juxtaposition and more.

Paul Auster's *City of Glass* is a text I use in other parts of the course that also addresses this question within fiction. It alludes to The Tower of Babel and Saussurian semiotics. If you are teaching this text later in the course, I recommend holding off on an explicit look at the question until that time. It would make a wonderful journal response, for example, or way to frame several passages of the text for Paper 1-style analysis.

Eduardo Galeano's *The Book of Embraces*, originally in Spanish, can be another example. Consisting of mixed-genre thoughts and fictions, it makes use of multilingualism and Sapir Whorf at many times. This example might be used as you tackle deconstruction with your students, or more simply with the idea of paradox.

■ Beauty (HL literature)

Here, I would look at the Wallace (or DFW, as many of his fans refer to him in fondness!) article I recommend, perhaps in conjunction with another one of his gems I have mentioned: 'Authority and American Usage'. If you want to stay within the topic of **beauty**, look at the Federer article after having read at least some of the other texts for the unit. Together try to understand how a feature article about a tennis player becomes a philosophical look at beauty and the power of humanity. It is a special piece and may help your students get excited about reading the newspaper; who would expect to find such joy and meaning from watching a tennis match until Wallace's language brings us these new discoveries?

CORE CONNECTIONS

TOK and EE – unpacking questions II

If you are interested in going outside of the **beauty** topic and doing something with more of a TOK connection as well, you can investigate the way structures of language create meaning and, therefore, knowledge. The personal knowledge becomes shared with the reader(s) of the text. You might even co-teach this lesson that deeply investigates a WOK (language) with a TOK teacher. Perhaps investigate the impact of this idea on translation, if you are studying a work in translation at this point. You might include a look at certain words or phrases that are untranslatable or are adopted within other languages. Or, look at excerpts of Noam Chomsky's *On Language,* including a focus on generative grammar that your math-minded students will love. Ask them to create their own mathematical formula for language construct. Reciprocal relationship between thinking and language: are ideas born from language use or do they exist without it?

Finally, if you are teaching in English, get your students to fondly embrace what it means to be a SNOOT (David Wallace's acronym for 'Sprachgefühl Necessitates Our Ongoing Tendance' or 'Syntax Nudniks of Our Time'), or at least understand it:

- 'Authority and American Usage', *Consider the Lobster and Other Essays by* David Foster Wallace (2005)

> There are lots of epithets for people like this—Grammar Nazis, Usage Nerds, Syntax Snobs, the Grammar Battalion, the Language Police. The term I was raised with is SNOOT. The word might be slightly self-mocking, but those other terms are outright dysphemisms. A SNOOT can be defined as somebody who knows what *dysphemism* means and doesn't mind letting you know it.
>
> I submit that we SNOOTs are just about the last remaining kind of truly elitist nerd. There are, granted, plenty of nerd-species in today's America, and some of these are elitist within their own nerdy purview (the skinny, carbuncular, semi-autistic Computer Nerd moves instantly up on the totem pole of status when your screen freezes and now you need his help, and the bland condescension with which he performs the two occult keystrokes that unfreeze your screen is both elitist and situationally valid). But the SNOOT's purview is interhuman social life itself. You don't, after all (despite withering cultural pressure), have to use a computer, but you can't escape language: Language is everything and everywhere; it's what lets us have anything to do with one another; it's what separates us from the animals; Genesis 11:7-10 and so on. And we SNOOTS know when and how to hyphenate phrasal adjectives and to keep participles from dangling, and we know that we know, and we know how very few other Americans know this stuff or even care, and we judge them accordingly.
>
> In ways that certain of us are uncomfortable about, SNOOTs' attitudes about contemporary usage resemble religious/political conservatives' attitudes about contemporary culture: We combine a missionary zeal and a near-neural faith in our beliefs' importance with a curmudgeonly hell-in-a-handbasket despair at the way English is routinely manhandled and corrupted by supposedly literate adults. Plus a dash of the elitism of, say, Billy Zane in *Titanic*—a fellow SNOOT I know likes to say that listening to most people's public English feels like watching somebody use a Stradivarius to pound nails. We are the Few, the Proud, the More or Less Constantly Appalled at Everyone Else.

Wallace's review of a dictionary turns into a beautiful look at the English language and why he finds it necessary to deeply understand the foundations of the language (including grammar and vocabulary, but also structures of text types) in order to then be more creative and adaptive with it. If you have more reluctant readers, maybe draw them in with the Federer essay first (also suits the sporty type). The writing is difficult, but before saying anything about the essay, try to ask each student to speak about their reaction to the text. Of course, let them have some time to brainstorm or free-write about their ideas first. I think you will be surprised and impressed by what they come up with.

■ Black in America (SL language and literature)

You can address this question again using Butler's philosophy. Both Twain and Baldwin give us explicit ideas about the construction of meaning through language in the core texts of the unit. You can extend this by looking at part or all of Baldwin's *Giovanni's Room* to see how he uses language to explore his gay identity in Paris. Meaning is also in the places and spaces he inhabits there, all expressed in his unique way. Alternatively, or in addition, look at Twain's satire: 'The Celebrated Jumping Frog of Calaveras County'. Begin trying to understand satire through this method – how is meaning constructed? How does verbal irony enhance the meaning? What is the danger of constructing meaning in this way? What purpose does satire serve to its readers? You can extend by looking at other satirical publications today, like *The Onion* (USA) and *Charlie Hebdo* (France). Perhaps get students to find their own and share in small groups.

You could lead into your #BlackLivesMatter media and social media study by looking at Kendrick Lamar's music and lyrics as well as the discourse surrounding his Pulitzer Prize. Some of the articles (*The Conversation*) offer dialogue about low and high art, and how Lamar uses both. Many look at his musical composition, others at his poetic lyrics and still more at his political discourse – in the lyrics, his speeches and the artistic projects he has been a part of or produced (the *Black Panther* film, for example). Still further, he has become an important figure in understanding #BlackLivesMatter beyond police/black citizen and black/white binaries and (re)defining blackness as an identity in America.

■ 4 How does language use vary among text types and among literary forms?

The next three questions I recommend addressing explicitly with students toward the end of your unit. By then, you will have studied a variety of text types and/or literary forms. A comparative approach will work well in response. Have the questions in mind as you conduct the learning throughout the unit, and simply hold off on an explicit conversation/ mind map/Padlet, etc, until you have enough in your arsenal. It might work well to divide the three questions among your students for group work and presentations. If you have a large class, either have some go back to the first three questions as well as synthesis, or create two groups for these last three, allowing them to compare ideas before sharing with the class.

For this question specifically, look at style, register, language choice, cultural language use, dialects and their relationships with the text type. Just think of the language of graphic novels vs. that of a formal essay vs. a satirical piece ... once we compare, it is not difficult to see the differences. *Why* may be more difficult than *how* in this case. The expectation of a particular type of language use can make us more aware, for example, when verbal irony is being used in satire. Subcultures or minor voices sometimes choose text types with a particular type of language in this way to construct meaning. The following are just a few examples from these sample units that would be useful.

■ Beauty (HL literature)

When we read about a subjective idea like definitions of beauty, it may be easy to compare the differences between texts. To stay within the realm of literature or artistic texts, you may want to use Morrison's novel *The Bluest Eye* or her short story 'Sweetness' in comparison to 'Ode on a Grecian Urn' by Keats to look at beauty. Discuss how the language is more abstract in poetry and how the references might be more layered. Then, take a look at an article, such as 'Beauty is in the Mind of the Beholder' (Wargo, 2011). Though this is a non-literary text and usually used for the other course, your students will use various types of articles for inquiry research, both in your class and as part of the EE.

Among these texts, you might ask students to compare:

- use of pronouns
- use of allusions or statistics
- register
- words used to describe beauty (make a list)
- language's connection to facts and truth.

They can use coloured highlighters or lists on the board or a shared digital space. The comparison of the above aspects should help make students more aware of language's impact in literary texts. You might go a step further to look at literary vs. non-literary non-fiction. If you look at the above article and then, for example, an excerpt on beauty from Diane Ackerman's *A Natural History of the Senses* (1990), you should see differences again in the use of language as listed above.

■ Black in America (SL language and literature)

A similar framing mechanism can be used for this conceptual unit, which draws on different text types even as core texts: fiction, essay and media. Try to go beyond generic text types, like novel vs. media. Even using 'social media' or 'newspaper articles' are too broad. The closer the text types, the more poignant the comparisons, like chiaroscuro where a painter places two shades of a particular colour in juxtaposition to highlight their uniqueness. For the #BlackLivesMatter movement, you can take an op-ed and a feature article, each about the same topic (perhaps a particular act of violence or a response to art, like Lamar's music or the Spike Lee film *BlacKkKlansman* (2018)). Look at how language shows bias in the op-ed and understand the use of adjectives in each text. Then, when your students are confronted with one or the other on Paper 1, they should know how to compare.

For this conceptual unit, we can also look at the question a slightly different way. We can look at 'Englishes' (a suggestion for another unit). We look at Black English or Ebonics in Baldwin's essay 'If Black English Isn't a Language, Then Tell Me, What Is?' After reading his essay and understanding his points about language and culture as well as certain places for different types of English and the power of different types, you can then look at uses of Black English in different texts – music, fiction, television – and have a philosophical discussion about why the language remains separate from standard conventions of academic English. Does this happen with other dialects? How so?

If you are instead engaged in the Englishes unit, or just have extra time, go further to look at different types in Anglophone countries, such as Scotland, South Africa, New Zealand,

Singapore and India. Then perhaps globally connect to dialects of French, Chinese and Spanish world-wide. A good article to include in discussion is 'What's a Language, Anyway?' (McWhorter, 2016).

> How do we define dialects vs. language?

> Does knowledge of standard English create power?

> Should we standardize language?

> What biases do we have when we hear or read certain dialects?

Sometimes even in fiction this dialogue about Englishes is made explicit. You can see the use of types of English for effect with comment from characters in novels such as *Huckleberry Finn*, *Super Sad True Love Story* (2010) and *Everything is Illuminated* (2003). Moving to India, the 'untouchable' caste unnamed protagonist in Adiga's *The White Tiger* (2008), begins his continued unanswered correspondence with the Chinese Premier by saying: 'Neither you nor I speak English, but there are some things that can be said only in English.' (page 1) English becomes a political text, one of the media, of colonization and of globalization.

■ 5 How does the structure or style of a text affect meaning?

Of course, this question is closely linked to the last. Looking at them together will be useful, but also understanding how they are different is important. Style can mean a lot of things, and you will see that I previously recommend using style of language use with the last question. However, style can also be font, colour, types of images or drawings, etc. In this way style can also be linked more closely to structure than language. You will need to help your students investigate both aspects.

You will look at both text type and genre – those who stick to conventions and those who break them. Transferable aspects of structure, such as juxtaposition and visual language, help with Paper 1 especially.

■ Beauty (HL literature)

It will be important to look at all four major forms in relation to this question as these will be needed for P1 and P2. If you haven't covered them all yet, you can still draw on students' middle school experiences and come back to the question toward the end of the course.

Again, look at distinctions within a literary genre here for a better comparison. For novels, this might be frame narration in *Frankenstein*, changing narrative voice in *The Bluest Eye* and the use of a preface in *The Picture of Dorian Gray*. Poetry of course has many structures to compare.

■ ATT & ATL

Using imagination

■ To teach this idea, you can ask students to imagine a new structure for a literary text type, still within the same genre. They can present their ideas to the rest of the class in groups for a discussion of how it would change the original text. How might the message change through a structural change?

■ Black in America (SL language and literature)

There is a bigger job here for the language and literature course. For Paper 1, students will need to be prepared to understand an arsenal of text types and how structure and style affect meaning. Though you may only have addressed a few text types here, it is useful to look at the question to show students that even if they do not know the specific text type well, they can transfer tools of analysing structure in this way.

■ ATT & ATL

Staying organized

- As you begin to explore different text types, and their subsets, I recommend you keep a running list. By now, students will have explored differences in language use, structure and style between text types with the previous two questions. You will have to keep coming back to these questions as you go through the course and expose students to many different types.

- How can you keep all the information organized? You could have a website updated with each text type covered and overviews as well as samples. I recommend you have this (and can use it year after year with examples used in your classroom), but that you also have a student-generated list. Of course, also refer to Purdue Owl, the AP Style Guide and any other useful standardizing resources of text types. I recommend there is a collaborative digital platform (Google docs or Padlet, perhaps) and/or work in student journals to address this. A sample template follows that you can use with your students.

■ Text type exploration cheat sheet

Text type (newspaper article, blog)	
Subset (feature, travel blog)	
Examples	1 2 3
Common layout features (headlines, columns, return address)	
Common visual features (images, colours)	
Common use of language (register, pronouns)	
Keywords of elements (bio, by line, caption, hyperlinks)	
Common audience (age group, culture)	
Common purpose (delivers information, motivates, sells product)	
History of the text type (why it was created, how it evolved, original use vs. now)	

■ 6 How do texts offer insights and challenges?

This question may seem a rather obvious one for a language A course – without insight and challenges in ways to view the world, what is the point of the texts we study? Should you take a text at face value or interpret for yourself? Of course, this is a reminder to look at the course conceptually.

The question asks us to consider a purpose beyond the text. Here, look at texts where the purpose is not so obvious. Tricks and subversion, parody or satire, politics, personal growth … these areas can all be explored in relation to this question.

■ Beauty (HL literature)

Rather than just a horror story, *Frankenstein* can challenge the way we understand genetic engineering (designer babies, cloning, etc) and the way we think about beauty (the Monster's ostracization by society). *The Picture of Dorian Gray* makes us consider how we view ourselves in terms of vanity, youth and desires. Are we all corruptible? *The Bluest Eye* offers a challenge to the way communities do little to help the weak, and create ideas of beauty that may be impossible to live up to.

CORE CONNECTIONS

CAS

Service is part of the CAS programme, and the ability to do this in connection to the classroom is encouraged. As ethical challenges are raised in the classroom, encourage students to go a step further by working in the community on an issue they feel passionately about. The work they do might even be through writing. They can write their opinion about one of the above topics in a school or local publication.

■ Black in America (SL language and literature)

Hold debates where students have to argue a side they may not agree with – should Ebonics be a language? Are police officers correct to draw on statistics if it discriminates? Use methods that I offer in the CBL lessons that follow to get kids talking about difficult topics in structured ways. They must use the texts to discuss the ideas, and therefore will understand the way a text can create an insight.

Time and space

For the IB definition of this area of exploration refer back to Chapter 2, page 21.

You could look at topics such as parallel universes, Nietzsche's eternal return or spatial reflections of identity in domestic spaces. However, as summarized in the last chapter, IB is mostly talking about what was previously referred to as context here. Essentially, this includes history, culture, language, politics – basically what is going on around the text's production that perhaps make it a reflection of a part of humanity/society or even make it a political text. Some may consider all texts reflections of culture; all texts political. The New Historicism lens in the next chapter will be useful in this regard.

You probably always contextualize the texts in your classroom to some extent, but here the conceptual questions help us to focus on contextual reference points that will cause your students to inquire, research and make connections. For many, it can make literature seem more purposeful, especially if we consider fiction's connection to the real world. Even non-literary texts that may seem to have obvious connections to time and space need further analysis, for example to understand their place within perspectives or how the connotation of language used is dependent on the producing and receiving culture.

We place this area of exploration second, as IB suggests but does not require, because it is a good way to approach the IO and HL essay. Both elements of the course focus on inquiry and global issues. Although neither are considered research papers, both allow students to research context for deeper understanding and possibly reference other sources or historical information as needed.

For this area of exploration, we take a closer look at the HL language and literature sample syllabus units: **writing the city** and **civil disobedience**, dividing the questions between the two. However, each of these, and especially the first topic, can easily be adapted to the literature course. Use some of the texts listed in extension as other core literary texts. Some of these will be mentioned in later lesson ideas connected to CBL pedagogy, creativity and assessment.

Alternatively, you could develop the **topographies** topic suggested in the HL literature sample syllabus for either course (page 34). It may depend on where you live or what your students are interested in. If you want more of a variety that includes elements like the Romantics' or Transcendentalists' view of nature or Gaston Bachelard's idea of 'intimate immensity' or more of a focus on the journey, and travel's impact on the individual, you may want to include a more diverse spatial element. We begin with the sample unit plans on the suggested template. Here, the first three questions relate to the first unit, so we break up the explanations in this way. Remember that the critical theory and assessment connections will be the subject of later chapters.

 ### ■ 1 How important is cultural context to the production and reception of a text?

Although Paul Auster's *City of Glass* and its adaptation would be a great way to look at genre (novel, detective fiction) and adaptation (graphic novel), here we focus more on the contextual elements, including allusions and the Cold War literature element of the novel. In fact, you might investigate what Auster's interpretation of the genres has to do with context. Although the Cold War between the USA and the USSR is not explicitly discussed in the text, the context must be understood to appreciate the elements of suspicion and paranoia that the protagonist undergoes. At this point, you could skip ahead to the New Historicism literary lens in the next chapter and simply address this question while teaching the lens that essentially answers the same question.

■ HL language and literature

■ Conceptual unit planning template: Time and space

Area of exploration: Time and space Conceptual focus: Writing the city (*Creativity, Culture, Transformation*)	Conceptual questions: 1 How important is cultural context to the production and reception of a text? 2 How do we approach texts from different times and cultures to our own? 3 To what extent do texts offer insight into another culture?			New York City at night
Core texts	**Extension texts**	**Critical theory**	**Formative assessments**	**Summative assessments**
City of Glass, Paul Auster plus graphic novel adaptation NL travel writing: essays and blogs	**Fiction:** *Dubliners*, James Joyce; *Invisible Cities*, Italo Calvino; *Open City*, Teju Cole; *NW*, Zadie Smith; *The Age of Innocence*, Edith Wharton; *The Great Gatsby*, F. Scott Fitzgerald; *A Tale of Two Cities*, Charles Dickens **Mixed genre:** *City Voices: Hong Kong Writing in English, 1945 to the present*, edited by Xu Xi **Films:** *Metropolis* (1927); *Bladerunner* (1982); *Lost in Translation* (2003); *Wall Street* (1987); *Paris, je t'aime* (2006); *Chungking Express* (1994); *Rear Window* (1954) Jean Baudrillard: 'hyperreality' – excerpts from *Fatal Strategies* (1990) and *The Spirit of Terrorism: And Requiem for the Twin Towers* (2002) Ackbar Abbas: 'cultural creation' – excerpts from *Hong Kong: Culture and the Politics of Disappearance* (1997) Robert Stam: 'Beyond Fidelity: The Dialogics of Adaptation' (2000)	Deconstruction New Historicism Marxist	Learner portfolio – focus on inquiry Pastiche (of literary or non-literary text) Visual adaptation Group close analysis (P1 style) Self-assessed recorded mock IO Peer mock IO	Mock IO LP mark

Focus questions: Where do cities come from? Where does the word come from? Why do we have cities? What are your feelings about cities? How do the big cities of the world compare and contrast? How do we see this reflected in literature? What is the city's relationship with modernity? What is the city's relationship with community and isolation? What is an urban landscape and how does it enter texts? How do writers use the city to show aspects of humanity? What is the relationship between the media and cities? How do texts create layers of meaning about a city and what does that have to do with human imagination? What does the city have to do with the ghostly or with tracings of the past?

Core connections: The inquiry work done in this unit will help students think about contextualizing and researching their EE topics. For TOK, the unit has explicit elements of the WOK language, memory and imagination and the AOK arts, history and mathematics (architecture).

ATT & ATL: Differentiation through many extra short texts, co-design curriculum based on individuals' experiences in the classroom, analytical skills of different genres and text types, organization of IO.

International mindedness: 'Visit' a range of cities, even if your focus is on one. Investigate the way international perspectives are contained, and change, within global cities.

Global issues: One's relationship with their surroundings, the city and cultural production, a city's reflection of shared traumas, etc.

Although the story is largely one about an individual's trauma over losing his family, the story is dependent on a relationship the individual has with New York City. We literally see him walking the city streets and mapping out the labyrinth of his travels in his drawings.

Places and spaces that are intrinsic to New York are part of the story: small apartments in close proximity with neighbours, the street grid, Central Park and metro stations. Perhaps look at film clips to enhance the effect – *Rear Window, Wall Street, Taxi Driver, Ghostbusters* – any iconic films would work well if you show clips of the panorama and street views or apartment scenes. When you add the layer of Auster's own relationship with the city, which he speaks and writes of often, you have many aspects of space and time to investigate. Indeed, this early novella of his has generated many secondary sources from academics as well as being the subject of his interviews. Further, there is a great YouTube video of the graphic novel adapters and the original author speaking at the Comic Arts Brooklyn Festival in 2013 (**www.youtube.com/watch?v=fM9S9cU_xkY**). It is useful to choose texts for this area of exploration that you know have interesting secondary sources of this nature.

Further allusions to the bible, specifically the Tower of Babel, contribute to a different reception of the text. It is a good starting point of discussion about the ways that religious perspective or knowledge can change the way we read a text and the way it is read by different communities. This question assumes some inquiry research by the student; the methods of which shall be discussed in the next sections.

Another good text type to investigate here would be advertising, considering the way its reception changes over time. Advertising is hugely dependent on cultural reception: what is *in*, what is cool, what is socially acceptable? Look at old advertisements that depict the joys of women doing housework, the need for the man of the house to be the breadwinner or the way smoking makes you a cool rebel. Students will identify some elements as 'wrong' and dated. What do the ads tell you about society at that time or in that place? Why has society evolved in this way? What changes to the adverts of those products do we see now? Do you still see problems with modern advertisements in terms of depicting stereotypes or leaving out certain perspectives? Feminist theory is one way to look at some of these ads, depending on the subjects. Try to go beyond the subject of the ads and closely analyse the specific language used (perhaps gendered) and layout or other visual elements on the page. How do they impact the reader and how are they subjects of their context?

■ 2 How do we approach texts from different times and cultures to our own?

Here, you may want to look specifically at works in translation, but of course anything outside of your school's context will work. Again, the New Historicism can be useful here. Be sure to use the keywords of perspective and international mindedness as you address the question.

Auster's novel is a strong one for this question because even within the fiction he includes allusions and excerpts from literature in different cultures. Beyond the Tower of Babel, he mentions other literary figures either implicitly or explicitly. One such is Baudelaire, whom he quotes in French: '*Il me semble que je serais toujours bien là où je ne suis pas*'. In other words: 'It seems to me that I will always be happy in the place where I am not'. The Spanish Cervantes' Don Quixote is mentioned several times as well, especially in discussion of translation (to Arabic then back to Spanish).

For this unit, you can also look at the way a city becomes a global city, and how we are bombarded with texts from different cultures within a single place. You could investigate Cold War ideology and how it shaped the way people may have read Auster at that time compared to now, or how they might read it in Russia, Cuba or Romania. Hypothesize what would change then try to understand what the students in the room can get out of it now in relation to time and place.

Then, of course, looking at travel writing should, by definition, open us up to different cultures. It would be interesting to look at the way different writers tackle a particular place. How do Charles Dickens and Zadie Smith write of London in fiction compared to contemporary bloggers like Jenny Nguyen-Barron ('Melting Butter') or Evelyn Hannon ('Journeywoman')? How is culture represented? If this is not your or the students' culture, investigate how these blogs and others portray different cultures through the travel experience.

For a different unit, another good novel to use for this question is *The Sailor who Fell from Grace with the Sea* by Mishima. The approaches in the text to masculinity, honour, family and shame are all dependent on an understanding of the Bushido Code of the Japanese Samurai. The definitions of these terms are different in different cultures; as we read this novel, we may approach it with our own biases that make the actions of the characters difficult to understand. We can add Mishima's political biography and harakiri, the commitment of ritual suicide, to the discussion. You might watch any version of *47 Ronin*, though the Keanu Reeves version will likely hold your students' attention the longest. Also bring in an expert if you can find a Japanese teacher or researcher with a background in this area.

Achebe's *Things Fall Apart* would also work well here. In both this novel and the former, students will be faced with ideas and behaviours they may see as strange unless they understand the cultural and historic contexts.

■ 3 To what extent do texts offer insight into another culture?

This question is similar to the previous one but takes out the comparative aspect. Instead, it asks us to question 'to what extent' this can happen: can we truly understand culture via texts?

The unit can look at cities as meccas of cultures. You can also *read* the city itself as a text. Ask your students to do a little project if you live in a city. In 20 minutes, what can they find out about the city's culture just by observing what they see around them? How do texts, such as blogs and novels, enhance or change the perspective of the culture? Again, you may draw on film clips as a starting point here.

Allow students to bring in short texts from their own cultures. Even if your students are largely local, they will have individual family cultures. These texts might be in a different language and you can ask them to translate if necessary. Get them to share in a small group, then ask the group to try to determine as much as they can about the culture through the text. Allow the original student to respond only after feedback has been given. You can use this in combination with a Paper 1 practice I suggest in Chapter 6, where students generate the multicultural and multilingual examples that you can analyse together.

■ HL language and literature

■ Conceptual unit planning template: Time and space

Pussy Riot invading the pitch during the World Cup final

Area of exploration: Time and space	Conceptual questions:
Conceptual focus: Civil disobedience (*Identity, Communication*)	4 How does the meaning and impact of a text change over time? 5 How do texts reflect, represent or form a part of cultural practices? 6 How does language represent social distinctions and identities?

Core texts	Extension texts	Critical theory	Formative assessments	Summative assessments
Yesi's poetry NL essays on passive resistance over time: 'Civil Disobedience', Henry David Thoreau 'Letter from Birmingham Jail', Martin Luther King, Jr. 'The Practice of Satyagraha', Mahatma Gandhi NL social media campaigns: Arab Spring, HK Umbrella Movement, Pussy Riot, etc (choose two for whole class or divide among groups)	Speeches from leaders of passive resistance (Gandhi, King, contemporary) Media on Rosa Parks (and civil rights music, OutKast's 'Rosa Parks') **Excerpts:** *The Thief and the Dogs*, Naguib Mahfouz Youtube.com campaigns (including the rap that sparked the Arab Spring: El Général's 'the voice of Tunisia') Twitter history and campaigns Philosophical essays	Marxist Neo-historical Formalist	Journal responses in learner portfolio: ■ inquiry ■ commentary analysis ■ personal opinion Class debate Peer individual oral mocks Disobedient music: share findings Finding a line of inquiry for the HL essay Outlining the essay	Mock P1 (on one of the speeches or media texts or unseen) **IO (IA)** HL essay draft

Focus questions: What does it mean to object politically? What is the purpose of free speech? What can people use besides violence to show outrage with a government? Why do people protest? What is the history of passive resistance? Why do people do something they know they will go to jail/prison for? Is it wrong to break the law? How has social media changed civil disobedience? What is the importance of language(s) and literature in civil disobedience?

Core connections: TOK – History and Ethics AOK, perspectives (government, rebels, ages, races …); EE – developing a line of inquiry, writing a useful outline, developing purposeful research questions and thesis statements.

International mindedness: Unit has many texts from around the world and in translation; how has civil disobedience travelled around the globe at different time periods? How has it changed?

ATT & ATL: Developing a line of inquiry, debate, outlines.

Global issues: Human rights, power structures in society, issues about violence, ethical issues.

■ 4 How does the meaning and impact of a text change over time?

For this question, it is useful to look at an older text that can be traced to explicit responses over time. **Civil disobedience** can be traced over time and rooted in the essay from Thoreau in response to American slavery. In this way, it is easy for students to see figures who have directly used his terminology and ideology in subsequent work (King, Gandhi, contemporary activists). The issues of pure government rebellion vs. non-violent resistance vs. breaking the law on purpose have been responded to over time in terms of their effectiveness. Gandhi added the aspect of Satyagraha, which is about holding onto the truth. Layers added can enhance the discourse that Thoreau originally set up in his essay and his action.

Of course, you can do this with literary texts as well. If Thoreau's other transcendentalist nature writings (*Walden, The Maine Woods*) interest you more, look at how Annie Dillard responds in *Pilgrim at Tinker Creek* (1974) and how it connects to the movement against climate change today.

Most of the literary texts I suggest in this book that are at least 50 years old can be looked at with this question. *Frankenstein* can be viewed in light of genetic modification and other advances in science that make the story more real than imaginary. *The Crucible*'s allegorical nature can now be transferred to the terrorist witch hunt rather than McCarthyism. There must be some reason we are still looking at an 'old' book in a classroom, so after assuming it is relevant, we address whether something has changed in its reception. Responses should vary in genre and text type, giving you a rich inventory to add to your syllabus.

GLOBAL ISSUES

Then and now

Take any timeless tale; perhaps link this question to the one about reading the classics. Shakespeare, Tolstoy and Dante are timeless for a reason. They have been read by different generations in different ways. Firstly, the global issues related to the personal human experience may be told in different time periods and different cultures or societies. Secondly, those that relate to a particular historical struggle may be transferrable to the contemporary struggles that the reader's world faces.

■ 5 How do texts reflect, represent or form a part of cultural practices?

The last global issues connection of course leads us straight into this question and can really be used as a frame of looking at either or both conceptual questions. There is a lot you can do in this unit in relation to the question. But first let's have a quick look more generally.

The question suggests that culture is not static and that its changes may be reflected in texts. The texts may either demonstrate culture or be a part of the change itself. You can also investigate the style and genre of writing as a cultural practice itself, drawing on the first area of exploration but historicizing these elements.

It might be useful to also think about this question in terms of the global and local; a dichotomy the IB encourages us to investigate. Global issues may have different cultural manifestations locally. For example, in looking at any type of media texts, see how news agencies make a global issue (such as the refugee 'crisis' or global warming) locally relevant and therefore demonstrate or impact cultural responses.

Any fictional text that is purposefully placeless also makes a good text to investigate here. By leaving out the setting, the narrative becomes transferable, allowing us to play with culture. Take Kafka's short story 'In the Penal Colony', for example. He certainly is not talking about his home city of Prague. This strange colonized island can be linked to historical penal colonies, like Australia, the Isla Maria Madre or Xinjiang province, but it might also be looked at in terms of more general body politics related to debates about using torture today.

Yesi's poetry, one of our core texts for this sample unit, is a nice bridge to *Writing the City* if you should choose to use both. His poetry comes from Hong Kong, but also from his travels. It engages with localized spaces, like the 'Old Colonial Building' at The University of Hong Kong, 'North Point Car Ferry', 'Ap-liu Street' and 'Fabric Alley'. However, it also talks about abstract concepts in poems such as 'Cloud Travel'. Then there is the discussion of other places: 'Postcards from Prague', '*Brecht-haus* Berlin' and 'Tokyo Story'. What do the local and global themes tell us about culture? How do the poems demonstrate the sometimes elusive Hong Kong culture, one that is much more than 'east meets west'? How does his local identity interact with the other spaces in the poems?

You can look at the creation of a Hong Kong culture through his poetry (see the Abbas reading in the previous unit) that would help students to understand current politics that include **civil disobedience**. He has a lot to say about language and culture. Yesi tells us he is talking *about* culture, but indeed some of the poems become a method of defining cultural practice. Some of it is included in his interview with Gordon T. Osing in *City at the End of Time* (2012).

■ Extracts from *City at the End of Time: Poems by Leung Ping-Kwan* by PK Leung (also known as Yesi outside Hong Kong) and G. Osing (2012)

I began writing stories when I first started working in the newspaper. I had since written several volumes of short stories and novels, starting with early magical realist stories about Hong Kong, and moving on to stories about the relationship between Hong Kong and China (*Islands and Continents*, 1987), investigating other cultures so as to look back at my own (*Postcards from Prague*, 1990) … [Recently, I wrote a novel called] *Changing Home* … about a Hong Kong person looking for a 'home' in present-day Hong Kong.' (page 218)

Even nowadays, in some of the programs in the public media that teach people to speak English, it seems that they always teach people to speak like Westerners in a Western situation … It is a pity that people do not teach the student as a Hong Kong person to express himself in an indigenous situation.' (page 221)

Through translation of 'works from Central and South America, as well as from Eastern Europe [for the Chinese public] … these alternative models suggested to me other ways to balance art and politics … In the late sixties, I subscribed to … underground magazines [from the Americas]. It seems strange now, but the poetry I wrote during those days was more in line with classical Chinese landscape poetry. I was looking for possible ways to write about my city, and had even tried to adapt the classical method in a new way to write about this modern city of Hong Kong.' (page 213)

■ 6 How does language represent social distinctions and identities?

For this question, you might look at the social media campaigns you have selected. Through various perspectives, different social distinctions and identities can be identified and then linked with language. A few readings from *Language, Society and Power: An Introduction* (2011), such as 'Language and the Media' (Anthea Irwin) and 'Language and Gender' (Pia Pichler and Sian Preece), can help you or your students get started with these ideas and related keywords for analysis. Or take a look at Alan Durant and Marina Lambrou's *Language and Media: a resource book for students* (2009), especially 'Media language and social change' (pages 233–37). Further, you can investigate any text through the Marxist lens, which we shall further explore in the next chapter, to analyse socioeconomic differences or the feminist and queer lenses to look at identity's relationships with language.

We have also previously discussed dialects. How do these distinctions of language change our understanding of the identity of the speaker? How are languages used for social power? You can also see this in Shakespearean texts and the way he moves between verse and prose to articulate a point about characters, whether it be madness, class or their ability to see the truth. See the Porter in *Macbeth* or the way Hamlet switches back and forth.

Additionally, the language conversations of Yesi and Osing pertain to a local and global discourse. In Hong Kong, where the official languages are Chinese and English, Cantonese is the common spoken language and the one Yesi writes in (though he also spoke English and Mandarin). In what way does it add to constructs of his local city?

with Virginia Woolf's 'A Room of One's Own' to explicitly tackle women's place in the writing and publishing world. Likewise, why and how is queer literature minor, and does it have a language of its own? Some of these questions can be looked at in conjunction with Marxist, postcolonial, feminist or queer theories, especially, although these scholars were mainly part of the post-structuralist movement.

Intertextuality: connecting texts

For the IB definition of this area of exploration refer back to Chapter 2, page 22.

Here, IB presents an **intertextuality** that goes beyond the written word, like Kristeva's views represented in her doughnut hole (page 23). The definition supposes a wider interplay of ideas in the world and anything that can be read for meaning, which may include a culture, a city, a person – really anything with meaning. However, though the ideas can go deeply in a variety of directions, what will help you anchor and focus this section for the purposes of your course is in one main idea: the dialogue of literature. This dialogue necessitates a look at the evolution of text types in connection to context, whether it be historical, philosophical or personal factors, and the ability for students to compare texts to one another to find meaning. In this way, the structural, linguistic and idea-based similarities and differences among texts help us to find the absent centre: the doughnut hole.

The symbol is a bit silly, but it helps us visualize the point. That is, the intertext is found from that negative space between texts. It is a separate thing; it is a new idea created from looking at both (or all) the texts. Of course, that idea will be rooted in the other texts, but different perspectives or genres or something else that is different allows us to see a bigger picture, a **global issue**.

To unpack this area of exploration's questions further, we shall look more closely at one unit from HL language and literature and one from HL literature. Again, both can be applied to either course and the second one is completely transferable if you choose to focus on literary texts at the end of the language and literature course. If you go back to page 37, you will see that I suggest this approach as a way to prepare for the Paper 2, which focuses only on literary texts for both courses. Here, I have mixed up the questions for what works better with each unit focus. We address 1, 2 and 5 for **truth and lies** and 3, 4 and 6 for **identity**. The rest of these questions have been presented in the order of the guide, but this is another reminder that you can look at them in any order you choose. You could even have students responsible for certain questions that you come back to orally, on bulletin boards and online Padlets or in journals.

■ HL language and literature

■ Conceptual unit planning template: Intertextuality

Area of exploration:
Intertextuality

Conceptual focus:
Truth and lies
(Representation, Perspective, Communication)

Conceptual questions:
1 How do texts adhere to and deviate from conventions associated with literary forms or text types?
2 How do conventions and systems of reference evolve over time?
5 How can texts offer multiple perspectives of a single issue, topic or theme?

The new catfish: someone who creates a fake online identity

Core texts	Extension texts	Critical theory	Formative assessments	Summative assessments
NL Social media as reality	Articles on fake social media	Formalist	Learner portfolio	HL essay
Catfish film	Articles on social media and identity (bridge to next unit)	Deconstruction	Social media self-study	Mock P1
NL fake news/political texts	Fiction: *The Circle*, Dave Eggers; *The Reverberator*, Henry James	Marxist	Group P1 outlines	
	Editorials	Intertextual	Presentations on elements of the commentary wheel	
	Satire		Debate	
	The Death of Truth, Michiko Kakutani, and related articles			
	Doctored visuals (Alexa Keefe: 'How the ultimate shark photo went viral', *National Geographic*; Colin Horgan: 'The Acosta Video Debate is the Future of Fake News', *Medium*)			
	Political speeches/tweets			

Focus questions: Is there more truth written in fiction or non-fiction texts? Why did the term 'fake news' arise and what does it mean about our world? What obligation does the media have to tell the truth? What checks and balances are in place to make sure the news reported is true? How do different journalistic text types have different roles to play in opinion and fact? What is the role of citizen journalism in depicting the truth? To what extent does social media reflect identity? Is social media a positive way to play with identity or a hindrance on our freedoms? In what ways does social media lie or tell the truth? How has social media changed the way the mainstream media report the news? How do journalists also use social media to get their messages across; is there a conflict of interest?

International mindedness: Media and political texts from around the world; how media discourse travels; censorship and propaganda around the world.

Core connections: TOK – an essential question in TOK is our understanding of where knowledge comes from and if that knowledge is 'true'. It also looks at fallacious reasoning, which can be drawn on here, to discover where lies or false claims may be made in the media or by politicians.

Global issues: Personal relationships with information we receive in media, how social media affects individuals, importance of maintaining the truth and how it can happen.

ATT & ATL: Writing process – revision, debate skills, analytical skills of new textualities.

■ 1 How do texts adhere to and deviate from conventions associated with literary forms or text types?

For this question, we cycle back to the first area of exploration's questions, especially numbers 3–5, that deal with understanding the way language and structure shape meaning in a text. Here, the investigation of text type and genre is spelled out. You will need to look at forms that are adhered to 'by the book' (or even those texts that helped to define a form) as well as those that reinvent a text type or perhaps merge several into one. It would make sense to consider the second question about the evolution of text types simultaneously with this one. Sometimes, you will find aberrations for purpose, but often we study these aberrations to also understand a change.

How might we approach this question? Of course, the possibilities are vast. It should happen each time you look at a text with students. Go back to the text type cheat sheets you have created with them (page 69) to understand how something fits or deviates, and then discuss why. We have already looked at this question through the first area of exploration. Its link to **intertextuality** should allow you to cycle back and investigate through comparison and the dialogue of literature.

For literature, you might approach this idea through modernism, using several genres and even other mediums of art. Modernism is many things, but one of its main aspects is the way it responds to the classics. Often this response is structural, so we see reinvented novels as well as sonnets, pastoral paintings and sculptures of human figures alongside comments on modernity and all that it encompasses. Or you might tackle this through poetry – Garcia Lorca, Elizabeth Bishop and William Carlos Williams are all sound choices. How do they use and change the sonnet form or other forms of Renaissance poetry?

For non-literary texts, let us consider them with the next question in mind.

■ 2 How do conventions and systems of reference evolve over time?

While both literary and non-literary texts do change over time, those not included as much in the dialogue of the arts evolve in a functional way, rarely jumping back and forth between styles and structures. Look at the news, for example. Readers have some expectation in terms of what they will read and what the layout is like on the page. Although web-based journalism has a greater diversity of formats, styles and experimentation than we ever saw in the print era, people still learn to understand the message in a certain way. They do not like when it changes unexpectedly! Even take social media and email interfaces. Small changes like font and colour or larger changes such as additional types of emotional buttons (Facebook, Twitter) or algorithms changing the information we see (from chronological to pre-determining for us what we may want to see, for example) cause uproar when they first appear. Once people slowly adapt to them (which does not take long if you spend enough time on your screen everyday), they just *cannot* go back to the old archaic interface.

At first some of these changes may seem petty and inconsequential, but if we consider themes like the funneling of information, merging of advertisement and individual social media posts and formations of personal identity, we begin to have an important dialogue about text type conventions.

In looking at the *Catfish* example, we see how people can manipulate social media for personal gain – on Facebook in this case. More recently, companies and governments have been exposed for doing the same. How does this change the way we use and read our 'newsfeeds'? How has Facebook changed it?

When we look at mainstream journalism, there is also a lot to investigate. The conversation should include elements such as bias, power, economics, advertising, perspective, internationalism and more as you investigate changes in journalistic format and style. Front page content, headlines, captions, hyperlinks, the placing of editorials and juxtaposition all inform readers differently in different contexts. The passive reader consumes it without realizing the ways their opinions are being shaped. Your students will become active readers and more readily discern their media content.

To look at the evolution of journalism, you may want to use inquiry strategies that I shall soon discuss (page 97). It is important that students understand the roots of both journalism and other types of media, including social media, to fully understand their influence and use today.

■ 5 How can texts offer multiple perspectives of a single issue, topic or theme?

You can look at this in terms of ways of looking at truth and lies or look at a particular issue. For example, to better understand the truth about climate change, you might listen to politicians, read a variety of news sources and listen to scientific podcasts. You may then need to make choices about what you believe. You will have to think about the motivations of the writer or speaker to help you understand this. You would also want to be aware of fallacious reasoning.

CORE CONNECTIONS

TOK – fallacious reasoning

Most TOK teachers will do some work with fallacious reasoning as they investigate the WOK of Reason with students. These areas include things like straw man, post hoc, hasty generalization, etc. You can find different lists and handouts online, including a good one on the University of North Carolina *The Writing Center* website, or you can ask the TOK teachers at your school for a copy of what they use with students. These will be valuable ways to address the analysis of media texts in your classroom.

Use of perspective can further be investigated in literature. Single texts can offer different voices within them if the narration changes (*As I lay Dying*, *Frankenstein*, *The Bluest Eye*). Similarly, in journalistic pieces, a writer will often include quotes from different angles and opinions. But the topic can also be addressed by different writers in different ways. This is the idea behind the pairing of texts on a more concentrated conceptual level. You can look at literary responses to texts (*Heart of Darkness*, *Things Fall Apart*, *Half of a Yellow Sun*) or the way different types of media in different places or with different politics address the same topic. A strong way to begin this dialogue is through Twitter, with the understanding that it was set up by journalists to do just that. Follow a hashtag around the globe to understand all the perspectives that can be had about it.

■ HL literature

■ Conceptual unit planning template: Intertextuality

Area of exploration: Intertextuality	Conceptual questions:		How does literature explore human identity?
Conceptual focus: Identity *(Identity, Communication, Creativity)*	**3** In what ways can diverse texts share points of similarity? **4** How valid is the notion of a classic text? **6** In what ways can comparison and interpretation be transformative?		

Core texts	Extension texts	Critical theory	Formative assessments	Summative assessments
Orlando, Virginia Woolf *The Unbearable Lightness of Being*, Milan Kundera *Hamlet*, William Shakespeare	**Excerpts:** Woolf's 'A Room of One's Own' (speech/essay); Nietzsche's 'Eternal Return' (in *The Gay Science*) or explanation on Thoughtco.com; Foucault's *History of Sexuality* Inquiry texts on Prague 1968 Film adaptations of all three texts **Novels:** *Middlesex*, Jeffrey Eugenides; *Giovanni's Room*, James Baldwin; *The Black Prince*, Iris Murdoch; *Gertrude and Claudius*, John Updike **Drama:** *Rosencrantz and Guildenstern are Dead*, Tom Stoppard	Queer Feminist Psychoanalytic Intertextual	Learner portfolio Group critical theory charts and presentations Comparative charts Unpacking P2 questions with mind maps P2 group outlines	Mock P1 Mock P2 **Paper 1 and Paper 2 exams**

Focus questions: How does literature explore human identity? What can we find out about our own identities by reading literature? How do texts over time show a universal human identity? To what extent is identity connected to context? Can we change our identities; how does literature reflect this idea? To what extent are identities performative? What do our beliefs about fate and free will have to do with our identities? To what extent is our gender identity a part of who we are? What is the relationship between sex and sexual identity with our overall identities? What aspects of identity are biological and which ones can we choose? In what ways does society inhibit or support different identities? What do we need – what freedoms or human rights – to be able to assert our identities fully?

Core connections: TOK – students should be able to draw on conversations and research about ways of looking at fate and free will in the TOK course in connection to this unit. Students should also have practice from the TOK essay (completed by now) to consider several texts and ideas to write about a single main idea or thesis statement. Similarly, their EE (also completed) will use a variety of sources, sometimes even of a comparative nature like the Paper 2.

International mindedness: Work in translation, inquiry into other cultures and historical events; writing in exile.

ATT & ATL: Literary theory to compare texts, outlining and timed-exam planning techniques.

Global issues: Personal identity in connection to sexuality, gender, history, birth rights; identity formation through societal structures; life choices and the meaning of life ('eternal return' and existentialism).

■ 3 In what ways can diverse texts share points of similarity?

Texts looking at identity from different time periods and genres can still help us to come to similar conclusions. Consider how the language we use for identities changes over time. The way we use pronouns has changed; where once 'he' was used as the default, now we have many choices and preferences that are still changing as this text is printed. Gendered language in different languages is an interesting discussion point if you are looking at a work in translation that deals with the topic of gender.

Any conceptual focus should give you the point of looking at the 'similarity' within them. However, a way to do this clearly and in preparation for the Paper 2 comparative essay is through the literary lenses in the next chapter. Keep in mind that you can use mixed literary forms to compare (unlike the old literature course), which is one way to understand the diversity of texts in the question. But diversity might also include time period or narrative voice.

Diversity toward similarity basically prepares students to use different texts in comparison for their Paper 2 and to be able to settle on a single thesis that purposefully brings together the texts. *Hamlet*, *Orlando* and *The Unbearable Lightness of Being* can all lead us to ideas about the named global issues in the planner, but in different ways. Notice in the following passages how each text grapples with notions of identity and how students might find comparative ideas. You can start by looking at short passages with students in this way, seeking similarities of ideas in the intertext as you compare.

■ Extract from Virginia Woolf's fictional mock-biography *Orlando* (1928)

> The whole of her darkened and settled, as when some foil whose addition makes the round and solidity of a surface is added to it, and the shallow becomes deep and the near distant; and all is contained as water is contained by the sides of a well. So she was now darkened, stilled, and become, with the addition of this Orlando, what is called, rightly or wrongly, a single self, a real self. And she fell silent. For it is probable that when people talk aloud, the selves (of which there may be more than two thousand) are conscious of disseverment, and are trying to communicate, but when communication is established they fall silent.

■ Extract from *The Unbearable Lightness of Being* by Milan Kundera (1984)

> If eternal return is the heaviest of burdens, then our lives can stand out against it in all their splendid lightness.
>
> But is heaviness truly deplorable and lightness splendid?
>
> The heaviest of burdens crushes us, we sink beneath it, it pins us to the ground. But in the love poetry of every age, the woman longs to be weighed down by the man's body. The heaviest of burdens is therefore simultaneously an image of life's most intense fulfillment. The heavier the burden, the closer our lives come to the earth, the more real and truthful they become.
>
> Conversely, the absolute absence of a burden causes man to be lighter than air, to soar into the heights, take leave of the earth and his earthly being, and become only half real, his movements as free as they are insignificant.
>
> What then shall we choose? Weight or lightness?

■ Extract from William Shakespeare's dramatic tragedy *Hamlet* (Act 5, Scene 2, 194–8)

(You could easily use the famous 'To be, or not to be' soliloquy as well.)

> Not a whit, we defy augury: there's a special
> providence in the fall of a sparrow. If it be now,
> 'tis not to come; if it be not to come, it will be
> now; if it be not now, yet it will come: the
> readiness is all: since no man has aught of what he
> leaves, what is't to leave betimes?

■ 4 How valid is the notion of a classic text?

Hamlet is surely classic, but some would add Kundera and Woolf to that list; they are on the IB text lists after all. *Hamlet* becomes universal – it transcends time and place. In a similar way, so do the other two core texts here, even though they are each so closely linked to historical events.

Although we have started to look at many more texts from 'minor' voices and different perspectives over the last few decades, there is still importance in teaching classical or canonical texts. They help us achieve cultural reference points and understand how other literature responds in a dialogue. Usually the work has achieved its status due to a kind of identified intrinsic beauty, a provocative understanding of humanity and/or a meaningful historical reference point.

Of course, we know that the publishing world has curated voices out of existence for us. Woolf goes on an interesting tangent about this in 'A Room of One's Own' when she talks about Shakespeare's fictional sister, Judith, and how we would be denied her voice. Women have had to take on pen names and, even now, the publishing world chooses what we see and what earns the prizes.

There is much more diversity in publishing now but in a recent piece of research, we found that it is still significantly harder to be published as a woman (Flood, 2015). Many women still use their first initials to remain nominally androgynous (JK Rowling, for example). We have self-publishing, so anyone can give it a go, but can they really reach a big audience? Sometimes it does not matter, but when we talk about what becomes part of the classroom experience, it does matter.

CORE CONNECTION: TOK

Canonical texts as shared cultural knowledge?

As you choose a combination of canonical or classical literature and minor voices, personal passions or contemporary texts, it may help to both do some extra reading on what the point of reading classical literature is yourself and to share some of these ideas or essays with your students.

Howard Bloom's *The Western Canon* and the *Norton Anthology of English Literature* have opinions that you have probably come across before. They attempt to choose the best literature from an aesthetic perspective that allows readers to have cultural knowledge of the *most important* texts. These are texts they would come across in cultural references and literary allusions.

However, some contemporary writers like David Foster Wallace ('Some Remarks on Kafka's Funniness', 'Borges on the Couch') and Zadie Smith ('Middlemarch and

everybody', 'E.M. Forster, middle manager'), perhaps authors you are using elsewhere on your syllabus, also have some great things to say about the canon.

Bloom is right to argue that we need to understand classics to be a part of the dialogue of literature ourselves. As readers and writers, we draw on this dialogue and add our own ideas and language to it. It is empowering to understand this concept. However, he made the mistake of leaving out 'minor' voices that have become classics as well. *The New York Times* revisited his *Western Canon* 20 years later and noted that "... he could not see that intellectual and cultural life in the West since the 1969s has been enriched by the representatives of a long invisible majority" (Mishra and Mendelsohn, 2014) and that the experiences of this group has ameliorated our understanding of the arts.

Perhaps Calvino's book *Why Read the Classics?* (2009) offers a better definition, even if most of the chapters are about the same names that Bloom lists in his text. Calvino offers fresh and dynamic reads, which he claims is part of the definition of a 'classic': one that can be read over and over with new interpretations.

You can use Calvino's initial 14-point definition of a classic in his first chapter as a test for students to help them understand the importance of a text (note that here I only reproduce the 14 points; Calvino provides a longer explanation of each in his book). Notice how the definitions are largely about seeking personal pleasure and understanding, supposing a lack of a fixed interpretation of a text. Ask students to what extent each of the three core texts in this unit fit each of the 14 definitions:

■ Extract from *Why Read the Classics?* by Italo Calvino (2009)

1   The classics are those books about which you usually hear people saying: 'I'm rereading ...', never 'I'm reading ...'

2   The classics are those books which constitute a treasured experience for those who have read and loved them; but they remain just as rich an experience for those who reserve the chance to read them for when they are in the best condition to enjoy them.

3   The classics are books which exercise a particular influence, both when they imprint themselves on our imagination as unforgettable, and when they hide in the layers of memory disguised as the individual's or the collective unconscious.

4   A classic is a book which with each rereading offers as much of a sense of discovery as the first reading.

5   A classic is a book which even when we read it for the first time gives the sense of rereading something we have read before.

6   A classic is a book which has never exhausted all it has to say to its readers.

7   The classics are those books which come to us bearing the aura of previous interpretations, and trailing behind them the traces they have left in the culture or cultures (or just in the languages and customs) through which they have passed.

8   A classic is a work which constantly generates a pulviscular cloud of critical discourse around it, but which always shakes the particles off.

9   Classics are books which, the more we think we know them through hearsay, the more original, unexpected, and innovative we find them when we actually read them.

10   A classic is the term given to any book which comes to represent the whole universe, a book on a par with ancient talismans.

11   'Your' classic is a book to which you cannot remain indifferent, and which helps you define yourself in relation or even in opposition to it.

12   A classic is a work that comes before other classics; but those who have read other classics first immediately recognize its place in the genealogy of classic works.

13   A classic is a work which relegates the noise of the present to a background hum, which at the same time the classics cannot exist without.

14   A classic is a work which persists as a background noise even when a present that is totally incompatible with it holds sway.

■ 6 In what ways can comparison and interpretation be transformative?

The answer should be obvious at this point: by creating an intertext, of course!

Ask your students how they see a text differently once they look at it next to another. Consider new interpretations together – they may have heard the 'To be or not to be …' soliloquy since their young school days, but now that they have interpreted it in a new way, how has it changed? How has looking at identity in several texts changed the way you see that soliloquy and Hamlet's character? Looking at a topic from different angles can make the initial reading clearer, even if it conflicts with those views.

With this question, and those going back to reader response and interpretation with the first concept, we want to be careful that students are writing about *ideas found in the text*. This is, of course, a danger of going beyond the text if students do not understand their tasks well enough.

If comparison and interpretation use skills and content for the groundwork, you should be able to keep the conclusions conceptually based. Texts that directly respond are different but just as useful. However, you need to be careful if you use these with students for comparative purposes.

For example, you can look at *Rosencrantz and Guildenstern are Dead* alongside *Hamlet*. Of course, the former drama is a direct response, using the characters from Shakespeare's text to tell it from a different perspective with humour and a focus on existentialist philosophy. It can make a strong companion text, but students may find it difficult to write about these two in comparison for Paper 2. Likewise, allegorical texts (*Kafka on the Shore* and *Oedipus*, for example) are rich ways to understand the dialogue of literature, but more difficult for students to write about conceptual intertexts. Instead, looking at the core texts of this unit takes texts with similar focus areas without the distraction of trying to understand how the texts fit together.

Conceptual lessons: pre, during, post

All of the previous ideas for framing the IB conceptual questions are methods of using CBL explicitly in your classroom. However, you and your students will find value in going beyond these framing ideas. This section proposes several explicit lesson ideas for CBL that can be applied to the language A DP classroom. The focus will always be on helping students arrive at and understand 'big ideas' with 'real world' relevance (Erickson, 2011).

■ ATT & ATL

CBL pre-unit lessons

- Many teachers use their own kind of pre-lessons or pre-assessments already. Some of these might be tweaked to be more conceptual. The reason for a pre-lesson of any kind is to activate previous student knowledge and get a better idea of what students already know about a topic, text or skill. The reasoning here is the same. Students need content and skills to understand concepts, so anything you have done previously should work. However, a stronger focus on purposeful ideas and their applications, including transference, helps students to be more motivated for the upcoming unit by giving it relevancy and creativity in thought. They are given more agency to reflect and think about the emerging ideas posed.

■ Take a Stand!

This is one of the favourite activities of my students of all ages. Many of you may have come across it in your teacher training or workshops, but perhaps not with a conceptual angle. Essentially this activity allows students to talk through opinions while moving through the room. I could say a lot more about the mind–body connection; essentially though, most of us know it is beneficial to include some movement in our classrooms, especially if we have long teaching periods.

You will need four signs in four distinct quadrants of the room: 'Strongly agree', 'Somewhat agree', 'Strongly disagree' and 'Somewhat disagree'.

When I am teaching in my own classroom, these signs are a permanent fixture. Since I currently share several classrooms, I keep them as laminated, sticky-tacked signs in my box of tricks. It is important that there is no neutral territory here! A student who is stuck should simply choose a side for the sake of argument. However, all students can move freely through the room as the debate ensues if they are persuaded by others' arguments and evidence.

To play the game, start with somewhere between three and ten statements related to a concept, or subtopic, you are exploring. The statements should be provocative and conceptual. In other words, they should relate to the real world and be what most would consider big ideas. Include some that you yourself strongly disagree with.

■ Example: Take a Stand! concept: beauty

Directions to students: Write to what extent you agree with the following statements or not. Explain your thoughts and try to add an example to better explain. We will then take a stand around the room based on our responses and pass the ball to facilitate debate. We shall allow up to four comments per item to start discussion, but the topics will be brought up again as we study the texts for the conceptual unit.

1 Beauty is in the eye of the beholder.

2 People should use science to make themselves more beautiful.

3 Deformities or abnormalities on people's physique should be fixed when possible.

4 How you look can keep you from getting a job.

5 Aesthetic beauty comes with no downside.

6 Parents are bound to love their children, no matter what.

I ask students to respond to these statements first on their own, without the influence of others. This is usually done at the start of a lesson in students' journals but could also be homework or something to do at the end of a lesson the day before. They do not need full responses to each topic and can pick and choose freely the order of their responses. I tell them it can be useful to start with a gut response of simply agree/disagree, then dive into a free-write or mind map of reasons and evidence, drawing on literature but also knowledge from other subjects and from their lives.

Next, you take the statements one-by-one: project it for the whole room and read it aloud two or three times. Ask students to get up and move to where they feel they should be in terms of their opinions. They can bring their notes if it helps them articulate their ideas. Ask one student to start the discussion by passing them a soft ball (or whatever you use for the speaker in the room). Allow them to speak and bite your tongue, only inserting yourself if you need to ask students to use more evidence or if the sides are heavily lopsided in ideas. Relatedly, if all students are on one side of the room, ask for some devil's advocate volunteers.

You may only have time for a few comments on each statement, but that is ok. Assure students that the conversation will continue throughout the unit and that if they are antsy, they can continue at lunch! You could also explicitly come back to the same statements at the end of the unit and ask how opinions have changed or what evidence from the texts they have studied they can add.

Through conceptual understanding with this activity, you also engage prior knowledge, work on oral language skills and develop conversational listen and respond skills. After students have completed this activity a few times, they might also be able to write the provocative statements themselves (though this would be a during- or post-reading activity; you write statements that engage with what will be debates or perspectives of the texts that will be studied). They should also start using devil's advocate on their own and accessing examples from different disciplines or research completed in the prep time without your prompts. In other words, they will internalize conceptual learning if they can see the benefits.

■ Question wall

Harvard University's Project Zero talks a lot about the idea of making learning visible. We all do this to some extent, but they have some great strategies on their website if you are unfamiliar. The question wall is not a specific Project Zero idea, but links to their suggested activities, such as See-Think-Wonder, which is wonderful to use when you are engaging with visual texts.

The question wall is simple. As you begin looking at a conceptual focus, get students to first come up with questions they have about the concept. Let's take Identity for this one. Students might first ask:

> Is identity a product of nature or nurture?

> How does cultural identity inform personal identity?

> Can we change our identities?

Then you can look at the opening passages of your core texts. The first scene of *Hamlet* might make students continue with:

> How does class or rank influence identity?

> Do our identities last beyond death? (As ghosts?)

The Unbearable Lightness of Being starts with an explicit discussion of Nietzsche's 'eternal return' and asking what the 'mad myth signif[ies]'? through connections to 'African kingdoms', the 'French revolution' and 'Hitler'. Through the labyrinth of ideas about morals and perspectives in this start, the students might further ask:

> Are people inherently evil or good?

> Are our identities formations of past (or future) events?

Finally, with *Orlando*, we are introduced to the young boy ('for there could be no doubt of his sex') and his inclinations toward poetry and solitude as well as an understanding of his physical description. Student questions may include:

> How does sex shape identity?

> How do people explore identity through the arts?

Now you have to capture the questions because you are not done with them! You ask the questions now, but you answer them as you move through the texts. Perhaps you also do some inquiry research about aspects that require it. Use a bulletin board in the room with sticky notes or tacked up questions, or digitally create a Padlet or Google doc with the questions. Keep everything visible and return to it at moments that will advance the students' understanding of the concept. As they answer the questions later in the unit, they will have found the formations of 'big ideas'.

■ Freewriting

Let students process what they already think about a topic, before studying it with you and being influenced by others. They may already draw on what they have learned in previous language A classes or other subjects or from their own experience. This brings us into the real world immediately before getting lost in books. In this way, it is easier to go back and forth.

I mentioned that you can use freewriting to start the 'Take a Stand!' activity, but you can make it even freer than that. Use a single word or the phrase that is the conceptual topic of your unit. Give students **beauty, Black in America** or **truth and lies** and they are sure to have associations and opinions already. Some students might respond through a poem, visual notetaking, a letter or a fictional story. Allow them to do this. Allow them to engage with the topic in whatever way makes sense to them on that day. You might choose to have them share in pairs or small groups and then allow anyone who wants to share with the class to do so, or you might simply respond to their journals later. It depends on your class, how much time you have and what you want to accomplish that day.

■ ATT & ATL

CBL during unit lessons

■ During the unit, students will start to use the variety of content you have introduced in combination with skills (mainly analytical at this point) to begin understanding the concept. You are working on synergistic thinking throughout the unit, helping students make connections. Every lesson should include some element of addressing: 'So what? Why are we learning this or reading that?' Though you may not have the answers until the end of the unit, it is important to at least begin posing the questions along the way, so students are motivated to continue.

■ Lexicons

Lexicons are the most simple and effective way to focus a lesson. We use them all the time in my classroom, and I ask students to keep their own running lexicons in their journals. Etymologically, a lexicon is simply a list of words, a type of word-association brainstorm. On the board, we constantly make lexicons – emerging themes or sometimes lists of characters or terminology.

In my own learning at university, one professor of mine, Celeste Goodridge, nearly always started our lessons with a lexicon. We had to read at least one book, usually a novel, for every single lesson, and to start to make sense of the large reading list we created lexicons and wrote down keywords: emerging themes, stylistic devices, allegorical connections, repeated phrases. Somehow the lesson (which had to have been both planned and spontaneous to work!) would take us back in circles to the words we had put on the board. Sometimes it turned into a web. Often a word became the object of further investigation by an individual or pair to report back in the next lesson. Sometimes a word turned into a thesis. Most importantly though, getting up and writing simple words on the board for about ten minutes opened up a world and gave us a voice. By moving through the space of the lecture hall or seminar room, I felt vivaciously alive and a part of my learning experience. I felt empowered and expressive while enjoying the learning.

You can use this activity once you have read a whole text or just the first chapter, or also later when you have read several texts. Try to understand what is going on by looking at the list of words. Nothing is 'wrong' if it has been activated in the student's mind, but some words you may want to highlight orally or visually (circling them, for example) if they link directly to a conceptual understanding. Ask how it relates to other texts they have read or to the real world.

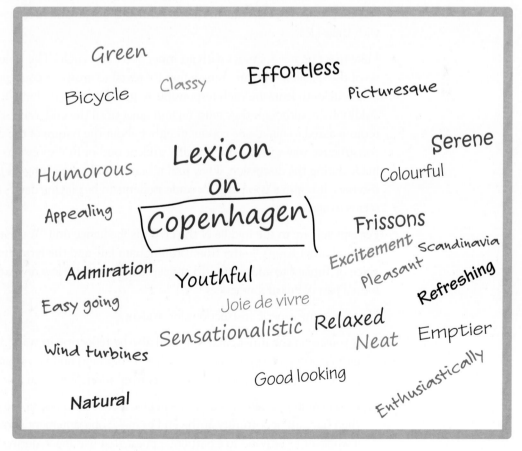

Class lexicon of 'Copenhagen' by Bill Bryson (Travel writing)

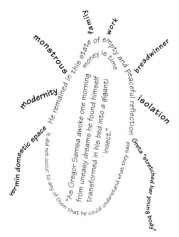

Student lexicon of Kafka's *Metamorphosis*

Keep these lists – in student journals or perhaps as photos on your website (or whatever type of saving device you use) – and build on them. They are just emerging ideas to begin with; they are not fully-fledged themes with verbs that say something about the world. Later you can go back to the lists to make the themes, or big ideas. What have we learned here? How can we use the texts to prove it?

If you have had a tough morning or you have nothing planned … just make a lexicon. The students can start on their own while you orient yourself. Then, they (and you) make good use of moving around the room as they get up to write on the board. The discussion will be natural and you can quickly get into the text itself, doing a close read together while referring back to the lexicon or asking students to come up with related quotes. Who said good teaching had to be complicated? As long as you are prepared with the text and where you want to go in the unit, you can make your lessons spontaneous.

■ Journal questions

I will not go into detail now as we will investigate journals in Chapter 5, but how you frame your questions can make them more conceptual. Use the actual IB questions, but also use questions related to your topics. These can include the focus questions proposed on the sample unit planners in this book.

■ Socratic seminars

Many language A teachers use Socratic seminars, though they may do so in slightly different ways. These are discussions based on a text where the main idea is that the students should be able to have a round table discussion *without* prompts from the teacher, and they should be referring to the text through quotes and specifics and digging deep with their ideas.

I like to set up my Socratics with an inner and outer circle. The inner circle is made up of the speakers who are using a text (or texts) to answer a conceptual question. The outer circle students are each responsible to give feedback to a single inner circle speaker. Additionally, although they must remain quiet until the end, each student around the room is asked to make one comment either about the nature of the discussion (in a constructive way without singling any student out) or in response to a point that was made during the discussion. They find it hard to hold their tongues but become excellent listeners. It is also a good idea for some students to be playing devil's advocate if everyone seems to agree.

Perhaps you are in the middle of the **civil disobedience** unit. You can ask students to use Martin Luther King's 'Letter from Birmingham Jail' and the lyrics from El Général's 'the voice of Tunisia' to address the IB conceptual question: 'How do texts reflect, represent or form a part of cultural practices?'

Here are some generic instructions for students:

- If you are in the inner circle, you will also be reflecting in your journal about your participation: Did you listen carefully to others and build on what they said? Were you polite? Did you assert yourself in the conversation? Were you able to resolve conflict?

- If you are in the outer circle, you will give feedback to one of the speakers. You will then have an opportunity at the end to make one statement about the conversation as a whole or to respond to a particular point that was made during the discussion.

■ Feedback sheet

Speaker:	
Student giving feedback:	
Moments of insight:	

How did the speaker advance the discussion? (Circle all that apply, then add comment)	Brought up controversial points
	Added evidence from the text
	Looked at different perspectives
	Played devil's advocate
	Included others in conversation
	Other:

What advice do you have to help the speaker? (Circle all that apply, then add comment)	Be more involved
	Don't talk over people
	Ask questions
	Include others in conversation
	Look at different perspectives
	Use evidence
	Other:

■ Padlets

Although an organizational tool, this web-based interactive platform can extend the life of your classroom ideas. The question wall and lexicons can be part of this – so can journal questions. If you are unfamiliar with the website, have a look at its easy-to-use interface and play around with a trial page yourself.

You do not have to use the Padlet website for these activities – you can use paper just as easily or maybe other webtools, like collaborative Google docs or something new that comes along. However, Padlet is fun and easy. You can set the page to private and you can choose for students to write anonymously or logged in (very easy if they have Google accounts at school). Your Padlet can pose the conceptual and topic questions, allowing students to not only answer in class but whenever an idea comes to them. Students work better in different settings or at different times. They can also draw pictures or mindmaps and post them to the Padlet or upload documents from their Google drives or directly from computers. They can add links to text examples or inquiry findings.

You can focus your Padlet for a unit directly on the conceptual topic (**beauty, civil disobedience**) or more largely on the IB area of exploration (**time and space**). It can be a play area that you return to when you have time or when students perhaps finish some work in class early. You might give more specific directions (for example, answer this question; post your drawing of the topic lexicon) in the first semester or year and move toward more student-directed posts. They can respond directly to each other. For this reason, if you are using the Padlet beyond one day in class, I think it is useful if students sign in. Anonymous online activity is not a great way to hold students responsible for their questioning or criticism of others. We also want to give others in the room credit for their great ideas!

By beginning with more structured posting, you can also work on bringing together skills and content. Learning specific analytical or writing skills can be a part of the Padlet. For example, ask students to find specific figurative language in a text that relates to a topic's focus question, or post pictures of characterization posters that allow students to show their understanding of the relationship between character development and conceptual perspective. At the end, make a post that asks students to create sample conceptual thesis statements related to earlier posts. Maybe follow with a posted sample outline strategy or template, or even a graphic organizer, that students can fill out in pairs and post to the group. The thesis statements and outlines should have big ideas (do they?) and then a discussion of real-world application can ensue.

■ ATT & ATL

CBL post-lessons

- At the end of the unit, a synthesis of conceptual learning is key and helps students prepare for assessments. This is where they find the thesis statements they need for any of the assessments from IB or any other presentations or essays you might assign. Additionally, they form the big takeaways that will hopefully last well beyond your completion of the course. You are helping students find the skills they need to read a variety of texts and genres to make meaning of the world.

■ 'Big ideas' chart and group presentations

You can make a chart of your conceptual questions for students to fill out which helps them easily identify big ideas on their own. They should come to some ideas you had in mind and perhaps others you would not have thought about. This exercise is simple and can be done individually or collaboratively. It works well on a Google doc where students can all write on the same document or simply on a large sheet of paper or the white board.

The activity can be a rather brief way to identify conceptual understanding or one that leads to writing or presentations that include examples from texts you have studied. You may want to identify big ideas after each core text (or set of short texts) and then look at them together at the end of a unit with the purpose of writing the HL essay or Paper 2. Further, you might choose to include visual notetaking or mindmapping from students. They can (perhaps as a group) identify a given big idea to explore in a visual way: collages, sketches of scenes and characters from texts, associated language, emotional connections … the possibilities are endless. Allow students to include material from other subjects, even other language A courses they might be taking, before later identifying what specifically from the course core texts led toward the idea, and can therefore be used as an example in assessments. If you keep the activity rather open and creative, then restructure it toward thesis writing or an organized debate, it will take on a focused purpose.

Though you can likewise use the focus questions, for the synthesis part of your unit, I recommend going back to the IB conceptual questions and dividing by major core text or group of texts. The initial boxes are a brainstorm related to that text leading toward a more general big idea that plays with several texts studied in the unit. Here is an example of a big ideas chart:

■ Big ideas chart – truth and lies conceptual unit

Conceptual questions	1 How do texts adhere to and deviate from conventions associated with literary forms or text types?	2 How do conventions and systems of reference evolve over time?	5 How can texts offer multiple perspectives of a single issue, topic or theme?
Social media (and *Catfish* film)	Facebook was made to connect people; now a political tool. Twitter created for/by journalists – now largely social. Users/public largely in charge of these platforms.	New textuality – social media has become connected with identity. Without checks and balances, can 'trick' people. More ways to connect with people and ideas around the world.	Allows many sources (searchable by hashtag). Can funnel information from one perspective.
Journalism (related to politics)	It is through deviation that New Journalism was formed and now new textualities are mixed in with journalism. Important to know if something is 'real journalism' with standards of fact checking, etc, or just some citizen journalism or a satire. Maintenance of different text types within journalism helps us know if something is meant to be unbiased or opinionated.	Print to online – changes timing, can use hyperlinks, more easily available, less likely to read full article, searchable. Standards of 'truth' and fact checking have changed; vary in different countries. Citizen Journalism – keeps in check but also adds fake news.	Should be unbiased perspective in theory. Different versions of 'truth'.

Conceptual questions	1 How do texts adhere to and deviate from conventions associated with literary forms or text types?	2 How do conventions and systems of reference evolve over time?	5 How can texts offer multiple perspectives of a single issue, topic or theme?
Political speeches	Public expects a certain standard and professionalism. Donald Trump has created sensationalist type of speech/ rally to connect with TV. Politicians need to weigh convention for believability/ reliability and doing something to make the public notice.	Contemporary leaders draw on rhetorical devices from past. TV speeches add the visual – sound bites shared on social media. Fact checking can now be immediate.	Personal view to sell an idea/vision. Need to compare several speeches to view different perspectives.
Big ideas about truth and lies	Certain text types give a standard of reliability that the public trusts. Text types that deviate from the norm catch the attention of the public, either creating believability by catching them off guard or making them reject the claims as gimmicky.	While we are more connected to different sources and able to fact check information today, fabrication of information is also more easily spread. Contemporary medias have created greater transparency of knowledge exchange and less ability for censorship.	Truth can be found by comparing multiple sources from different political and cultural views. We need to be careful that we are not swayed by information that claims to deliver the truth.

Once students have completed the chart, have small group presentations on their findings. You will see some conclusions here that negate each other. This is ok as long as students use evidence. Students should use at least two texts from the unit to support their ideas and you should request that they use specific quotes and analytical terminology to connect the texts to the big idea.

You can also use this chart in relation to several units, either to prepare for the IO or Paper 2. For example, with the chart above, you might add the Albanian novel *Broken April* by Ismail Kadare (1978) and the Indian novel *The White Tiger* by Aravind Adiga. Kadare's novel shows multiple perspectives about traditions in rural Albania. Although it largely adheres to novel convention, the perspective changes as well as the perspective of a killer allow us to consider the way truths are created in small communities within Communist-controlled countries. Adiga's novel also implies another perspective, since the novel is written as a letter to the Chinese premier Wen Jiabao. By playing with genre and using the epistolary form to the real leader of China (at the time of publication), Adiga adds an element of playing with the truth. The narrator's direct engagement with the premier as a man of the untouchable caste adds layers that cause the audience to question 'typical' media that might not give them the full picture. Both of these novels could be added to the dialogue above and possibly be used as comparative texts for the IB assessments.

■ Debate

Focus on debatable questions and use of the texts studied here. A debate in your classroom might bring in other real-world examples, but try to keep the focus on using examples from your texts. You can do this by using a single text or small sampling of short texts from different perspectives for students to draw on in debate.

I will not go into the details of how to set up a debate here, because many of you have your own methods that work. However, one thing I highly recommend is to get at least some students to argue the opposite of the side they believe in. I recommend also getting students to predetermine several point-based speakers after an opening statement speaker and before a concluding point. In this way, the whole class will have set up an essay of at least five paragraphs to be delivered orally. We look at this structure in Chapter 5.

Inquiry's place in CBL

■ What does inquiry have to do with CBL?

Use the student-generated factual/conceptual/debatable questions you came up with in the pre-unit lesson (question wall) for the inquiry. These should be written somewhere for student access, perhaps on Managebac, if your school uses this online organizational tool for IB, or another online curriculum platform your school has decided on. Alternatively, it might be on a unit overview like the ones in this book, either displayed on a wall or through an online medium. While I do like paper-based planners and overviews for many reasons, these questions might do well digitally for several reasons. It will be easier to add or adjust the questions with student input and to build up your course components in one place that is easily changeable. The platform need not be fancy; the focus should be on accessibility and ease of use, though a little color and creativity can go a long way to motivate students.

Students at all stages of the IB curriculum should be using the inquiry cycle. Students who come to you from PYP and MYP should already be familiar with this cycle, allowing you to draw on it easily. Most of you may know the circular diagram from Kathleen Murdoch: Tuning In, Finding Out, Sorting Out, Going Further, Making Conclusions, Taking Action. It is important that the circle is a continuum and the process is never truly finished.

I like to show students this circle and discuss how even though it is designed for primary-age students, professors use a similar model. Make it a process that students can replicate on their own by breaking down parts together as a class, giving your students tools to conduct effective research and draw their own conclusions. Once you and your students understand the inquiry cycle, it is something that can be used easily for a variety of situations, including the HL essay and the EE.

■ Scaffolding inquiry

It is easy to say: 'Inquiry is so easy! Get the kids to just decide what they want to know and go for it …'. Yes, you want to get them to that level, but even DP students need help to get there. They need some structure and pointers, some curating and motivating to get to a level of inquiry where more freedom leads to clarity rather than chaos.

Part of the structure can be in using the inquiry cycle as well. All of these structural components also fall under skills development, which for CBL should work in conjunction with content. You may want to explicitly tell your students when they are working on a skill or content, or both, and how these things will help them move toward conceptual understandings.

Kathleen Murdoch has done the most explicit and useful pedagogical work on this topic. She gives a succinct overview of what it is and what it should not be in 'What does it mean to be an inquiry teacher?' (**www.youtube.com/watch?v=xlX32gB_e-w**). Here she explains that the educator is an expert and guide, a co-designer of the student's learning experience. For inquiry to work, scaffolding must be clear and effective, and the teacher must have the knowledge to guide the student correctly.

■ Inquiry lesson ideas

■ Curated reading lists

Students can collect other texts they find through their own guided research. They might be referencing or printing/copying these into their journal. Alternatively, they might curate on a digital platform like Scoop.it or Diigo where they can tag by keyword to create an ongoing platform, one where they can interact with the real-world curating on this topic (if your school allows) or at least within the classroom.

You can start with your own curated lists, as these can be the basis for your first semester group projects. Initially, you may even print a single article per group, then move toward a page with limited choice, followed by a combination of teacher curation and free student investigation and finally completely free student investigation. By that time, students should have also talked about what makes a good source in their TOK and individuals and societies classes. Pointing out this transference again shows real-world possibilities in using the skills *and* the content generated in the inquiry work.

■ Group presentations

Although there is no longer a required IB DP presentation in front of the class, it is still valuable to get students up in front of the classroom as much as possible. When students present, they synthesize information and perform. They use creative thinking skills, metacognition and collaboration (if a group project) to do so. Even activities that ask students to present after 15 minutes with a partner or group can be valuable. Tableaux, summaries, visual depictions of ideas – these tasks all accomplish the skills above and help students to understand the content differently. It can certainly help students feel comfortable and gain skills for the individual oral assessment. The truth is that the more people try out their public speaking skills, the more confidence they will have.

A caveat: students need to have meaningful, immediate, positive reinforcement for this to be true. By creating your classroom to be one of risk and respect, students will encourage each other as much as you encourage them. They will model creative strategies in accomplishing your formative tasks. You can indicate students to give the following specific feedback after a group presentation:

■ comment on a specific aspect you liked and why

■ give a specific area where the student(s) can improve

■ ask a specific question.

All of these should be framed positively and can be either about the content or style of the presentation. You can, of course, follow with your own comments and questions as well as possibly asking students to give feedback on paper. In addition, you could have a CBL moment on the spot by asking the class to engage themselves with the presentation through finding a big idea or real-world application connected to the delivery.

■ Extension reading

Extension reading can mean a lot of different things. Essentially, it is any reading done beyond the core requirements. Sometimes, the extension material differentiates by allowing students to access a topic through more challenging texts or by providing easier-to-read explanatory information. You might assign different extension reading to different students or allow them to choose freely. You might have set text lists, perhaps created with other teachers or the librarian at your school, or there may be a few suggestions with the option to conference with you for more ideas. These can be physically available or listed and curated online.

Extension texts might include scholarly writing, related novels from the library, media sources, texts in different disciplines – in this way it becomes real world through the transference. You might be surprised that your weak or average students are interested in a topic that takes them to some challenging extension texts. If you incorporate these additions as requirements in your early inquiry activities, then students are more likely to access them on their own later. If you want to use longer texts but students are struggling, use these as summer or holiday reading – it should not feel like work!

One way you might structure extension reading into your first unit is through book circles. Depending on your class and your unit, you might either choose a limited selection of scholarly articles, historical texts or novels (for example) for the groups to focus on.

Let us suppose you are beginning with the **beauty** unit in your literature class. If you use my suggested texts, you have nothing from this century. You could ask students to select from three to five novels, depending on the class size, from this century that relate to the topic. You might select from the suggested texts in the chart or choose your own, especially if you want to look at particular cultural perspectives. So then you might have four groups looking at Zadie Smith's *On Beauty*, Arundhati Roy's *The God of Small Things* (1996, but perhaps contemporary enough), Milan Kundera's *The Festival of Insignificance* (2013), and Raphael Selbourne's *Beauty* (2009). Alternatively, for the **Black in America** unit, students might select from novels written by Black American authors over the last century, including Ralph Ellison's *Invisible Man* (1952), Zora Neal Hurston's *Their Eyes were Watching God* (1937), Richard Wright's *Black Boy* (1945, though it is a memoir), Paul Beatty's *The Sellout* (2016) and anything by Toni Morrison. Another option would be to select related poets or worthy films for each unit if you think your students would struggle with the extra reading.

Each small group of two to five students will then choose a focus question from the unit after previewing the book. As they read the text, they will annotate related passages and write down their ideas in their journals. As they come together to discuss at the end, they will then develop a further inquiry question by first brainstorming many and finally selecting one to go deeper with. The question should have real-world significance. In other words, it should not be about a character or element of the plot. Instead, it should take the author's ideas and extend them outward to psychology, nature and biology, philosophy or perhaps ethical concerns in the news.

In the next step, each student finds one related source. You could have a mini lesson from yourself or the librarian on accessing resources through your school library and online databases, as well as how to effectively research through open online search engines. By finally bringing these sources together toward the end of the unit, students should have some conclusions, but they will not stop there. They can now bring in the core texts to help understand the initial focus question and the inquiry question. Finally, they can synthesize their information in a five-minute presentation or informal discussion with the rest of the class.

In the above activity, you have helped motivate students beyond the classroom, worked on collaborative skills, engaged with conceptual questions, worked on research skills, practiced synthesizing and summarizing and developed a line of inquiry, skills which will be needed for the HL essay.

■ Role-play activities

We often ask students to think from different perspectives, but how often do we really make them own that role? As Atticus explains to Scout in *To Kill a Mockingbird*: 'You never really understand a person until you consider things from his point of view … until you climb in his skin and walk around in it.'

For students to understand an issue from different angles, I often either have them role play as characters or authors from the works we are studying, or as real-world figures who relate to the topic. The role play can eventually take different formats: a debate, forum, trial, television show and more. However, the preparation and outcomes are similar in each case.

As an example, I used the Umbrella Revolution in Hong Kong as a case study to look at **civil disobedience** and the related textual discourse. For this topic, role play was hugely important. I decided to look at it with my students in Hong Kong in the middle of the protests, as news was unfolding while we were in the classroom. It had generated many emotional responses about identity, economics, immigration, language and more within the school grounds. After initially overhearing students talk about the issues with differing levels of being informed, with some students relying only on 'what their parents said', I thought it was something we should look at more carefully. On top of that, there were students in the room who were planning to head to the protests. I knew that some of my Cantonese and Mandarin speakers would also have access to different information than others of us. We set out to first understand how citizen journalism works and how Twitter hashtags help us to get immediate information from different sources. However, we also investigated reliability. Which sources could we trust? Which images even? How could bias or censorship be included in different mediums? How did the coverage from the rest of the world differ from that within Hong Kong? How did it differ between languages of publication? Who had even heard different reports from friends, taxi drivers or the next table at the café that had not been reported?

To sort through the information, I asked students to take on different roles: journalists from different sources in Hong Kong and the rest of the world, poor protestors, rich university student protesters, an immigrant from the Mainland, a CEO of a Hong Kong bank, a survivor of Tianamen, a taxi driver, a Triad (Hong Kong gang) member, someone whose commute had become 40 minutes longer, the head of the British Council and President Xi. We were going to have a forum, since there were not clearly only two sides, but many. The students had to determine what their character's main issue was with the protests (whether for, against or indifferent) and why they felt that way. They had to do this through inquiry and then through thinking creatively about how to present their fictional perspective. In this way, a topic that was so heated became a performance. Students could speak freely as someone else, acknowledging that their words might not be their own perspectives. We did not set out to solve the problem! However, we did set out to try to understand on a deeper level what was going on and how to get the information through texts.

INTERNATIONAL MINDEDNESS

Perspectives

Role play helps students to develop their skills from the inquiry cycle while also focusing on different perspectives. In this way, they can begin to consider different international perspectives as well, and become more comfortable with this idea anytime they read literature or news from around the world.

■ Journal investigations

Again, more on the journals later, but the journal, as part of the learner portfolio, can be a dynamic force in student-led inquiry. This is where I would ask students to really experiment. Later, I will show you how to work toward more independent journal investigations. First you will begin by directing students toward inquiry and limiting their scope. Later, you will encourage them to do their own investigations. In the journals, you can also include responses to group inquiry work in the classroom.

Using critical theory

The importance of critical theory in language A

Literary or critical theory and its use in academia has gone through ebbs and flows in terms of its value as a way of looking at a text. However, its use in the secondary classroom has been growing. Rather than adhering to what is more popular or current, recent work with young adults has included reference to several schools of thought in an effort to expand perspectives and layers of meaning, rather than limit them. Similarly, in academia, research often now considers several theories to ultimately say something purposeful. As early as 1969, Henry Levin 'urg[ed] more practical work [in comparative literature] and less agonizing about theory' (Bassnett, 1993, page 5). Comparative literature departments that used to focus on translation now are places of dynamic cross-theoretical, and often cross-disciplinary, study. For that reason, they make a closer model to your mixed-genre, interdisciplinary-linked, international classroom than a classical literature department (even if you are teaching the literature course). The idea is that these lenses can help us discover; for students, a simplified version of the theories create angles of analysis that can be used to unpack and create meaning from a text. Through comparison, both as part of daily lessons and in working toward the Paper 2 assessment, we can find universal human truths and big ideas about global issues.

Gone are the purely formalist days of the 20th-century English classroom. The IB curriculum has expanded to include works from different places and a broad range of people that beg to move into a contextual analysis, one that can be focused through a particular lens. Using theory is about revealing hidden truths, or hidden possibilities at least. It should be easy to see by now how important revelation of different perspectives and truths is to a CBL classroom structure, even though it is not a requirement from IB.

Although close textual analysis is an essential skill for your students, when classrooms became heavily based on formalism (with some historical reference points), they turned into stagnated dialogues. If you hear students who have been turned off by overanalysing texts and 'taking the fun out of reading', this approach has likely been utilized. There is a narrowing rather than an opening of understanding. The CBL approach with the added use of critical theory does not mean they can say *whatever they want*. It instead allows a more focused approach to uncovering real purpose(s) of a text in the world today.

This chapter offers several theories to introduce to your students as tools for analysis and discovering big ideas. For each theory, several related articles or essays are suggested, providing further background for you or your students. They are by no means exhaustive, and you may want to keep both *The Norton Anthology of Theory and Criticism* and *Literary Theory: An Anthology* by Julie Rivkin and Michael Ryan within close reach if you want to investigate further in this area. Easy-to-use online resources include *Owl Purdue's Writing Lab*, which has a great section on 'Literary theory and schools of criticism', and the *Stanford Encyclopedia of Philosophy*.

After framing the theory, we look at practical ways to use it and approach its teaching in your classroom. Each theory is followed by a table you can weave into your course. These can be used for collaborative Google docs, part of student journals or part of a carousel classroom exercise. I usually start with isolated lenses early in the course for particular texts, or a particular section of a literary text. Then, as students become more comfortable, they can more dexterously apply the table questions and sometimes even the philosophical ideas of theorists themselves. They can use the charts to make comparisons between texts, which will be useful for your Paper 2 preparation work.

Alternatively, you can introduce all the theories you plan to use throughout the course early, and follow by coming back and fleshing out the ideas more carefully. You might choose a core text where you could apply any of the theories: *The Great Gatsby*, *Things Fall Apart* or *A Doll's House* would work well. One creative colleague of mine also uses children's books for this purpose at the start. If you are teaching *The Bluest Eye*, you could start with a theoretical analysis of a children's reading primer, since the allusion to this text is used throughout the novel, or you might choose a different text type, such as a newspaper. Take in a full print newspaper for each pair of students or ask them to bring in their own. You can make this activity multilingual with newspapers in other languages they speak. For each theory, they should be able to find an article where the application is relevant. Then, ask them to try to apply another theory that did not seem to obviously go along with the subject. See if they can unpack more from the text through Marxist theory, or apply New Historicism to *Crime and Punishment* to learn about culture.

With an emphasis on discovery rather than limitation, you cannot go wrong with critical theory. It does not really matter how many theories you cover (and the list here is not exhaustive); better to do a few well. Make sure students understand that critical theories are not meant to limit their analysis but open it up; they need not refer to theories in their assessments, but using them explicitly is possible. The more you can talk about critical theories in a colloquial way in the classroom, the more students will have confidence to apply them to the texts you study or the texts they are faced with in Paper 1.

Literary theory is designed, of course, with literary texts in mind. However, transference to other text types is relatively easy. In order to discover and unpack global issues for the IO, for example, literary theory will be useful for language and literature students as well. However, most examples I explain here relate to literary texts and will be useful strategies for either course's Paper 2 preparation.

Finally, you can of course use theories implicitly in your classroom as well. Your own knowledge of these lenses and theorists that interest you might inform the way you approach a particular text, set up formative work for your students, or generally guide questions and discussion of a text. You may find some of the theorists offer you a needed challenge to stay fresh in the classroom. You have taught *Hamlet* 20 times, but now you have some fresh reading on it and can think about new approaches to the text.

Again, the point is to *discover* rather than limit. This goes for both the students and the teacher. Keep exploring and become part of this dialogue of literature yourself.

Formalist theory

There is still a place for formalism; it provides the groundwork for any analysis your students will do in your classroom. Hopefully they have been building these skills of formal analysis throughout MYP or whatever system they were in before the DP.

Use some parts of this type of analysis for everything so students can perform well on Paper 1, which remains a large component of either course (35 per cent of the overall mark). However, Paper 1 responses can draw on other lenses, and this lens can be used for other course components as a building block. I often start with at least some close analysis of this nature before doing any contextual work with students. In fact, this is often how many of us read. I love to go into a bookstore or library and simply immerse myself in the prose without looking at the back or looking up information about the book.

Formalist theory supposes your head is in the text in a very 'old school' kind of way. For a purist, the only 'research' one should conduct is with a dictionary. One might equate this theory with an old library, where concentration is purely textual. (Vienna National Library)

We immerse ourselves in the text. We analyse the first page or the first poem. How does it affect you? What is the language doing? Is there anything unusual about it? How does the text look on the page? This is the idea behind Roland Barthes' 'Death of the Author' (1967), which connects 'author' to 'authority', allowing readers to take over the authority in reading the text. Formalism began even earlier in the 1930s, around the ideas that valued the aesthetic and, specifically, the form and structure of a text. Theorists often draw on Aristotle's *Poetics;* parts of this text can be interesting and manageable when students first investigate the nature of tragedy. Drawing on this process of investigation forms a good basis for formalist work in the classroom.

You can use a commentary wheel (something you can find easily online) or other teachers' charts for 'what to look for' in a piece of unseen writing. There are many forms that try to categorize the areas a student should look for in a commentary. What is sometimes missing is the link to purpose. Students get so good at identifying pieces and parts that they do not tie it all together to solve the puzzle. Even if we stay isolated within formalism's limitations, we can find purpose.

Of course, you may have to break it apart first before you can put it together. But what if you could show that both formalism and purpose have reciprocal aspects of analysis? The table on page 106 attempts to do just this. We can never make something that is fully exhaustive. Instead, this table is meant to be something both useful and memorable in helping students identify many formalist aspects of the text while constantly thinking about purpose, even if it is not yet identified.

Rather than a thematic question-style table that you will see for the other theories, this one specifically asks students to flow toward a purpose that might otherwise be left out. It mimics the kind of discussion you might have with a student: 'You've spotted a simile. Ok, so what? Why is it there and what purpose does it help us understand? If you don't know yet, that's ok. As you uncover more details in the text, you should be able to find the big idea.' Here the flow enables the student to have the same outcome.

For this exercise, we will take short excerpts from Borges' 'Funes, his Memory' and Dillard's *Pilgrim at Tinker Creek.* Each are a different literary form: fictional short story and non-fiction memoir, respectively. This is the type of pairing you might see on a literature Paper 1, but they are likewise texts (in full) that a language and literature student could pair for a Paper 2.

Let us say you are looking at the concept focus of **memory**. In fact, there would be many passages in each of these texts that could investigate the concept. Likewise, if these were unseen texts, there would be a variety of concepts (place, time, etc) that could be drawn out from the texts. Although both might be texts where you would look at a lot of contextual elements and even conduct an inquiry, they are also the types of texts you are likely to see in an unseen commentary due to their rich literary devices.

The table contains building blocks toward a conceptual understanding and big idea (present in the thesis statement). The areas of analysis become the foundation of common topics that you can lead students toward identifying, followed by an overall big idea. This lesson makes a memorable device for students to use throughout the course, something that should become second nature.

Try out the same process with non-literary texts (we will do the same in Chapter 6 when we look at assessment). Here, you might even add one on that has to do with **memory**, like a blog entry or a published letter that deals with the concept. Again, this chapter largely focuses on literary texts only because the messages are often less explicit and the use of lenses is especially helpful for Paper 2, but you can adapt them to any part of the course.

■ Extract from *Pilgrim at Tinker Creek* by Annie Dillard

I remembered the ocean, and I seemed to be in the ocean myself, swimming over orange crabs that looked like coral, or off the deep Atlantic banks where whitefish school. Or again I saw the tops of poplars, and the whole sky brushed with clouds in pallid streaks, under which wild ducks flew with outstretched necks, and called, one by one, and flew on.

All these things I saw. Scenes grew in depth and sunlit detail before my eyes, and were replaced by ever more scenes, as I remembered the life of my time with increasing feeling.

At last I saw the earth as a globe in space, and I recalled the ocean's shape and the form of continents, saying to myself with surprise as I looked at the planet. 'Yes, that's how it was then; that part there we called … "France".' I was filled with the deep affection of nostalgia – and then I opened my eyes.

We all ought to be able to conjure up sights like these at will, so that we can keep in mind the scope of texture's motion in time. It is a pity we can't watch it on a screen. John Dee, the Elizabethan geographer and mathematician, dreamed up a great idea, which is just what we need. You shoot a mirror up into space so that it is traveling faster than the speed of light (there's the rub). Then you can look in the mirror and watch all the earth's previous history unfolding as on a movie screen. Those people who shoot endless time-lapse films of unfurling roses and tulips have the wrong idea. They should train their cameras instead on the melting pack of ice, the green filling of ponds, the tidal swing of the Severn Bore*. They should film the glaciers of Greenland, some of which creak along at such a fast clip that even the dogs bark at them. They should film the invasion of southernmost Canadian tundra by the northern-most spruce-fir-forest, which is happening right now at the rate of a mile every ten years. When the last ice sheet receded from the North American continent, the earth rebounded ten feet. Wouldn't that have been a sight to see?

People say that a good seat in the backyard affords as accurate and aspiring a vantage point on the planet earth as any observation tower on Alpha Centauri**. They are wrong. We see through a glass darkly. We find ourselves in the middle of a movie, or, Gold help us, a take for a movie. And we don't know what's on the rest of the film.

Say you could look through John Dee's mirror whizzing through space; say you could heave our relief globe into motion like a giant top and breathe life on its surface; say you could view a time-lapse film of our planet: What would you see? Transparent images moving through light, 'an infinite storm of beauty'.

*Severn Bore – tidal wave that flows against the direction of the River Severn (UK)
**Alpha Centauri – star system closest to our solar system

■ Extract from *Fictions,* from the short story 'Funes, his Memory' by Jorge Luis Borges (1941)

I recall him (though I have no right to speak the sacred verb—only one man on earth did, and that man is dead) holding a dark passionflower in his hand, seeing it as it had never been seen, even had it been stared at from the first light of dawn till the last light of evening for an entire lifetime. I recall him—his taciturn face, its Indian features, its extraordinary *remoteness*—behind the cigarette. I recall (I think) the slender, leather-braider's fingers. I recall near those hands a *mate* cup, with the coat of arms of the Banda Oriental*. I recall, in the window of his house, a yellow straw blind with some vague painted lake scene. I clearly recall his voice—the slow, resentful, nasal voice of the toughs of those days, without the Italian sibilants one hears today. I saw him no more than three times, the last time in 1887 ... I applaud the idea that all of us who had dealings with the man should write something about him; my testimony will perhaps be the briefest (and certainly slightest) account in the volume that you are to publish, but it can hardly be the least impartial. Unfortunately I am Argentine. And so congenitally unable to produce the dithyramb that is the obligatory genre in Uruguay, especially when the subject is Uruguayan. *Highbrow, dandy, city slicker*—Funes did not utter those insulting words, but I know with reasonable clarity that to him I represented those misfortunes. Pedro Leandro Ipuche** has written that Funes was a precursor of the race of supermen—'a maverick and vernacular Zarathustra'—and I will not argue the point, but one must not forget that he was also a street tough from Fray Bentos***, with certain incorrigible limitations.

My first recollection of Funes is quite clear. I see him one afternoon in March or February of '84. That year, my father had taken me to spend the summer in Fray Bentos. I was coming back from the ranch in San Francisco with my cousin Bernardo Haedo. We were riding along on our horses, singing merrily—and being on horseback was not the only reason for my cheerfulness. After a sultry day, a huge slate-colored storm, fanned by the south wind, had curtained the sky. The wind flailed the trees wildly, and I was filled with the fear (the hope) that we would be surprised in the open countryside by the elemental water. We ran a kind of race against the storm. We turned into the deep bed of a narrow street that ran between two brick sidewalks built high up off the ground. It had suddenly got dark; I heard quick, almost secret footsteps above me—I raised my eyes and saw a boy running along the narrow, broken sidewalk high above, as though running along the top of a narrow, broken wall. I recall the short, baggy trousers—like a gaucho's—that he wore, the straw-soled cotton slippers, the cigarette in the hard visage, all stark against the now limitless storm cloud. Unexpectedly, Bernardo shouted out to him—*What's the time, Ireneo?* Without consulting the sky, without a second's pause, the boy replied, *Four minutes till eight, young Bernardo Juan Francisco.* The voice was shrill and mocking.

I am so absentminded that I would never have given a second thought to the exchange I've just reported had my attention not been called to it by my cousin, who was prompted by a certain local pride and desire to seem unfazed by the other boy's trinomial response.

He told me that the boy in the narrow street was one Ireneo Funes, and that he was known for certain eccentricities, among them shying away from people and always knowing what time it was, like a clock. He added that Ireneo was the son of a village ironing woman, Maria Clementina Funes, and that while some people said his father was a doctor in the salting house (an Englishman named O'Connor), others said he broke horses or drove oxcarts for a living over in the department of Salto. The boy lived with this mother, my cousin told me, around the corner from Villa Los Laureles.

* The Banda Oriental – old name of Uruguay before it became a country
** Pedro Leandro Ipuche – Uruguayan literary figure
*** Fray Bentos – small town on the banks of Uruguay River, famous for canned meats

■ Formalist theory: building toward a big idea

Subheadings	Dillard excerpt	Borges excerpt
Text type/genre	Non-fiction, memoir (nature writing).	Fiction, short story.
Structure/form/layout	Prose paragraphs. Space separation where voice changes.	Prose paragraphs – long. Start of first three paragraphs is the narrator talking of memory: 'I recall'/'My first recollection'/'I am so absentminded'.
Title(s)/publication/audience	'Pilgrim at Tinker Creek'/'Intricacies' – about perplexing things. Seems universal audience interested in philosophy and nature.	'Funes, His Memory' (translator has changed title from previous translation 'Funes the Memorious' – can discuss separately). Memory central to story. Personal memory, though fiction – both of narrator and of Funes. Faux 'testimony' – makes mysterious – there is a fake law/police audience.
Setting/place and time of publication	Tinker Creek, Virginia, USA. 1998 Pastoral	Uruguay (Fray Bentos vs. city). Small streets, 'Villa Los Laureles'. 1942
Narrator(s)/character(s)/persona(s)	Author's voice, past tense. Includes collective 'we' – humans – changes to present tense. Nature as character.	First person account – fictional memory of a memory. Funes, his and narrator's families. Changes between past and present tense.
Diction/register/mood/tone	More specific imagery changes to more general, worldly observation. Personal changes to world refs/allusions. Dreamlike → reflective, inquisitive. Nostalgic → philosophical.	Many words related to memory. Colloquial though high level of diction. Mysterious though explanatory.
Sentence or line structure/rhythm	Part 1: long wistful sentences, ellipses and dashes. Part 2: less poetic, rhetorical questions.	Dashes and ellipses – shows stream of consciousness. It's a recall but also pensive.

Subheadings	Dillard excerpt	Borges excerpt
Sensory imagery	In memory: ocean – crabs, poplars … sees whole globe … focus on imagery later as 'film' as if we can replay the 'beauty' in our minds – imagines sights before humans were even around.	Description of Funes ('taciturn' 'remoteness', etc) and his voice. Description of place: the house, the 'broken sidewalk' and 'broken wall'.
Figurative language	Comparisons used to link one natural element with another ('crabs that looked like coral') – cycle of life; film metaphor to human memory.	Funes compared to 'clock'. Hyperbole 'race of supermen'. Supernatural nature elements – man vs. nature 'race against the storm'.
Symbols/connotations/allusions	Allusions in part 2 when less personal; about places on the globe to witness change; John Dee's idea.	Place seems important (rural vs. city and connotations). Real places and literary figure.
Comparative topics	Switching back and forth between past and present. Man's relation with nature. Breaks in natural prose (dashes, ellipses). Importance of time. Allusions.	
Thesis statement	Humans use memory to relate to the natural world.	

You can then get students to colour code their topic ideas when they identify patterns. They can colour both the chart and the original passage. These should all lead to themes. These themes will be conceptual big ideas. With the use of a predicate in their formation, the theme is a clear point emerging from a formalist reading of the text. From the information in the table, students might come up with a list of comparative topics (see this row in the table). Through these topics, we find the thesis, where the topics represent areas the students will explore in paragraphs that link back to the thesis (more on this in Chapter 6).

In the chart, we came up with a simple thesis: Humans use memory to relate to the natural world. Orally, or on paper, students can then expand on what they mean and how it would become part of a written or oral introduction. It might look something like this:

The excerpts from Annie Dillard's 'Pilgrim at Tinker Creek' and Jorge Luis Borges' 'Funes, his Memory' explore how humans use memory to relate to the natural world. The narrators in both texts move between past and present tense while emphasizing the importance of passing time in considering a philosophical view of humanity's connection to place, animals and the universe at large. They each further use breaks in formal prose to present a more colloquial and unfixed view of the world, one that the reader can intercept and become a part of. Although one is a personal account and the other a fictional story, both use allusions in combination with a personal experience to connect individual readers with their place in the reflection, ultimately allowing a faulty or imaginative memory to become a living connection with the natural world.

By starting with the simple thesis, students understand the conceptual nature that must go beyond the texts themselves. Additionally or alternatively, you can use guiding questions, such as:

- What conventions of structure does the novel (or dramatic tragedy or blog post) employ?

- How does the layout contribute to your understanding of the text?

- How does a close reading of the text reveal subtexts?

- How does a change in form connect to a change in mood, narration or action?

- What language has alternative meanings and how does that shape the overall purpose?

- How are symbols developed through the text?

- How would you describe the aesthetic quality of the work and what role does that play in interpretation?

- What are the keywords in the text? Do their connotations change by the end of the reading?

Either way, you should move toward thematic big ideas that link to your conceptual focus. The conceptual focus can move beyond that of your semester focus. Perhaps you might cycle back to one that you looked at previously, or expand to a different area of comparison for a lesson. The idea is that students find versatile ways to arrive at purposeful ideas through the texts. The theme can become a thesis statement that will be easily backed up through the features already identified.

You might want to begin with a formalist approach followed by another layer of interpretation that contextualizes the texts further. That way we can see how students can uncover ideas about something like gender without the specific context, as will be necessary during the Paper 1 commentary exam.

A further area of consideration present on the chart is the importance of titles (including headlines and subtitles or even visible publication titles). Although Jacques Derrida is in no way a formalist, his essay 'Before the Law' (2018), which makes great use of Kafka's similarly named parable, talks about these titles as initial entries into texts. As we become more conscious of the layers created to enter a text, of course we have to look outward beyond formalism. But as a starting point, just investigating the language of the entry is an important focus, particularly in media studies. A headline can create a sneaky bias or perspective. In poetry, the title is often a separate or repeated line of the poem, giving us clues about the overall meaning. In discussion of titles with your students, be sure to include a discussion about their own use of titles for assessments.

New Historicism

New Historicism brings back the author and context as important tools in understanding culture through history. It supposes the importance of minor voices and the arts in telling the story of history, adding a richer cultural perspective to this view. Sometimes scholars use the term 'cultural studies' to provide a similar meaning to New Historicism.

To understand this theory better, you may want to look at Stephen Greenblatt's 'Invisible Bullets', which analyses Machiavelli and Shakespeare as discourses of their times, or Louis Montrose's 'Professing the Renaissance: The Poetics and Politics of Culture', which offers a different reading of the 'historicity of texts', one of 'cultural specificity' that includes 'textual traces' as they appear in analysis after the initial text (Rivkin and Ryan, page 781, 1998). You might also consider lengthier texts by Michel Foucault, such as *Language, Counter-memory, Practice* (1977), or Pierre Bourdieu, including *The Field of Cultural Production* (1993). Rather than reading literature as a pure historical document, this theory sees these documents as elements in a continuous dialogue that have also been reshaped from the perspective of the current reader.

You would likely consider using elements of the inquiry cycle to investigate the time period and politics of the author here. Some amount of research may be needed to fill out even the basics of the chart that follows. You might have small groups do so, then divide the class into lines of inquiry or allow for lines of inquiry that could be investigated further in student journals or an HL essay. However, be careful that at least for the IB assessment, you do not want this to become a history paper. In fact, if the student understands the elements of cultural production, they will use the text as artistic evidence of an idea.

INTERNATIONAL MINDEDNESS

The New Historicism theory allows for inquiry into different international perspectives, and assumes that the perspective is essential in understanding the text.

For the texts on the following chart, we will continue to look at the conceptual focus of **memory**. Sometimes the ideas about memory in these texts are on a very individual level, but the use of this theoretical lens allows us to think of shared knowledge and collective memories of places and cultures.

■ New Historicism theory

Questions	*City of Glass*	*A Tale of Two Cities*	*Frankenstein*
What is the setting of the text?	New York City – Cold War period. Uses NYC apartment building and labyrinth of city streets; reference to real places in NYC.	Paris and London from 1778 to 1790. During the French Revolution. Uses homes of aristocracy and lower class to tell story; places of law – prison and courtroom; city streets and real buildings or monuments.	The Monster was built/created in Ingolstadt, Germany. Victor goes to Switzerland, leaving the Monster in Germany. The Monster follows Victor to Switzerland, London (England), Holland, Paris (France) and Russia, as well as to a small unnamed town by the Mediterranean Sea. Journey goes to Mont Blanc and then the Arctic. Uses science lab, aristocratic home and ship as parts of setting.
During what time was the text written? Where?	1985, USA.	1859, England. Published as separate chapters in Dickens' London literary periodical, 'All the Year Round'.	1818, England. Written during a holiday in Geneva.

Questions	*City of Glass*	*A Tale of Two Cities*	*Frankenstein*
Is there any connection to real-world activity in the text such as allegory or allusion?	Suspicion, mystery, isolation, identity and impact of memories are all connected to Cold War era. Tower of Babel.	Strongly connected to the events of the French Revolution. Connects Paris and London though no revolution in England; implicit allegorical links to American Revolution against the British. Biblical allusions (resurrection, wine/blood, etc).	Allusions: Biblical – Monster compares himself to Adam in Genesis and Victor to God. Prometheus – Victor could be seen as a modern-day Prometheus (original title). He created the Monster as Prometheus created man. He reached too far and died/suffered as a result. Allegory: 'Paradise Lost' – The relations between the Monster and Satan. 'Don't play God'. Explicit allusions included when Monster reads it.
Do you think this text pushed for change at the time of its publication?	What could happen to the country as a whole if they stay in the same 'Cold War environment' – the way individuals are impacted by it.	Deconstructed gender norms. Questioned fault in revolution. Showed class movement as positive.	The text was mainly a shock to society because of Mary Shelley's age, and sparked controversy. People used to think it must be written by her husband. The text encouraged scientific adventure as well as a warning to not take things too far ... be careful. Foreword talks about this.
How might the text be received differently today vs. its original publication date?	Post-Cold War, but might question if USA is still somewhat influenced by it (Russia and US elections; fears of neighbours = terrorists). More texts also play with detective genre in new ways; changes way we see it as a serious text.	Feminism isn't as unusual as it was at the time of publication. Questions the death penalty – could use in current debate.	Science has changed – links to genetic engineering, cloning, etc. We see female authors differently now. Arctic discovery might now be metaphor for going into space. Abortion debate connects to Victor's destruction of second monster.

When looking at historical context, one might also bring in postcolonial theory if this context is relevant to the text. You might look at core texts, such as: *Sea of Poppies*, 'In the Penal Colony', *The Outsider* or *Things Fall Apart*. Or look at shorter texts, such as Charles Philip Martin's mock letters to a subscriber of the magazine *Colonial Life* 'Colonial Life and Times' (1997) and Xu Xi's short story 'Until the Next Century' (2001), both in *City Voices: Hong Kong Writing in English, 1945 to the present*, edited by Xu Xi. Political speeches or news reports from changes in colonial status would be great non-literary texts. These short text examples would work well if you are using a place as a concept that has a relationship with postcolonial discourse: Nigeria, Hong Kong, India, Uruguay, Algeria. Of course, there are many other choices, but rich texts from these places are mentioned in this book. Edward Said, Gayatri Spivak, Frantz Fanon and Homi Bhabha all have excellent and accessible scholarly work on postcolonial theory that you or your students may want to look up.

There is a link between New Historicism and Marxist theory, our next lens, in that we are inherently talking about power relationships. For example, Greenblatt makes great emphasis on power and class when discussing Shakespeare's plays in this context. However, the unique relationships in postcolonial studies could make for a strong theoretical lens or conceptual focus.

Marxist theory

Deborah Appleman's *Critical Encounters in High School English* (2000) has a clear one-page overview of key terms directly from Karl Marx that might help students unpack works according to this theory. You might find this and other approaches she includes useful. However, I tend to introduce an even more reduced Marxist theory to students that rather sharply focuses on power and money. I like to think of texts in this way:

- Who's got the money?

- Who's got the power?

- How does it change (and why)?

What teenager cannot relate to money and power? Perhaps start with music that talks about money and power explicitly: *Money* (Pink Floyd, 1973), *Mo Money Mo Problems* (Notorious B.I.G., 1997), C.R.E.A.M. (Wu-Tang Clan, 1994) or *Billionaire* (Travie McCoy and Bruno Mars, 2010). The list goes on and I'm sure students will have their own to share. Music is a great entry point for any topic in your classroom to get students interested. If you have a class that need extra help for motivation, you can also trick them into analysing lyrics (a.k.a. poetry!) this way.

You could follow it with a short writing activity or journal entry where students discuss their own relationships with money. Does money control aspects of their lives? Does money control their daily decisions? Their future ambitions? How do they plan to make money in the future? What problems regarding money do they see for their generation? Do they work for money? How do people who have money (parents, employers, the state) control them?

Just like with other lenses, you might already see several overlaps. Postcolonial theory will deal heavily with power relationships and the matrix of how this power dynamic changes as governments seize or relinquish power. When we look at feminist and queer theory, we shall see how power dynamics in society create a matrix of the treatment of different sexes as well as gender and sexual identity in society.

Marxist theory can be a lot of things in this way, but what it should *not* be is a study of Marx and communism. It does not hurt, though, for your students to read *The Communist Manifesto* or to understand Karl Marx, and perhaps Friedrich Engels, as a historical figure whose ideologies are still at play in the world today. You might suggest these areas as extension work or draw on students' knowledge from their history classes. Further, if you are studying texts that deal explicitly with communism, now or in the past, you might do a more contextual inquiry investigation that includes Marx.

It would be helpful for students to at least understand the idea of the material dialectic, that the socio-economic base of society drives actions and, therefore, history. It values this base over ideologies. For secondary sources that may be easier to understand or to take a quicker look at, you might start with a couple of classic texts: Walter Benjamin's 'The Work of Art in the Age of Mechanical Reproduction' (1999, pages 282–89) and Frederic Jameson's *Marxism and Form: 20th Century Dialectical Theories of Literature* (1974) and *The Political Unconscious: Narrative as a Socially Symbolic Act* (2002). A few others stand out as interesting focus areas that could be used to inform your teaching or to allow for students to extend their understanding. VN Volosinov's 'Marxism and the Philosophy of Language' (Rivkin and Ryan, pages 278–81) links dialects and accents as well as any type of language 'dynamism' with 'social struggle', which would be an interesting connection to the 'Englishes' unit proposed, or any look at semiotics (with *City of Glass,* for example, which makes explicit use of it). Terry Eagleton is another academic who deals with Marxist theory in a way that is easier to understand on a practical level. A chapter from *Marxism and Literary Criticism* (1976) called 'Literature and History' helps us understand 'literary forms, styles, and meaning "as products of a particular history"' (Keesey, page 460). These articles might lead to lines of inquiry from your students or allow you to gain deeper knowledge.

However, to work with the theory as a whole class, it is more about understanding and tracking the connections between money, power and behaviour in texts. Almost any literary text will include elements of power at play, even if simply between two characters rather than as a whole society. It is an easy way for students to look at advertising or Instagram feeds analytically as well. How do material goods that cost money tell a story and create power and influence? They can look at fashion in this way, but the item being sold might not be the clothing or jewellery. Instead, the fashion might be selling a car, household items or non-material goods. In newspapers or any form of online media, students can also attempt to understand how money and power control the message of the paper. How are biases contained within 'unbiased reporting'? Why are some news stories covered and others not? Who decides? Why and how are journalists censored?

Although like other literary criticism, they are traditionally used with literary texts, a move toward transference can apply to text types as well. Marxist theory can easily be adapted to look at other text types, including propaganda posters, news articles and the epistolary form (where the power relationships between the writer and audience can be investigated through language and form). Advertisements are another strong non-literary text type that can be further analysed through Marxist theory with your students. Nearly all ads use some kind of power dynamic (if you include desire as power, as Foucault does) to ask their readers to spend money on something. This is an easy power and money reduction activity.

■ Marxist theory across text types

Clearly, many text types would lend themselves to a Marxist interpretation. Let us look at a couple of examples to use the question chart with your students. Use the QR code to look at Donald and Ivanka Trump's 1995 Pizza Hut ad – do power or money make pizza taste better? Will eating at Pizza Hut raise your class status? Students should be aware that it is money and power selling the product; though many love him or hate him, Trump has never (to my knowledge) been seen as a symbol of *beauty* (another way to sell products), which is why he makes a good example. His businesses cover a wide range, so there is no specific desire for anything other than the money and power he represents. You can also look at his spouse (whom many would call beautiful) as a *prize* for his status.

You might ask students to bring in ads they discover, since almost any should work well here. There is a relevant article in the *Journal of Business Ethics*: 'Persuasive Advertising,

Autonomy, and the Creation of Desire' by Roger Crisp, which essentially argues that all forms of advertising (which by definition creates desire for a product) are 'morally wrong'. This could be a good starting point for a Take a Stand! activity (page 88).

You can use the literary chart on page 114 or simply ask students to first analyse how power and desire are used in the text. Then, together consider how the ad attempts to trick consumers. Is it morally wrong to do so?

Next in the chart, we see a passage from *The Crucible* where the power relationships of the community are at play within the confines of a domestic space. This text is a wonderful one to use with Marxist theory. The basis of the text is a witch hunt and trial in a small theocratic community in Salem, Massachusetts. The underlying reasons revealed for accusations are often linked with money or class. Sometimes there is a land dispute, other times the village slave or mad homeless woman makes an easy target. Sex and sexuality are often part of the matrix; we shall see in queer theory how Foucault links these aspects directly to power in society. In the play, we see positional power in the judges (backed by the church) and power through knowledge. A great activity is to have students track the power of different characters through each act. You should end up with a graph of hierarchies that changes over the course of the play. Here is a sample of what it might look like:

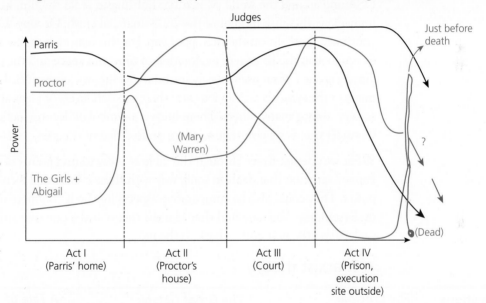

Sketch showing the changing power dynamics in *The Crucible*

I will not go into a detailed explanation of the sketch above; you will see some ideas in the table that follows. What might be interesting to overlay is the idea that the acts change setting. How does the transition from the minister Parris' house to John Proctor house to the courtroom, then the prison and finally outdoors change the power dynamics of the characters? Miller even includes several interesting stage directions about the positions of characters, how they come down or go up, to show directions of power dynamics. You can also look at the flow of knowledge in the text, shown symbolically in Hale's books (he first appears 'loaded down with half a dozen heavy books' and later both he and other characters refer to these books' contents as 'authority'), and its connection with power. Alternatively, overlay the feminist theory lens to understand why women of this society would have felt desperate for power or attention due to the fact they could not own anything, were not allowed to learn to read and had little say in their fates.

Know also that there are ways to include other minor characters at pivot points:

- Giles Corey at one point feels jealousy of his wife's ability to read; look at knowledge as power.

- Land wars that go back generations show the way a few minor characters might lash out due to money/power dynamics.

- Tituba is the only foreign and Black character, a slave of Parris, and her inclusion is a reminder of the power structures of slavery that the US was at one time built upon.

You could likewise do this activity with other texts. In the **India** unit suggested, *The White Tiger* and *The God of Small Things* deal with the caste system and its effect on character behaviour. *Balzac and the Little Chinese Seamstress* looks specifically at the Cultural Revolution and communism, but also includes a look at how knowledge is linked to power. *Hamlet*'s protagonist questions the role of the monarchy and if he wants to be a part of it; he looks at people dying for no reason other than glory or due to the orders of those in power. The scene where Hamlet speaks to the deceased court jester Yorrick's skull, or when he reflects in soliloquy on the war with Norway are especially poignant.

In the table that follows, we compare *The Crucible*, *A Tale of Two Cities* and *The Great Gatsby*. We looked at *A Tale of Two Cities* with New Historicism, so you should start to see how you can add depth to texts by looking at them through several lenses. The last novel by Fitzgerald is a classic that would also work well; it is often taught both in the USA and around the world. When Baz Luhrmann redid the film in 2013, it became an immediate discourse in light of the 2008 financial crash, Occupy Wall Street and the continued spotlight on the rich–poor gap. For this reason, it makes an interesting text as you look at the IB area of exploration of **time and space** and the questions they pose. *Gatsby* is one I often use to easily introduce *all* literary lenses. While the message is deep, many of the symbols are obvious and there are rich layers of ideas about class, gender and society, among many others. There is even a symbol of deconstruction in the crashed car. Consider this as we continue to move on to different theories.

What we attempt to see through the table is a way to find points of comparison for a Paper 2 question that deals in some way with these conceptual focus areas of money and power. They could also be comparative aspects for the IO or, more universally, conceptual understanding. You may find that Marxist theory is the one that students tend to understand the best and go back to the most.

■ Marxist theory

Questions	*The Crucible*	*The Great Gatsby*	*A Tale of Two Cities*
Who has the power in the text and how does it change?	Parris/religious figures. Court – Danforth/theocracy. Abigail has power over the girls by making them help her denounce Mary Warren. Proctor attempts to take the court's power away from them; partly leads to his imprisonment. Knowledge drives power but is manipulated (Hale, Proctor ...).	Those with money have power – especially Gatsby and Tom – it is a competition to gain Daisy's affection. More power in the 'stable' marriage – Tom and Daisy. Power in elusiveness and being new in town with big mansion (Gatsby). Jordan has more power or autonomy than Daisy in being single.	Starts with royalty in charge (queens and kings of England and France). Shifts to Bourgeois and peasants (people of kingdoms). Courtroom also shown as place of power (London has legal system in place; in Paris it is confusing due to revolution and changing power dynamics).

Questions	*The Crucible*	*The Great Gatsby*	*A Tale of Two Cities*
Who has the money in the text and how does it change?	Parris has money though should be poor (golden candlesticks, etc). Landowners – lose rights if accused of being witches.	Gatsby and Tom especially; Meyer Wolfsheim also highlights the underground economic system in NYC. Poor men shown as miserable and can't attract women (Wilson).	Money stays in the upper classes for the majority, but it redistributes due to the fact that many members of the upper class are killed.
What does the text reveal about social classes?	Conflict between master–servant relationship. Reflected in how laymen must revere and obey religious figures. Theocratic hierarchy. If Indian or Black, you are a lower social class automatically. Unmarried women are lower class.	Shows mobility of classes. Big rich-poor gap and ways things can change quickly (Valley of Ashes). Shallow desire for money (Daisy). Downtown NYC classes mix more (the apartment party).	Differences and unfairness between social classes has severe and unnecessary consequences.
Does the text push for or against any political ideologies?	Critiques theocracy and fascism (allegory).	Highlights problems with capitalism but also positive how people can move 'up the ladder'. Fitzgerald seems to critique the surplus/excess of the 1920s even before the big crash (pub in 1925).	Dickens was always critical of the upper classes. Uses Revolutionary ideology to make point, but then also points out hypocrisy in the revolutionaries. Clearly shows benefits of democracy over monarchy, but also how democracy can be corrupt.
What is the role of society in the development of the protagonist?	(Allegorical as well.) Refutes value system of society – John, Abigail. The protagonist revolts against society. It shapes the outcome of the play, but the character is only 'free' and 'powerful' in death (Proctor follows teachings of Rebecca Nurse, shows women can be wise). But does he get caught up in pride? Leaves pregnant wife and kids in wake of his death – Hale thinks life is more important.	Nick as narrator acts like observer on the way society affects Gatsby – the crime world, the war, the way richness could get him love and power – he is really focused on winning Daisy's love so we see how empty having all that money in that huge mansion really is.	The role of society is a significant one, due to the fact the society is constantly critical of the protagonist, for being the heir of all the money. It also plays a big role in all of the significant power shifts in the book. Uses comparison of two societies implicitly to show both need to change and that revolution/democracy is a start but not the full answer.

The next step can again take several shapes in your classroom. One concretely useful exercise is to ask each student or pair to then use the chart to create a single thesis and find one quote from each text to support their idea.

They can present this information to the class in a one-minute pop-up recap to finish your class for the day. The more students can synthesize toward big ideas that require evidence in this way, the more comfortable they will be both with the details of the texts and the ability to come up with purposeful statements. By requiring the thesis to cover several texts, it is easier to focus on a big worldly purpose rather than sticking to what happens inside of a particular text's reality.

Feminist theory

Some students might be averse to feminist theory when you first mention it, because they think of it as 'women are better', and some think it is not relevant anymore. Of course, recent #MeToo discourse and projects like 'Day of the Girl Child' from the UN have helped to publicize why women can still be looked at as minor voices in a patriarchal system.

Still you may have students who say: what is the point? This might be the case especially if you live in a country with equality laws for women in the workplace or in sport, for example. However, we only need to look at some statistics such as the absence of female authors in the literary cannon to convince students that the minor voice of women is relevant. Several research projects and personal investigations have found the difficulty women still have in getting published today ('Sexism in Publishing: my novel wasn't the problem, it was me, Catherine', Flood, 2015).

We will talk briefly about the three waves of feminism and feminist theory to bring us toward an understanding that it has evolved into a more dynamic look at sex and gender in society. Some would disagree, but I include a careful look at masculinity with this theory. We will look at 'heteronormative' approaches to gender in this theory and then look at discourse that goes against the 'norm' in queer theory. I find talking about masculinity at this juncture also makes boys feel more comfortable becoming part of the discussion.

There are a few key texts you might find useful to use yourself or to mention to students as extension. If you are reading *Frankenstein*, have a brief look at Shelley's mother, Mary Wollestonecraft's *A Vindication on the Rights of Women* (1792). Follow historically by looking at part of Simone de Beauvoir's *The Second Sex* (1949), which starts a new type of criticism, and Julia Kristeva's 'Women's Time' (1993), which questions the three waves of feminism and the way the lens is used. Finally, 'Toward a Feminist Narratology', by Susan S. Lanser (1986) is likewise both critical of feminism and takes useful aspects of the lens into the reader's reality.

Together, you might first discover what 'normative' masculinity and femininity means. How is the definition different in different cultures and how has it changed over time? You can use music, such as 'Girls', by The Beastie Boys and 'Macho Man' by The Village People, as starting points. Then, update the conversation through Alicia Keys' 'Superwoman' or Ariana Grande's 'God is a Woman' and Chance the Rapper's 'Paranoia' or J Cole's 'Lost Ones'. Another approach would be to use advertising over time – those cowboys in the old Marlboro cigarette ads or housewives with cleaning products and supermodels laying across car hoods. Look at how some contemporary ads combat gender stereotypes (Nike's 'Play like a girl' campaign and the Dove 'self-esteem project') but how others perpetuate them (such as the 'Are you beach body ready?' ad in the London Underground that went viral).

Also look at texts that investigate gender from different cultures. *Kafka on the Shore* looks at masculinity in a striking way that would make a great pairing with *Half of a Yellow Sun*. *American Psycho* questions the way Wall Street asks men to behave. Patricia Highsmith and Mary McCarthy have many interesting novels that deal with the changing shape of women's role in Western society during the first feminist movement, as does Sylvia Plath's tragic novel that mimics her life, *The Bell Jar*.

Alternatively, you might look at the play between genders and the constructs of femininity, masculinity and anything in between. You might use both the feminist and queer lenses to do so – what definitions are seen as normative and which veer from it? Within the similar conceptual focus of **identity**, here specifically gender identity, you can look at a literary passage from Woolf's *Orlando* (with a protagonist who changes gender and explicitly discusses the implications) and a non-literary journalistic piece in *Vanity Fair* on 'Bruce Jenner's journey from Olympic icon to transgender woman' in 'Caitlyn Jenner: The Full Story' (Bissinger, 2015). Further, you can look at constructs of masculinity in texts like *The Things they Carried*, *Fight Club* or *Things Fall Apart*.

For the table here, we can again use many different texts, but I select several that are part of our conceptual units to build on them. Here, we can use **beauty** as the concept.

■ Feminist theory

Questions	*The Bluest Eye*	*Frankenstein*	*A Streetcar Named Desire*
Who are the female characters in the text?	Pecola, Frieda, Claudia, Pauline, Aunt Jimmy.	Caroline, Justine, Elizabeth, Margaret, Agatha, Safie. Female monster (destroyed).	Blanche, Stella, Eunice, 'Negro woman'.
Do the female characters push for a more modern or independent view of women?	The female characters do not greatly push for gender equality. However, the narration looking back by Pecola adds a layer that things might change and women can become more independent. Female characters do have depth but they are oppressed.	No, it is the contrary because Elizabeth was quite the opposite of her foster mother Caroline. Victor's 'possession' of Elizabeth has no female equals.	All of them are pushing for a life of comfort and it is not important whether it brings independence or whether they stay in traditional positions. Stella goes against tradition by marrying a person who is not in her class, but the relationship she has with Stanley is a traditional patriarchal one (she is abused physically and mentally and just takes it). Criticizes the traditional society and pushes for modern view. Blanche is attempting to be an independent woman, however she is so judged that she goes mad (we don't know about her morals but others judge her even though they also don't really know). Use of rape shows the inequality of power, even in a domestic space, used against women.

Questions	*The Bluest Eye*	*Frankenstein*	*A Streetcar Named Desire*
Does the text push for gender equality or not?	The text portrays a society with little gender equality and criticizes this. So, it pushes the reader to want it. It links a big problem with the way women feel they need to be beautiful to be accepted and how women are abused even in their own families.	It does not push for gender equality, since all of the female characters have a selfless nature, where they are in a constant position to make others around them happy and are not particularly focused on themselves.	The text pushes for equality. It shows how Blanche is judged and victimized and how Stanley gets power by being manly.
In what ways does the text portray the performance of gender?	Women are not given many options on what to do with their lives: they can work for white families, get married and have children or work as prostitutes. This is true especially for Black women in the text.	Women were kept in their traditional role, they serve as a means for males to gain knowledge and experience.	Women are portrayed as weak and downtrodden. Men shown as caretakers but at the same time are abusive (this is accepted); hyper-masculinity. Mitch has the chance to subvert this but fails.
What is the role of the female author in the text's message?	The female author witnessed the inequality. The culture of women is a very significant theme in the novel. She emphasizes playing with dolls, beauty magazines, celebrities. She connects it to what kids are taught in school (school primer allusions).	Women can create just as good or maybe even better written pieces than men. Author was aged 18 – some people believe that her husband had written it. Connects to her mother the feminist writer.	None, however, because it is a play the actors for the female roles have some kind of authorship and the director could be female.

Queer theory

Queer theory is essentially a look at otherness. It is a look at what is not considered 'normal' by society, but it also looks specifically at the LGBTQ+ discourse, especially since the 1980s. Queer theory draws on the power relationships considered in Marxist theory and gender criticism in feminist theory, but it also draws on psychoanalysis and deconstruction theory in the way it investigates individual psyches and personality construction, as well as the breakdown of binaries in society.

Judith Butler talks about gender as performance in 'Imitation and Gender Insubordination' (1991). Most people are now familiar with the concept of performative gender, but the way she politicizes gender identity and attempts to separate sexuality from gender is avant-garde for the time. Likewise, Foucault politicizes sexuality as a power structure in society and interpersonal relationships in *The History of Sexuality: 1* (1980). Both of these theorists cross several lenses. While Foucault's understanding of sexuality as part of the hierarchical structure of the world (Marxist theory) and focus on a breakdown of pre-set dichotomies (deconstruction theory), he ultimately helps the reader understand that 'Sex is worth dying for' (page 156). In other words, sexuality is identity, and without it, we are nothing. In looking at the 'perpetual spirals of power and pleasure' (page 45), Foucault understands the way desire works in a system, but understands it from the reference point of the individual, which is one that cannot nor should be fixed. In other words, queerness is essential in this articulation of a world filled with all types of desires.

CORE CONNECTIONS

TOK

Foucault looks carefully at the 'interplay of knowledge and pleasure' and works toward an idea of the 'will to knowledge' (pages 72, 73). He talks further about the connections between sex and truth, but highlights the dangers in government bodies defining 'something called "sexuality" to embody the truth of sex and its pleasures' (page 68). Many texts place sexual identity exploration in juxtaposition with political ideologies, allowing the reader to understand these questions as queer, even if the acts are not necessarily classified as 'gay' or 'bisexual', terms we use as non-heteronormative sexual identities.

In Gayle Rubin's 'Sexual Transformations', she theorizes that 'sexual arrangements have a distinctive character which sets them apart from pre-existing systems' (1998, page 679) and concludes that 'perversions', or queer identities, are not becoming greater but that existing people who identify as such 'are attempting to acquire social space, small businesses, political resources, and a measure of relief from the penalties for sexual heresy' (page 681). Her short text can help you or your students explicitly identify the connections between queer theory and either Marxist or New Historicism theories, while allowing us to see more purposefully beyond identification. Some students think the theory, in relation to older texts where, for example, gay and transgender identities might only be implicit, is more just about identifying them as such. Is Holden Caulfield's teacher in *Catcher in the Rye* gay? Does Dorian Gray murder because of his suppressed homoerotic desires? The questions should not be whether characters have any LGBTQ+ identity, but why it might matter if they do. How would it change our reading of the text in regard to the author's intentions about identity or as commentary on the time period?

The difficult thing about defining queer theory is that the more it is defined, the more it becomes what it is not. This is an idea addressed in the autumn 2005 issue of *Social Text*, where the editors posit in the introduction to 'What's Queer about Queer studies now?' (Eng, 2005) that if we normalize or standardize what queerness is, then it becomes 'unqueer'. This is a fun paradox for students! But in fact, they can probably see through contemporary media and political discourse that queerness is always changing.

Because of this paradox, it is often useful to look at individuals rather than types of queerness. A former student of mine at The University of Hong Kong, Siufung Law, has made a name for himself in world-class body building as a 'genderqueer' but nonoperative female-born individual living as a man. What is interesting about him is that he is also a scholar, currently a teaching assistant who gives academic lectures about his personal journey's relationship with scholarly discourse. Recently, he facilitated several discussions for the Hong Kong Lesbian and Gay Film Festival and has featured in several interviews around the world. His story is not one of trying to normalize himself as a trope but to help people understand and accept him. (See, for example, the *SCMP* article: 'Genderqueer Bodybuilder Siufung Law Is Both He and She (and Could Still Kick Your Ass)', 19 October 2016.)

Studying queer theory through literature and media can be powerful in its allowance of your students to assert their identities. However, the discourse can sometimes uncover difficult situations for people who identify as queer. It has to be something you feel comfortable discussing to allow your students to also feel at ease. Looking at a few real individuals will help students understand more deeply what authors working in fiction or poetry are trying to achieve, and it will also allow you to investigate other text types.

We can create a spectrum and question heteronormative scripts. In this way it is a type of deconstruction, but we focus on gender and sexuality to find answers about human behaviour. You could start with a clip from the original vogueing (á la Madonna) of the New York queer community in Jenny Livingston's documentary *Paris is Burning* (1990) or media articles about gay marriage in a particular country.

Gay Pride in Paris: some of the world's most provocative and philosophical writing explicitly about queerness comes from Paris. Not only French authors, but also those in exile over the years have found freedom and *juissance* (life affirming joy) on the Parisian streets

In more canonical literature, you do find novels, memoirs and plays that deal with queerness, although some more explicitly than others. *Orlando, Kafka on the Shore* and Paul Auster's *Invisible* (2009) are all literary texts you might explore in this way. A strong example is Kundera's *The Unbearable Lightness of Being*, where sexual 'deviance' and intimacy is explored in conjunction with a response to the Prague Spring (political liberalization from the Soviet Union) as Kundera wrote from exile in Paris on the wings of the May 1968 civil disobedience that included a new look at sexual freedom.

The two central characters, Tereza and Tomas, have a somewhat tumultuous relationship due to Tomas' affairs, which Tereza is aware of. Her ideas about sex are also different, as she thinks about entering the world of the affairs, having an audience for sex and considers the philosophical and artistic value of her body in relation to her soul.

■ Extract from *The Unbearable Lightness of Being* by Milan Kundera (1984)

'I want to make love to you in my studio. It will be like a stage surrounded by people. The audience won't be allowed up close, but they won't be able to take their eyes off us ...'

As time passed, the image lost some of its original cruelty and began to excite Tereza. She would whisper the details to him while they made love.

Then it occurred to her that there might be a way to avoid the condemnation she saw in Tomas's infidelities: all he had to do was take her along, take her with him when he went to see his mistresses! Maybe then her body would again become the first and only among all others. Her body would become his second, his assistant, his *alter ego*.

I'll undress them for you, give them a bath, bring them in to you ... she would whisper to him as they pressed together. She yearned for the two of them to merge into a hermaphrodite. Then the other women's bodies would be their playthings.

Oh, to be the *alter ego* of his polygamous life! Tomas refused to understand, but she could not get it out of her head, and tried to cultivate her friendship with Sabina. Tereza began by offering to do a series of photographs of Sabina.

We shall now look at how we can use short excerpts to begin to use theory rather than the whole text. Here we use the Kundera excerpt along with part of a Carol Ann Duffy poem that appeared in *The Guardian* in 2016 (after the Orlando nightclub shooting that targeted LGBTQ+ youth) and an excerpt from Yoshimoto's *Kitchen* (in which a transgender father addresses his son). After filling in the chart, students should be able to find common understandings and big ideas. Here, these may include an understanding of acceptance and non-acceptance of queerness in society and within families.

■ Extract from the novella *Kitchen* by Banana Yoshimoto (1988) – a letter sent following Eriko's murder, which is likely a hate crime at her gay bar

Yuichi,

I feel very odd writing a letter to my own child. But because lately I've been feeling somehow I might be in danger, I'm writing you this on the one chance in a million that something might happen to me. No, just kidding. One of these days we'll read this together and laugh.

Yuichi, think about what I'm about to say. If I should die, you will be left all alone. But you have Mikage, don't you? I'm not joking about that girl. We have no relatives. When I married your mother, her parents cut off relations entirely. And then, when I became a woman, they cursed me. So I'm asking you, DON'T, whatever you do, DO NOT contact them, ever. Do you understand me?

Yes, Yuichi, in this world there are all kinds of people. There are people who choose to live their lives in filth; this is hard for me to understand. People who purposely do abhorrent things, just for the attention it draws to them, until they themselves are trapped. I cannot understand it, and no matter how much they suffer I cannot feel pity for them. But I have cheerfully chosen to make my body my fortune. I am *beautiful*! I am *dazzling*! If people I don't care for are attracted to me, I accept it as the wages of beauty. So, if I should be killed, it will be an accident. Don't get any strange ideas. Believe in the name that you knew.

Just this once I wanted to write using men's language, and I've really tried. But it's funny – I get embarrassed and the pen won't go. I guess I thought that even though I've lived all these years as a woman, somewhere inside me was my male self, that I've been playing a role all these years. But I find that I'm body and soul a woman. A mother in name and in fact. I have to laugh.

I have loved my life. My years as a man, my years married to your mother, and after she died, becoming and living as a woman, watching you grow up, living together so happily, and – oh! taking Mikage in!! That was the most fun of all, wasn't it? I yearn to see her again. She, too, is a very precious child of mine.

Sentimental of me, isn't it?

Please tell her I said hi. And tell her to stop bleaching the hair on her legs in front of boys. It's indecent. Don't you think so?

You'll find enclosed the papers detailing all my assets. I know you can't make heads or tails of all that legalese. Call the lawyer, okay? In any case, I've left everything to you except the club. Isn't it great being an only child?

XXX

Eriko

■ 'After Orlando: Gay Love' by Carol Ann Duffy (2016)

This writer is gay,
and the priest, in the old love of his church,
kneeling to pray.
The farmer is gay, baling the gold hay
out in the fields,
and the teacher, cycling to school each day.
The politician is gay,
though he fears to say,
knotting his tongue, his tie;
and the doctor is gay,
taking your human pulse in her calm way.
The scientist is gay,
folding the origami of DNA,
and the judge, in his grey wig, is gay.
The actress is gay,
spotlit in the smash-hit play;
the butcher, the baker, the candlestick-maker,
our children, are gay.
And God is gay.

■ Queer theory

Questions	Kundera excerpt (novel)	Yoshimoto excerpt (letter in novella)	Duffy excerpt (poem)
What are the issues surrounding sexuality and gender identity in the text?	Infidelity. Exhibitionism. Trust.	Transgender. Gay bar. Danger connected to queerness.	Suggests that many 'normal' people all around can be gay. Violence against LGBTQ+.
When does a character exhibit non-heteronormative behaviour?	Tomas' affairs. Tereza's desire to make love in public and to be in a polygamous relationship. Tereza's desire to 'merge into a hermaphrodite' with Tomas.	Eriko (Yuichi's dad) changes to a woman following Yuichi's mother's death. Eriko can't use 'man's language' anymore.	People are generalized by profession so they can be anyone in our communities. Ends with 'God' – questions identity of Him and also plays on word 'gay' as meaning happy.
What are the directions of desire in the text? (See 'the gaze' in psychoanalytic theory)	Tereza desires the gaze from the public on her love making. Tereza is intrigued by Tomas' lovers and will photograph Sabina.	Eriko's desire to be a woman. Eriko loves her son and vice versa. The man who kills Eriko has a desire for violence, maybe because he is suppressing something in himself like a desire for her.	There is a lack of desire. Maybe just a desire for being normal and also desire to let gay people do the important jobs they have, gain knowledge, etc.
Who is seen as 'other' in the text and why?	Tereza wants to be other: the 'alter ego'. Tomas could be an other – he initiates the 'deviance'. The lovers are also 'other' to the heterosexual relationship between Tomas and Tereza.	Eriko is seen as other and this is why she is killed.	Other is negated, making gayness normal. The politician still feels like he is other, since he 'fears to say'/'knotting his tongue'.
What do sexuality and relationships have to do with identity in the text?	Tereza mixes her sexual identity with her work as an artist.	Eriko feels like her real self as a woman – 'beautiful' and 'dazzling'.	Gayness here is just identity or being; link to the doctor studying 'DNA'. Separates love from sexuality (the priest).
What does sexuality have to do with power and/or politics in the text?	Being a photographer gives Tereza power and agency. The power is linked with Prague Spring due to her work as a photographer there as well.	Family: unacceptance from Eriko's in-laws; power in Yuichi keeping them cut off. Violence: the man who kills Eriko thinks he is controlling her; actually, she kills him, too, getting 'even' – she takes justice into her own hands.	Response to a violent act. Shows fear from some to be who they are (politician, maybe the priest). Gayness in justice system – 'judge', 'writer' as powerful way to have a voice as gay or queer.

Psychoanalytic theory

As mentioned in relation to Marxist theory, the goal here is not to become Freudian psychologists, but rather to understand how his psychological and literary theories have formed the basis for this lens in looking at literature. Psychoanalysis can be fun for students because it links greatly to the visual, the dream world, allegories and the *uncanny* (which they might not know is fun until they start to understand it).

You can start with a couple of excerpts from Freud and suggestions for further reading in 'The Uncanny' (1919) and *Interpretation of Dreams* (1899). Further, work from Lacan on *objet petit a* is an interesting and useful focus when looking at creating otherness and unattainable desires. You can look at this further in his *Four Fundamental Concepts of Psycho-Analysis* (1978).

Essentially, though, there are a few key terms that can be used for analysis and to help students approach texts creatively. Remember that they are literary tools rather than psychological terms here. You can use this overview as a handout for your students, or embed your own definitions of these terms as part of your course. Each term is followed by questions, which you could likewise use in a chart or keep as separate journal questions.

■ Trauma

Different psychologists look at trauma in different ways, but Freud and psychoanalytical theory considers trauma to be a driving force in people's emotions and actions. Unexplained behaviours can be attributed to traumas, which may in fact be supressed. Sometimes authors give us hints or small windows into characters' pasts to allow an explanation for their current behaviour or psyche. Holden Caulfield is suicidal and anti-society in *The Catcher in the Rye*. We have short flashbacks to his little brother's death and aftermath twice in the novel, most poignantly when Holden smashes his knuckles through the garage windows in frustration. JD Salinger allows us to think that this trauma has not been dealt with appropriately, and instead has been tucked away, resulting in anger and confusion within the teenager. His parents are distant and he is ostracized at school. Psychologists would understand how to help Holden in a variety of ways, but with psychoanalytic theory, we can at least piece together the parts of the novel more clearly.

Many texts that deal with war or violence also include traumas. Tim O'Brien's *The Things They Carried* (1990) is a fictional account that largely draws on his experiences in the Vietnam War. This excerpt from the similarly-named chapter exhibits the symbolic nature that people can carry traumas with them throughout their lives.

■ Extract from *The Things They Carried* by Tim O'Brien (1990)

They carried USO stationery and pencils and pens. They carried Sterno, safety pins, trip flares, signal flares, spools of wire, razor blades, chewing tobacco, liberated joss sticks and statuettes of the smiling Buddha, candles, grease pencils, *The Stars and Stripes*, fingernail clippers, Psy Ops leaflets, bush hats, bolos, and much more. Twice a week, when the resupply choppers came in, they carried hot chow in green mermite cans and large canvas bags filled with ice beer and soda pop. They carried plastic water containers, each with a 2-gallon capacity. Mitchell Sanders carried a set of starched tiger fatigues for special occasions. Henry Dobbins carried Black Flag insecticide. Dave Jensen carried empty sandbags that could be filled at night for added protection. Lee Strunk carried tanning lotion. Some things they carried in common. Taking turns, they carried the big PRC-77 scrambler radio, which weighed 30 pounds with its battery. They shared the weight of memory. They took up what others could no longer bear. Often, they carried each other, the wounded or weak. They carried infections. They carried chess sets, basketballs, Vietnamese–English dictionaries, insignia of rank, Bronze Stars and Purple Hearts, plastic cards imprinted with the Code of Conduct. They carried diseases, among them malaria and dysentery. They carried lice and ringworm and leeches and paddy algae and various rots and molds. They carried the land itself – Vietnam, the place, the soil – a powdery orange-red dust that covered their boots and fatigues and faces. They carried the sky. The whole atmosphere, they carried it, the humidity, the monsoons, the stink of fungus and decay, all of it, they carried gravity. They moved like mules. By daylight they took sniper fire, at night they were mortared, but it was not battle, it was just the endless march, village to village, without purpose, nothing won or lost. They marched for the sake of the march. They plodded along slowly, dumbly, leaning forward against the heat, unthinking, all blood and bone, simple grunts, soldiering with their legs, toiling up the hills and down into the paddies and across the rivers and up again and down, just humping, one step and then the next and then another, but no volition, no will, because it was automatic, it was anatomy, and the war was entirely a matter of posture and carriage, the hump was everything, a kind of inertia, a kind of emptiness, a dullness of desire and intellect and conscience and hope and human sensibility. Their principles were in their feet. Their calculations were biological. They had no sense of strategy or mission. They searched the villages without knowing what to look for, not caring, kicking over jars of rice, frisking children and old men, blowing tunnels, sometimes setting fires and sometimes not, then forming up and moving on to the next village, then other villages, where it would always be the same. They carried their own lives. The pressures were enormous. In the heat of the early afternoon they would remove their helmets and flak jackets, walking bare, which was dangerous but which helped ease the strain. They would often discard things along the route of march. Purely for comfort, they would throw away rations, blow their Claymores and grenades, no matter, because by nightfall the resupply choppers would arrive with more of the same, then a day or two later still more, fresh watermelons and crates of ammunition and sunglasses and woollen sweaters – the resources were stunning – sparklers for the Fourth of July , colored eggs for Easter – it was the great American war chest – the fruits of science, the smokestacks, the canneries, the arsenals of Hartford, the Minnesota forest, the machine shops, the vast fields of corn and wheat – they carried like freight trains; they carried it on their backs and shoulders – and for all the ambiguities of Vietnam, all the mysteries and unknowns, there was at least the single abiding certainty that they would never be at a loss for things to carry.

■ Questions

- How does trauma explain actions, thoughts or personalities in the text?

- How is trauma represented symbolically or metaphorically in the text?

- What is the author trying to help us understand through the inclusion of trauma?

■ The Oedipal complex

Freud privileges family relationships as reasons for personality development and behaviour, and draws on the story of Sophocles' *Oedipus Rex* to explain urges and desires within the family. Essentially, the complex assumes that everyone is born with a sexual desire toward the parent of the opposite sex and a desire to harm the parent of the same sex. Jealousy, power, desire – these can all come into play. When you use this concept with literature, be careful to discuss its metaphorical value rather than actually talking about incest. However, some stories (*Kafka on the Shore*, Auster's *Invisible*) use incest metaphorically to show a misunderstanding of, and yearning for, love. The characters who act on such impulses do not understand different forms of love and where sex fits in to all this. Of course, because *Oedipus* is a rich part of the literary canon, this complex is already in the literary dialogue and it is a useful one to try to make some sense of in your classroom. The complex tells us more about fate and the complexities of families and morals than it does about sexual desires and drives.

■ Guiding questions

- ■ How does the text draw on intertextual or allegorical connections with Sophocles' *Oedipus Rex*?

- ■ How does the character's relationship with his or her family affect his or her behaviour and personality?

- ■ What desires does the character have in regard to his or her parents and why?

■ The unconscious

For Freud, traumas, especially those from childhood, are often kept locked up in the unconscious and are carried with us every day, influencing our thoughts and actions. We often see the unconscious in a literary form as dreams, alternate realities or surreal stories. The stories are then metaphor for underlying problems a character faces. Kafka's *Metamorphosis* (1915) gives us a surreal story that starts with the character waking up as a bug. Any narrative that starts while a character is in bed should make us consider the aspect of dreaming. Laura Esquivel's *Like Water for Chocolate* (1989) and many stories from Jorge Luis Borges likewise have this motif of the dream world running through them, as do other surreal texts. Freud is often cited as a key influence of the work of surreal artists such as André Breton and Salvador Dalí.

■ Guiding questions

- ■ Is there evidence of the unconscious or subconscious at play in the text?

- ■ Are there any forms of dreams, alternate realities or surrealism in the text? Why are they used?

■ Id, Ego and Superego

The *Id* is the part of the person that is instinctive and led by desires. It is linked with the unconscious, where the driving forces are sometimes unknown even to that person. The *Ego* represents a reasoned view of the world, though it is still driven by the same desires as the Id. It is a kind of mediator between these desires and the world that must be navigated. The *Superego* is made of the conscience and the ideal self, drawing on learned morals to make decisions. The Superego controls the Ego's decision-making process as a result of this moral viewpoint. You might, for example, consider Victor Frankenstein's different motivations for his actions here (as well as those of the Monster).

■ **Guiding questions**

■ What instinctive desires does the character or author have and to what extent do they keep it in check or succumb to these desires?

■ To what extent does the character or author use reason and rationality to understand the world?

■ What is the moral compass of the character or author? Where does it come from?

■ Where do you see examples of tensions among the Id, Ego and Superego in the text?

■ The gaze

The gaze refers to the focus points both of the characters within a text and the audience outside of the text. Basically, who is looking at whom? Where are the directions of desire or intrigue? We can see this visually in paintings such as Diego Velázquez's *Las Meninas* ('The ladies-in-waiting', 1656), below. It shows layers of consciousness through the gaze of the painter, and the gaze of the young girl and others in the painting. The mirror and the paintings contained within also add layers of directional observation and desire in the text. In fact, it is the viewer (or reader) who is being gazed at by the painter and who should be represented in the mirror, thereby adding this viewer to the text itself.

Diego Velázquez's *Las Meninas* (1656). Where is everyone looking? Who has the power? How does the viewer fit in?

Paintings are often constructed to likewise lead our eyes around the image in a certain way. The gaze can be useful for visual analysis of advertisements or graphic novels in your course. The gaze of a woman selling a product can tell you whether she is a passive sexual object or an empowered female force in the same way that Edouard Manet's *Olympia* (1863) stares directly at the viewer, accessible to the man's gaze and unlike the Olympias of old who are demure and shy. In the extract from the graphic novel below, the character Persepolis, who grows up in Iran's Islamic Revolution, often looks out at the reader, as if in direct dialogue. It gives her power. *Persepolis* is a memoir of the author Marjane Satrapi's life. However, the interaction of the gaze with other characters in the text is telling of what is happening as well. Perhaps the gaze can also be linked with language, culture and audience. The translation from the original French text (rather than the author's native Persian) maintains some of the multilingualism that reflects the author's own skills and experiences.

■ Guiding questions

■ Who is looking at whom within the text?

■ How does the author create a focus for the reader or audience's eyes and thoughts?

■ What are the desires of the characters in the text? What are their goals?

■ Do the characters achieve their desires? How does it make them feel when they do?

■ The uncanny

The uncanny is *unheimlich* in Freud's original German, and its etymology is important. The German translates literally to 'unhomely'; when your familiar surroundings suddenly seem strange and unusual, this is the uncanny. The classroom should be a familiar setting; if it were suddenly empty on a weekday, this would be a simple example of an uncanny feeling that might arise. When a zombie apocalypse begins in a film and the familiar city streets are suddenly creepy, empty places, this is also the uncanny.

You can watch *Contagion* (2011) or several other short films in response to the SARS outbreak in Hong Kong as an eerie example of the way recognizable streets and landmarks take on new identities. Similarly, people can give you an uncanny feeling if they are known to you but are suddenly acting strange. When a friend turns you in to the authorities, you suddenly feel you do not know them anymore (among other problems you would then face). If your friend turns into a zombie or vampire, the same things happen. Cult classic *From Dusk Till Dawn* (1996) comes to mind.

■ Guiding questions

■ When does the text portray feelings of the uncanny?

■ What do the moments of uncanny feelings reveal about the characters or the context?

■ How do the feelings of uncanniness create tension for the reader? When does this lead to a deeper conceptual understanding?

■ The double

The Freudian double is a great metaphor for thinking about humanity's paradoxical nature. Shanghai and Paris

The Freudian double is a fun and useful motif to look for in literature. The easiest way to think of it is as an alter-ego or doppelganger. It can help us to understand two sides to a single character as well as the reasoning for paired characters in a text (such as protagonist/antagonist relationships). Robert Louis Stevenson's *Strange Case of Dr Jekyll*

and Mr Hyde (1886) is a clear example: the protagonist develops a chemical potion to turn into his alter-ego who subsequently murders, leading to his own self-destruction. It is a look at those mixed desires within us as well as the danger of keeping some desires suppressed. Similarly, Dr Frankenstein and his monster can be seen as doubles. You can link this motif to the previous aspect of the uncanny through setting, where Hyde's home contains dualities and Frankenstein's return to his own home becomes a haunting, rather than a familiar and comforting experience, but this might only be due to his own psychological changes.

There are many examples in both texts of mirrors and reflections, as is common when we look at the double. The idea, simply, is that this second person or second personality of one person is represented in the image, though it can be a more complex motif as well. As Utterson and Poole review Jekyll's chamber, they look deeply 'with an involuntary horror' into the 'cheval glass', which has 'seen some strange things' (page 54). Sydney Carton likewise has several mirror moments in *A Tale of Two Cities* (1859) and ends up taking the place of his look-alike Charles Darnay at the guillotine in an act of sacrifice for the woman he loves. Chuck Palahniuk's visceral novel *Fight Club* (1996) takes the idea one step further in tricking the reader into thinking there are two alter-ego characters, though we eventually find out there is just one who sometimes finds it easier to dissociate from parts of himself.

■ Guiding questions

- Who are the parallel characters in the text? What do they reveal about each other?

- Are there any further symbols of the double in the text, such as reflections or twins? When do they appear and why do you think so?

- Do any characters portray some sort of split personality? What triggers the changes in behaviour or thoughts?

■ Madness

'Madness' is not a Freudian term, but I like to include it here as an area for students to consider. What is madness really? We will all have different definitions. A lot of texts use madness to show the problems with 'normal' society: the normal character is deemed mad by society, because it is society in fact that has problems. You can use madness as a conceptual focus area as well. Many texts deal with it explicitly and can be useful points of comparison: *Hamlet, A Streetcar Named Desire*, Lu Xun's 'A Madman's Diary' (1918), *Madame Bovary* (1856), *One Flew over the Cuckoo's Nest* (1962) and Sylvia Plath's *The Bell Jar* (as well as her poetry). This topic might be a more general and ongoing conversation, but you can still use several focus questions.

■ Guiding questions

- Are any characters at odds with the community or society of the text? What bothers them about the group and vice versa?

- Are any characters labelled as mad or put into a mental institution? Is their madness questioned by the author?

- What do we learn from the 'mad' character(s) about the world?

- What aspects of madness in the text may be perpetuated or caused by society or interpersonal relationships?

Here are a few excerpts you might use in connection to the idea of madness above. You can then use the above questions to help students find big ideas from investigating this angle.

■ Extract from a Chinese short story, 'A Madman's Diary' by Lu Xun (translated by Yang Hsien-Yi), (Part III, 1918)

I can't sleep at night. Everything requires careful consideration if one is to understand it.

Those people, some of whom have been pilloried by the magistrate, slapped in the face by the local gentry, had their wives taken away by bailiffs, or their parents driven to suicide by creditors, never looked as frightened and as fierce then as they did yesterday.

The most extraordinary thing was that woman on the street yesterday who spanked her son and said, 'Little devil! I'd like to bite several mouthfuls out of you to work off my feelings!' Yet all the time she looked at me. I gave a start, unable to control myself; then all those green-faced, long-toothed people began to laugh derisively. Old Chen hurried forward and dragged me home.

He dragged me home. The folk at home all pretended not to know me; they had the same look in their eyes as all the others. When I went into the study, they locked the door outside as if cooping up a chicken or a duck. This incident left me even more bewildered.

A few days ago a tenant of ours from Wolf Cub Village came to report the failure of the crops, and told my elder brother that a notorious character in their village had been beaten to death; then some people had taken out his heart and liver, fried them in oil and eaten them, as a means of increasing their courage. When I interrupted, the tenant and my brother both stared at me. Only today have I realized that they had exactly the same look in their eyes as those people outside.

Just to think of it sets me shivering from the crown of my head to the soles of my feet.

They eat human beings, so they may eat me.

■ Extract from a Nigerian novel in English, *Things Fall Apart* by Chinua Achebe (1959)

There were many men and women in Umuofia who did not feel as strongly as Okonkwo about the new dispensation. The white man had indeed brought a lunatic religion, but he had also built a trading store and for the first time palm-oil and kernel became things of great price, and much money flowed into Umuofia.

And even in the matter of religion there was a growing feeling that there might be something in it after all, something vaguely akin to method in the overwhelming madness.

This growing feeling was due to Mr Brown, the white missionary, who was very firm in restraining his flock from provoking the wrath of the clan. One member in particular was very difficult to restrain. His name was Enoch and his father was the priest of the snake cult. The story went around that Enoch had killed and eaten the sacred python, and that his father had cursed him.

Mr Brown preached against such excess of zeal. Everything was possible, he told his energetic flock, but everything was not expedient. And so Mr Brown came to be respected even by the clan, because he trod softly on its faith. He made friends with some of the great men of the clan and on one of his frequent visits to the neighbouring villages he had been presented with a carved elephant tusk, which was a sign of dignity and rank. One of the great men in that village was called Akunna and he had given one of his sons to be taught the white man's knowledge in Mr Brown's school.

Whenever Mr Brown went to that village he spent long hours with Akunna in his obi talking through an interpreter about religion. Neither of them succeeded in converting the other but they learned more about their different beliefs.

■ Extract from French novel *Madame Bovary* by Gustave Flaubert (1856)

Madame Bovary senior, the evening before, passing along the passage, had surprised her in company of a man—a man with a brown collar, about forty years old, who, at the sound of her step, had quickly escaped through the kitchen. Then Emma began to laugh, but the good lady grew angry, declaring that unless morals were to be laughed at one ought to look after those of one's servants.

'Where were you brought up?' asked the daughter-in-law, with so impertinent a look that Madame Bovary asked her if she were not perhaps defending her own case.

'Leave the room!' said the young woman, springing up with a bound.

'Emma! Mamma!' cried Charles, trying to reconcile them.

But both had fled in their exasperation. Emma was stamping her feet as she repeated—

'Oh! what manners! What a peasant!'

He ran to his mother; she was beside herself. She stammered

'She is an insolent, giddy-headed thing, or perhaps worse!'

And she was for leaving at once if the other did not apologise. So Charles went back again to his wife and implored her to give way; he knelt to her; she ended by saying—

'Very well! I'll go to her.'

And in fact she held out her hand to her mother-in-law with the dignity of a marchioness as she said—

'Excuse me, madame.'

Although all three excerpts look at different ideas about madness, the use of this lens makes them easier to compare for a Paper 2 or IO, or just for general classroom discussion toward conceptual understandings. *Madame Bovary* may be best understood through the additional use of the feminist lens to understand her situation and the way people view her in society. Different views of Okonkwo and the missionaries as mad in *Things Fall Apart* can be understood through New Historicism as well, or more specifically postcolonial discourse. What are the boundaries of cultural relativity when understanding behaviour from a moral standpoint? Finally, Lu Xun takes us to China and helps us to understand how someone can be made a 'mad' outsider in a village where Communism is the pervading ideology. But this idea of the mad outsider need not be in a Communist society; one can make connections with Camus' *The Outsider* or Shirley Jackson's 'The Lottery' as well as any Dickens novel discussing group mentality (for example, in *A Tale of Two Cities*, the crowd outside the Old Bailey who are 'ghoulish' and likened to 'flies' looking for 'carrion').

Each text takes a different angle of madness, but a common thread is that a seemingly mad character in a work of fiction often tells us more about the shortcomings of society than of the individual him/herself.

Although one might consider New Historicism or Marxist theory here, the focus in each section is on the individuals at play, the way their independent psyches are affected and how they contribute to our ideas about madness, sanity and morality.

Deconstruction theory

We can get into a lot of fancy post-structural terminology when we look at deconstruction theory, but essentially we can see it reduced to:

- a questioning of the reality presented to us

- an understanding of how binaries and dichotomies create realities, but can be broken down

- a way of thinking and writing that often leaves more questions than answers.

We can help our students become comfortable in the ambiguities of existence by empowering them to see that there are different perspectives of looking at the world, given truths have changed over time, and authors often try to help find a new way of looking at some of the reductions the world has been broken down into, such as good and evil, black and white, man and woman, etc.

CORE CONNECTIONS

TOK

TOK asks us to question established truths, where knowledge comes from, and to consider shared and personal knowledge. A shared knowledge system would inherently contain ways of viewing the world through dichotomies. With deconstruction theory, we can then question this shared knowledge as absolute truth.

For your own interest, you might want to look at a closer level through Jacques Derrida and Gilles Deleuze especially. The most comprehensive to start with are Derrida's *Of Grammatology* (1967) and Deleuze's work with Félix Guattari on *Anti-Oedipus* (1972) and *What is Philosophy?* (1991). Postmodern 'theory' might be better discussed as a literary and artistic movement, especially in contrast to modernism, as both ideologies are still at play in the literary world today. A look at them can help your students debate the purpose of form in different texts, for example. You might also be interested in the concept of *difference*, but I find this is a tricky one to bring into the secondary school classroom. Instead, you can more generally talk about tensions in the text and a creation of cognitive dissonance through similarly developed ideas, characters or symbols. Minor differences are clearer in the proximity and similarity. Use musical dissonance as an example, where notes at intervals with undesirable pairing are played simultaneously to create a harsh sound, or chiaroscuro, where painters place different shades of a colour in juxtaposition to highlight their uniqueness.

'Binaries' and 'dichotomies' are slightly different in that dichotomies refer to anything divided in two (not necessarily opposites, but they may be used in opposition to each other), while binaries are things consisting of two or as a doubling. For this reason, although some teachers refer to binaries, I find the definition of dichotomy to be closer to what we are really looking at here.

Deconstruction can happen within a text through close analysis, or it can be explicitly discussed by the author. Often a subversive text is a good one to look at in that the reality presented can be deconstructed by the reader. This happens in *Huckleberry Finn* where Twain's view of Black men does not equate to Huck's, who is all for freedom but does not understand the superior intelligence of the former slave named Jim. Likewise, in Herman Melville's *Benito Cereno* (1855) the reader is at first unaware that the 'slaves' are in charge of the ship that we enter with the protagonist. They have already rebelled, and as their power is revealed toward the end of the novella, we can deconstruct the connotations of the language about both sides – black and white – on the ship.

Common dichotomies that arise in texts are:

- man/woman
- evil/good
- light/dark
- black/white
- life/death

- in/out
- us/them
- friend/stranger
- rich/poor
- love/hate.

Many other dichotomies go back to some of the ones above. They create associations of symbols or other elements of society with each side of the dichotomy until they are broken down. In this way, if the topic being broken down is related to another theory (for example, man/woman and feminist theory) there is good reason to intersect the use of the two theories. The media also uses these dichotomies, including the use of us/them in discourse, that can easily be explored.

Below, we have three excerpts of different text types and topics to investigate through deconstruction theory. You might start the first part of the table (identifying dichotomies) as a chart on the board or screen together. In fact, each question could be a step of formative work in the classroom rather than simply a table to fill out. The table instead might be used to synthesize information more concisely for review and comparison between texts.

- **Extract from 'A Room of One's Own' by Virginia Woolf (1929)**

At any rate, whether or not the blame rested on the old lady who was looking at the spaniel, there could be no doubt that for some reason or other our mothers had mismanaged their affairs very gravely. Not a penny could be spared for 'amenities'' for partridges and wine, beadles and turf, books and cigars, libraries and leisure. To raise bare walls out of bare earth was the utmost they could do.

So we talked standing at the window and looking, as so many thousands look every night, down on the domes and towers of the famous city beneath us. It was very beautiful, very mysterious in the autumn moonlight. The old stone looked very white and venerable. One thought of all the books that were assembled down there; of the pictures of old prelates and worthies hanging in the panelled rooms; of the painted windows that would be throwing strange globes and crescents on the pavement; of the tablets and memorials and inscriptions; of the fountains and the grass; of the quiet rooms looking across the quiet quadrangles. And (pardon me the thought) I thought, too, of the admirable smoke and drink and the deep armchairs and the pleasant carpets: of the urbanity, the geniality, the dignity which are the offspring of luxury and privacy and space. Certainly our mothers had not provided us with any thing comparable to all this—our mothers who found it difficult to scrape together thirty thousand pounds, our mothers who bore thirteen children to ministers of religion at St Andrews.

So I went back to my inn, and as I walked through the dark streets I pondered this and that, as one does at the end of the day's work. I pondered why it was that Mrs Seton had no money to leave us; and what effect poverty has on the mind; and what effect wealth has on the mind; and I thought of the queer old gentlemen I had seen that morning with tufts of fur upon their shoulders; and I remembered how if one whistled one of them ran; and I thought of the organ booming in the chapel and of the shut doors of the library; and I thought how unpleasant it is to be locked out; and I thought how it is worse perhaps to be locked in; and, thinking of the safety and prosperity of the one sex and of the poverty and insecurity of the other and of the effect of tradition and of the lack of tradition upon the mind of a writer, I thought at last that it was time to roll up the crumpled skin of the day, with its arguments and its impressions and its anger and its laughter, and cast it into the hedge. A thousand stars were flashing across the blue wastes of the sky. One seemed alone with an inscrutable society. All human beings were laid asleep—prone, horizontal, dumb. Nobody seemed stirring in the streets of Oxbridge. Even the door of the hotel sprang open at the touch of an invisible hand—not a boots was sitting up to light me to bed, it was so late.

■ 'An Old Man's Winter Night' by Robert Frost (1916)

All out-of-doors looked darkly in at him
Through the thin frost, almost in separate stars,
That gathers on the pane in empty rooms.
What kept his eyes from giving back the gaze
Was the lamp tilted near them in his hand.
What kept him from remembering what it was
That brought him to that creaking room was age.
He stood with barrels round him – at a loss.
And having scared the cellar under him
In clomping here, he scared it once again
In clomping off; – and scare the outer night,
Which has its sounds, familiar, like the roar
Of trees and crack of branches, common things,
But nothing so like beating on a box.
A light he was to no one but himself
Where now he sat, concerned with he knew what,
A quiet light, and then not even that.
He consigned to the moon, such as she was,
So late-arising, to the broken moon
As better than the sun in any case
For such a charge, his snow upon the roof,
His icicles along the wall to keep;
And slept. The log that shifted with a jolt
Once in the stove, disturbed him and he shifted,
And eased his heavy breathing, but still slept.
One aged man – one man – can't keep a house,
A farm, a countryside, or if he can,
It's thus he does it of a winter night.

■ Extract from 'Letter from a region in my mind' by James Baldwin, published in *The New Yorker* (17 November 1962)

The fear that I heard in my father's voice, for example, when he realized that I really believed I could do anything a white boy could do, and had every intention of proving it, was not at all like the fear I heard when one of us was ill or had fallen down the stairs or strayed too far from the house. It was another fear, a fear that the child, in challenging the white world's assumptions, was putting himself in the path of destruction …

In short, we, the black and the white, deeply need each other here if we are really to become a nation—if we are really, that is, to achieve our identity, our maturity, as men and women. To create one nation has proved to be a hideously difficult task; there is certainly no need now to create two, one black and one white …

When I was very young, and was dealing with my buddies in those wine- and urine-stained hallways, something in me wondered, *What will happen to all that beauty?* For black people, though I am aware that some of us, black and white, do not know it yet, are very beautiful. And when I sat at Elijah's table and watched the baby, the women, and the men, and we talked about God's—or Allah's—vengeance, I wondered, when that vengeance was achieved, *What will happen to all that beauty then?* I could also see that the intransigence and ignorance of the white world might make that vengeance inevitable—a vengeance that does not really depend on, and cannot really be executed by, any person or organization, and that cannot be prevented by any police force or army: historical vengeance, a cosmic vengeance, based on the law that we recognize when we say, 'Whatever goes up must come down.' And here we are, at the center of the arc, trapped in the gaudiest, most valuable, and most improbable water wheel the world has ever seen …

Everything now, we must assume, is in our hands; we have no right to assume otherwise. If we—and now I mean the relatively conscious whites and the relatively conscious blacks, who must, like lovers, insist on, or create, the consciousness of the others—do not falter in our duty now, we may be able, handful that we are, to end the racial nightmare, and achieve our country, and change the history of the world. If we do not now dare everything, the fulfillment of that prophecy, re-created from the Bible in song by a slave, is upon us: *God gave Noah the rainbow sign, No more water, the fire next time!*

■ Deconstruction theory

Questions	'A Room of One's Own'	'An Old Man's Winter Night'	'Letter from a region in my mind'
What are the dichotomies in the text?	Man/woman. Inside/outside. Locked in/locked out. Professional/mother. Rich/poor.	Inside/outside. Life/death. Light/dark. Survival/succumbing. Nature/human.	Black/white. Us/them. Conscious people/those who act by fear. Knowledge/ignorance. Beauty/blindness.
What dichotomies are deconstructed and what do they teach us?	Being locked out can give you freedom to do what you want. Maybe it's not worse to be a woman?	Inside/outside – though at the start the outdoors (unknown? afterlife?) seems something to be afraid of – the man 'scared it'; the inside – to show he is getting over his fears (solitude? death?).	'Maturity' as nation = black and white making one nation together. Creativity needed to deconstruct.
Is there a clear notion of good and bad in the text?	Not really; Woolf doesn't blame a particular person for the problems, rather patriarchal society as a whole, and then she prefers to be outside of it.	No, like a lot of Frost's poems, he leaves us with ambiguity.	Bad for the father = 'white world's assumptions' (dangerous for his son).
Is there a clear notion of us vs. them in the text?	Them: the scholars with access to the library can only be men; it is easier for men to make money as writers. Us: women without the same access and resources.	No, the man is isolated. Maybe he was against nature at the start, but he embraces it. However, maybe you can imagine society is something totally different than this man on his own.	Yes – 'us' are the people willing to be creative and help races work together.
How does the narration or voice aid in the deconstruction within the text?	The author is a clear character and gives us a conclusion: that as long as a woman has money and a room of her own, she can achieve success as a writer (but this is not always possible); it draws from Woolf's own experience.	Poetic voice leaves ambiguities and gives us symbols with mixed meanings ('consigned to the moon'/'log' and fire).	A clear voice of someone willing to take risk and face fears; calls on others to do the same.

Questions	'A Room of One's Own'	'An Old Man's Winter Night'	'Letter from a region in my mind'
What questions or ambiguities does the text leave us with? What is still open to interpretation?	Is it better to gain access even if women (and poor) would become institutionalized? Does creativity need an outsider perspective? How can women get published even if they have this creative space? To what extent was Shakespeare (and other famous male writers) influenced by women?	Unclear if the man has decided to live on or succumb peacefully to death and what will happen that night/tomorrow. Unclear if ending is negative or positive about the meaning of a man's life. Nature's role is ambiguous.	How this can happen exactly is unclear; it is more a general philosophy. Shows hope – 'whatever comes up must go down' – though a difficult time.

All three texts are about a kind of acceptance of something inadequate in the world: women's place in society, humanity's ultimate loneliness and a racially divided nation based on fear. None of the texts say we should accept them as inequalities or fears, but all three do show how there is hope and that in understanding these problems, one can be empowered and face fears head on. There are other interesting connections, like the inside/outside symbolism from Woolf and Frost or the force of creativity in Woolf and Baldwin's texts.

Although we did not start with a singular concept focus here, this exercise might be helpful in helping students find connections in their Paper 1 and even Paper 2 texts. Remember that the Paper 2 texts can come from different parts of the course. You might find it useful to re-connect texts from different conceptual focus areas as you prepare for the exams, helping students find a freshness in 'review' where they discover ideas about new concepts. Maybe these are concepts they have looked at in other classes, including TOK, or they note that a text from **Black in America** (Baldwin) actually has a lot to do with **beauty**. We shall come back to this notion in Chapter 6, but for now, try to consider the way that a course can be both conceptually designed and also deviate for the purpose of lessons that investigate through other skills or topics.

Intertextual theory

Intertextual theory is now a particular area of exploration that we study in the IB course. Therefore, it may not need the designation as a particular lens in your course. However, I think it is useful to continue to look at this theory as a tool rather than only a part. Students are then aware there is academic dialogue about it. Also, as a theory, it produces a more meaningful and structured approach to investigating the *in between* of texts; the dissonance created in looking at them together delivers truth. Although **intertextuality** is also about responses to literature, whether as pastiche, historical reference points, satire or other defined methods, the emphasis needs to be placed on how we look at the texts together to find meaning rather than simply understanding them on a continuum. We cannot dismiss earlier works, for example, as historically petrified truth tomes. They are still living, breathing art forms that can deliver ideas to us as we analyse, interpret and understand them.

We explored this lens as an entire area of exploration, a third of the course, in the last chapter. You may want to use the theory explicitly to emphasize the ideas that can come from the *in betweenness* of texts, or Kristeva's doughnut hole.

Using any of the lenses above can help with **intertextuality** and this third part of the course, due to the fact that the theories help us to compare the texts in each conceptual focus area. The IB give us certain questions to focus on in this part of the course:

- How do texts adhere to and deviate from conventions associated with literary forms or text types?

- How do conventions and systems of reference evolve over time?

- In what ways can diverse texts share points of similarity?

- How valid is the notion of a classic text?

- How can texts offer multiple perspectives of a single issue, topic or theme?

- In what ways can comparison and interpretation be transformative?

I recommend you go beyond these questions with the addition of the questions below, in order to use the theory itself more effectively:

- What new ideas can you discover from looking at two or more texts together?

- In what ways are texts responses to texts that have come before them?

- How do allegory and allusions create intertexts?

You may want to use some texts that explicitly draw on intertextuality. Pairings of this nature help students understand the dialogue of literature, as shown in the diagram below.

The voice of the American child and formation of new ideologies: *Huckleberry Finn, Invisible Man, Catcher in the Rye* and *Vernon God Little*

An Oedipal journey and the Westernization of Japan: *Oedipus Rex, Kafka on the Shore*, Kafka's short stories, Western advertising (Johnnie Walker and KFS)

The best and worst of times: *A Tale of Two Cities*, Julian Barnes' *The Noise of Time* (2016), Ali Smith's *Autumn* (2016), media articles that reference Dickens in relation to the rich-poor gap

Shakespearean texts and modern adaptations: *The Taming of the Shrew* and *Ten Things I Hate About You, Othello* and *O, Macbeth* and *Scotland PA*

Zen comes West: Japanese Haiku (Basho especially) and painted scrolls, Jack Kerouac's American Haiku, Kerouac's *On the Road*, Huxley's *Island*, Salinger's 'Teddy', Robert M. Pirsig's *Zen and the Art of Motorcycle Maintenance* (1974)

Bringing it together

Think of these theories as tools for your students rather than research strategies. When used effectively and in a focused way, they can offer your students methods of analysis that are neither high-brow nor esoteric but make sense on an everyday basis. Power, money, gender, sex, identity, dreams, sexuality, connotations, history … these are things that make sense to students.

Once students are comfortable looking at several theories, you can bring them together more loosely and dynamically. You can say things like: 'If we put on our queer theory hats now, how might you interpret the poem differently?' or, 'Can you think of what else might be revealed through this essay from a century ago if we consider a New Historic approach?' Simple prompts in the classroom or as feedback in journals can go a long way in this regard.

You can do class activities, like short presentations or creative pieces, to also bring theory together. The table below gives a sample of what you might do with Kafka's *The Metamorphosis*, for example.

■ Further considerations guided by literary theory

Franz Kafka's *The Metamorphosis*	
Lexicon (Formalism)	What are the roles of the following elements in the story and where do they come up in the text? ■ Hysteria, madness, rage ■ Expectations, fault ■ Subconscious, dreams, nightmares ■ Isolation ■ Money ■ Punishment, torture ■ Disgust, horror ■ Death ■ Absolute, complete, total
Authorship (New Historicism)	What does your knowledge of Kafka's biography add to our interpretation of the text? Describe Kafka's relationship with Prague and his family. Are there any connections to Gregor's character? What was happening in Prague at the time of his writing?
Power (Marxist theory)	Who is in power throughout the story? Who is in power before the story begins? What creates power within these relationships? Who works and why? What other working wages and financial exchanges come about over the course of the story?
Time (Intertextual connection to *The Outsider*)	Where do you see evidence of time in the text? Why do people always seem to be in a rush or working with a sense of urgency? How does Gregor view the passage of time? How does your understanding of time in *The Outsider* and now here change the way you see time as a whole?
Feminist theory	Is there a difference between the actions of the men and the women in the text? What does each gender act as a function of? How are the futures of Gregor and his sister linked with gender? Whom does Kafka give more power to? What happens to Greta at the end of the story and is it empowering or not?
Psychoanalytical theory	What does the metamorphosis (real or imagined) of Gregor's physical self have to do with his mental self? What does he find meaning in? What does he think of his parents? Could he have survived beyond his death? How do dreams enter into the story?

Franz Kafka's *The Metamorphosis*

Dichotomies (Deconstructionist theory)	What do the following dichotomies reveal and how do they aid our understanding of a message in the text? Do the dichotomies last or deconstruct? ■ Fate vs. free will ■ Private vs. public ■ Anxiety vs. calmness ■ Reality vs. imagination
Reader response	Do you see any aspects of Gregor's family reflected in your own? Does it make you want to change anything in your family life? What do you predict will happen at the end of the story?

Students can then do a short presentation on their topic using the lenses above. I would recommend requiring the use of at least three quotes from the original text as well as a requirement of one question from each group for the class to respond to. Further, you could ask students to select a single image to represent their responses or allow more creativity, like a tableau sequence.

For F. Scott Fitzgerald's *The Great Gatsby* (1925), you might instead ask students to investigate particular symbols to demonstrate how to approach the text from a particular lens. Students can create posters or models to show their points. The smashed up car might demonstrate deconstruction theory in the text and the breakdown of class binaries. The eyes of Dr TJ Eckleburg could help us understand the role of the Freudian gaze. Jordan as a character symbol can investigate queerness in her non-binary relationship with gender roles. She can also be looked at through the New Historicism lens to understand how her dress, behaviour and bold ideas would be part of a 1920s discourse about feminism. She was no saint, though. As a cheat and liar, her character could either be an indictment of such free women at the time or could show that women needed to be these things to beat the patriarchal system. What does her character say about women in the 1920s? What is Fitzgerald's intention in providing us with such a complex minor character? Jordan Baker, 'incurably dishonest', shows time and again through her actions and behaviour that she wants to be free and, thanks in part to the money she has and her status as single, is able to make choices, including whom to keep company with and how to spend her time: 'let's get out … this is much too polite for me' (page 45).

The character of Jordan Baker played with gender roles in many ways – at one point in the novel, she is playing golf in masculine clothing. Here, she embraces the flapper look like many feminists of the 1920s. This is a representation of her bold ideas and subversion of male attire

Use the above charts and activities, along with journals or preparation for Paper 2 (these will be discussed in the next couple of chapters), to get students interacting more with the texts and with each other. Get them excited also about academic studies in literature, the arts and media. The teaser of scholarly texts should not feel threatening in the way they are represented. Instead, they should offer to the student a window of what is to come should they dive into these disciplines. This window is often left out of reach to students, not allowing them to understand the greater intertextual dialogue of language that is out there, being studied and redefined.

You can go further into areas like postcolonialism, semiotics and race theories. Eco-criticism is a nice lens to use if you study American transcendentalism as a literary movement. If you are looking at film as well, perhaps look at work on adaptation (Robert Stam's 'Beyond Fidelity: The Dialogics of Adaptation', 2000) or anything in Thomas Elsaesser and Malte Hagener's *Film Theory: an introduction through the senses* (2010). The list goes on. You can even look at a short excerpt or more current events-based articles from Slavoj Žižek, a challenging author who plays around with and through different theories.

Challenge your students. Help them to think differently. Allow them to make conclusions themselves.

■ ATT & ATL

Giving students power

■ The methods of using theory in the classroom are all ATT, while the skills the students achieve are ATL, mostly about thinking strategies. The important thing to remember is that all theories in this chapter are things that you *can* use, not things you *must* use. None of it is a requirement of IB, but the use of theories will help students achieve conceptual understanding and become advanced tools in the skills area of their development. Try to encourage students that they are the philosophers (little 'p'!). Anyone can think for themselves and make their own conclusions about the world. They do not need to be a big 'P' Philosopher to do so!

Developing student writing and speaking

A unique voice

Everyone has a unique voice, everyone has something to say and everyone can find a way to be heard. Each August when I begin with my students, this is what I tell them: *I want to help you find your voice.* Finding it is about writing, speaking, reading ... and it's about identity. It's about power, perspectives, truth and beauty. It's about the future.

We often say that children are our future; we must cultivate the voices of children if they are to have anything to say. They must learn how to communicate with themselves and others. They must learn how not to be afraid to take a risk with an idea. To speak up for what they believe in and to question norms or arguments presented to them in a meaningful and purposeful way.

I tell my students they are philosophers: if you allow yourself to think freely, to use parts of others' perspectives to gain your own, by having a voice and cultivating that individuality, then you are a philosopher. Do not be intimidated by those who seem to have the answers – you have answers, too. You are an individual with ideas. You can agree or disagree with someone else. You can read others' thoughts and decide which parts to make your own, and which parts to respond vehemently against.

When we accept we are philosophers, we are no longer afraid to speak up in class. We are no longer afraid to share an opinion. This is a wonderful effect of conceptual learning. Students are empowered to come to conclusions and create ideas that they share through writing and speaking, using the skills and content of your course.

■ The one-minute challenge

One way to easily set up this idea is to force students to give their ideas in class. I use the word 'force' in a gentle and caring way! Directly talking with students and valuing their opinions will set up a sense of respect and trust in your classroom, but you will also have to set some boundaries. Once you feel you are at this point, you can do this activity. Set a challenging or controversial short text as homework reading. It might be a David Foster Wallace essay, an op-ed on Google Translate, replacing the need to learn other languages, or the opening page of *Chronicle of a Death Foretold*.

Next, in class preferably, ask students to spend about 15 minutes reflecting on an idea that interested them in the text. They can focus on a particular paragraph or even just a word. They might instead look at a subversive meaning, or perhaps investigate a symbol. Give them a few ideas but let them know it is open for them to explore. As you walk around the room, those who are stuck on blank paper can either just write a list of words that come to mind or make a drawing of their ideas.

When the 15 minutes end, the one-minute iPad begins. It does not have to be an iPad, but this has been my favourite, very simple, use of it that I picked up at a Learning 2.0 conference in Bangkok, where we all, as curriculum leaders, spoke for one minute about our takeaways from the conference.

The one-minute challenge is a great way to prompt all your students to start thinking and sharing their thoughts positively with their peers

You put the timer to one minute on the iPad and stand it up facing the first student speaker. It can be a laptop or even a stopwatch or phone, but the iPad somehow seems both prominent and unintimidating. The speaker stands, we begin the time, and they start. They might ramble a little, but usually they then find their way. If they get stuck, you ask a question or ask for evidence from the text. Usually, though, the student gets to 59 seconds with a disappointed look because they want to keep speaking. When your alarm sounds (I like the dog bark) the student can only finish the sentence he or she is in the middle of.

Everyone in the class takes a turn. Everyone is validated with immediate positive feedback from the teacher and/or the other students. Most importantly, *everyone* in your classroom is listened to for a full minute. How often do people get to just say what is on their mind, what they think about something, without interruption? Those questions or prompting I mentioned are only for when a student gets stuck. This is rare, but it might happen. Otherwise, *let them be.* Some students talk and talk in class, but others will wait their turn in order to be polite, will try to not take too much time for the same reason, and will mostly simply listen and reflect. Good for them, but they deserve to be heard as well!

■ Encourage debate

In Chapter 3, we looked at different ways of engaging with concepts through debate. These included a structured court-style debate, Socratic seminars and 'Take a Stand!'. Each of them gives a voice to the students while being guided by your direction, including the structure, the prompts and the texts or content to include as evidence.

By nature, each of these activities are hands free, meaning that students decide when to speak and also encourage their classmates. Of course, you can ask directed questions to individual students to include them or to dig deeper as well. For Take a Stand!, I encourage you to use a soft ball or object to pass around the classroom, whereby the speaker must possess the ball. You could ask that students pass to someone who has not spoken yet or who is on the other side of the room (or both). Debates should be structured so that each student has a speaking role at a particular moment, but there might also be some time for open debate or follow-up questions. Socratics by nature should be free of teacher input, with students sharing ideas and pushing each other with questions and provocations at the centre of the room.

Depending on the size of your class and how they do with the above activities, you can go a step further to make a seminar-style class.

Value the multilingual voice

When we talk about student voice, we must think of valuing multilingualism. Research has shown that multilingual students process better; they develop unique cognitive skills. The one drawback is that they can have a smaller vocabulary due to interference from other language(s), but the benefits tend to outweigh this issue. In fact, they may understand more vocabulary that they read if the language(s) are more connected to each other. In any case, multiple studies show the vast benefits, which is why the IB values a multilingual learning environment in their language philosophy.

Many of you will have training or done research about ways to help students without native speaker language level in your classroom. If you have not, I encourage you to try to get some personal development through your school. There are also many books and websites out there you can go to for resources. One website that I find really useful is called *EAL-Time* from Joris Van den Bosch, an educator currently based in Brussels. His tools are easy, fun and effective to use in the classroom and can be transferred to language A courses other than English.

Your second- or third-language students may be the best in your class. With a slight tweak in attitude and approach, we can value their languages by asking for help with translations, looking at media in their mother tongue (or other language B) and discussing the etymology of words in the classroom. By reading PRL-t texts that include some of the original language, perhaps untranslatable due to Sapir Whorf theory, we again value other languages and multilingualism. This is especially important if you are a teacher of English A, since we all know that some kind of English is becoming the 'common language', as well as the the internet language. Looking at texts in different languages and valuing their use will allow you to have richer, deeper discussions in your classroom and encourage students to continue to seek different perspectives through languages.

You may have many in class with a similar, perhaps local, mother tongue. Are they taking that language A as well? If not, maybe teach some shorter text types and texts originally in that language, even if you do not speak the language yourself. Use it as an opportunity to learn. It is not selfish; students who teach you will internalize what they are telling you about language and writing. Further, links to the host culture are encouraged by IB for a variety of reasons. Quite practically, students may carry on living and working in the area, and you will have access to sites and resources in the museums, libraries or monuments that might link to what you are studying.

Encourage through feedback

Student voice will be developed in your classroom largely in writing as well, of course. We need to think about the way we give feedback to writing, whether a free write, journal entry, creative piece, IA draft or internal exam. At each of these levels, there is room for feedback from the student, peers and the teacher. We shall look at some self and peer assessment and feedback strategies in the next chapter, which will help students take ownership of their work and really internalize the most effective way to cultivate a voice through writing.

For you, the teacher, you have probably learned, discussed and reflected on your own strategies of giving feedback. However, it is easy for us to forget all this as we approach exams, thinking that we have a different goal in mind and we need to just red ink the heck out of student writing! We have probably all had experiences professionally when we would have also liked to receive more direct, constructive feedback; this is what we should channel as we respond to the work of the young people in our classrooms. It does not matter how 'tough' or 'mature' they are; they can hear the harsh truth framed in a supportive and directive way.

■ ATT & ATL

What kind of feedback is most useful?

■ Here, I condense proven effective ways to think about the feedback you give in the classroom. For many of you, this is just a reminder. Others may have different opinions, which might be more effective in different ways. Actually, much of what you see below are questions to help you reflect on your practice. I hope that this list will at least be a prompt to help you think about how you want to give feedback, perhaps to start a dialogue with other teachers at your school. Other subject teachers may also look for your guidance as the writing expert; don't be afraid to offer it. Marking papers can be the bane of the language A teacher's existence, or it can be something we see as a constructive tool toward student success.

Reflecting on your feedback	Potential solutions
What type of feedback do you give? Do you connect it to the rubric? Language features? The text type? The conceptual ideas? Student personal goals?	We don't want to overwhelm students or make them feel bad about their writing. We want to empower them, give them a voice and give them directed feedback to help them improve. Sometimes we add criticism to help students, but it turns them off from writing. Comments like: 'you don't sound like a native English speaker' can be very damaging. Instead, specific constructive criticism along with positive feedback is more useful for student motivation.
Can you think of examples where you could give specific constructive criticism? How do you ensure the right tone with students? Do you consider giving oral feedback instead, so the tone is clear?	Often, less is more (this is proven in research). It also speeds up your marking! For example: ■ You can mark the grammar/language features in only the first paragraph and ask students to continue to look for similar issues throughout. ■ You can use a simple formula for holistic feedback: one or two things that went well, one or two to improve and one question. For oral feedback, Feedback Studio or Google docs allow you to record your voice. John Hattie suggests you should combine how your student did with how they could do better, as shown in the artwork on the following page.
Can you think of meaningful ways to give immediate feedback? How can you facilitate easier/quicker methods of providing written feedback?	We are all super busy, but research shows that students respond better to feedback in a timely manner. This is why sometimes direct feedback in the classroom setting is even more useful than written comments, if they must come weeks later.
Feedback without grades	Feedback without numbers is also proven by research to have greater impact on students. We have all seen students who look at a number and then stop looking at feedback! How can you facilitate this in your classroom while still needing to provide summative marks? Of course, all of us give different types of formative assessment feedback without marks. We can try to use the language of our rubrics to help students see where the end mark is coming from. We can withhold marks and even marked/highlighted rubrics until after students have seen feedback and done some kind of reflection on the work. Only then do they receive the corresponding number. You can also use self-assessment with a rubric before revealing the mark.

Reflecting on your feedback	Potential solutions
Chance for revision?	Most researchers have found that the most effective strategy to help writers is to allow them to revise. Of course, sometimes we have to give a mark before revision. However, you can still allow for revising connected to student goals and specific learning goals (maybe for the whole class).
	Time is also important in allowing students to understand feedback and using that feedback. If you include time for reflection, revision or discussion while giving back work, it proves to be most useful in the learning process. You might have a type of assessment reflection sheet, perhaps digitally, that allows students to track their learning.
Can students give each other effective feedback?	Peer editing sounds like a shortcut to some people, but it's a great way for students to learn from each other. We often feel like we internalize something when we teach it. By allowing students to provide feedback, they have done the same.

Feedback **=** **How did your student do?** **+** **How could they do better?**

John Hattie model of feedback

You can think of giving the right feedback as a way of coaching your students and you can transfer this coaching also to the formats of peer- and self-editing by modelling the style you encourage students to use. Some strategies include online (public to the class) comments on each other's work, direct oral feedback, directed questioning, using a checklist, oral presentation or Socratic seminar feedback (also to keep students engaged during orals), etc.

■ **FEEDBACK CHECKLIST**

✔ Can you think of examples where you could give specific constructive criticism?
✔ Are you giving the right amount of feedback?
✔ Are you using the right tone?
✔ Are you feeding back in a timely manner?
✔ Can you feed back without grades or numbers first?
✔ Can you allow any time for revisions or reflection?
✔ Can students offer any feedback to their peers?

■ Pastoral care

As we discussed on page 141, I like to tell my students they are all philosophers (little 'p'). They should not assume they need a famous name like Plato to have something to say, but they are free to think and speak for themselves with an audience. This idea goes beyond the direct content and skills in the classroom; conceptual lessons are meant to help a student bring real life into the classroom, and vice versa.

Maybe they feel like they are not listened to at home. Encourage them to ask for one minute, or five, to just explain how they are feeling. As adults, we may think we are helping but sometimes we do not understand the real problem. I am constantly biting my tongue with teenagers when I think I know what is going on inside their head! Often, if I stay silent a bit longer, I find the real issue underneath. How many of us have jumped into water when we don't know how to swim, but reached the other side and succeeded by learning along the way? In this case, the question is not only metaphorical.

Watch short videos like David Foster Wallace's 'This is Water' graduation speech at Kenyon College to engage with the issues that might be on their minds right now. You can look

Writer David Foster Wallace

Sometimes we take our realities, our 'water', for granted: 'The point of the fish story is merely that the most obvious, important realities are often the ones that are hardest to see and talk about' (DFW)

at this video as a speech for another text type or connect to a conceptual focus area such as consciousness, transitions, society, etc. Another great one is an interview with John Connors after winning Best Actor at the IFTAs and discussing how anti-traveller (or Romani people) bias nearly led him to suicide before finding his voice through acting and the creative forces within him: 'I have a spotlight now. People listen to me.' (*The Guardian*, 27 February 2018). Use the Connors interview with something from Herta Muller, such as *The Land of Green Plums* (1994), to explore the context of Romania and its diaspora further.

Language A class and finding a voice means different things to different students. That is ok. Our job is also to listen to what they want to achieve in this course – a grade, an opportunity, skills – and also to offer further reasons to continue to develop their minds through reading and writing.

Journals and learning portfolios

The IB now requires what they are calling the learning portfolio (LP). Though it is unassessed, the IB can request these to determine authenticity of work and a school's practice. You have probably used some kind of folder or digital platform to help students track their progress or work in the past. This is no different, but its link to assessment (explicitly, the IO but also the HL essay) makes it a more integral part of the learning environment.

Many language A teachers also use some kind of journaling as part of their courses. I recommend here that you bring the LP and the journal together. This way, rather than separated drafts and assessments, the area of *play*, the journal, and the area working toward marks, the portfolio, come together as one.

■ What's the point of the LP and journal?

It is essential that students do not merely see the LP and journal as requirements but as places for experimentation and play with their ideas and individual voices. For this reason, we will talk about how you can assess this large piece of work without inhibiting students or creating fear about marks.

As my track coach used to say, 'Make practice feel like competition and competition like practice'. We take away the fear of assessment in this way and link it to the creative process with the use of content and skills learned in the course. Concepts can be linked to personal experiences and other subjects in juxtaposition with close analysis of a core text.

Students will be required to also use the journal in the process of formulating their ideas for the IO: the text selection, global issue and ideas to outline in preparation. We shall talk about this process in the next chapter. You can use a similar process for the HL essay with your HL students.

The 'point' of the LP and journal is beyond assessment; it is about the entire learning process – engaging with content as students learn skills. Students will:

- learn how to integrate quotes

- try out creative writing

- apply literary lenses to texts

- begin to compare texts to each other.

You will guide them through scaffolded assignments and questions, allowing constructive feedback and debate with their peers, and eventually enable them to fly free and flourish in DP language A and beyond.

■ Approaching your students' journals

I once had a professor at university, Michael Harper, who made our whole course into a journal investigation of the content he presented to us (as well as the content he encouraged us to look at beyond the classroom). He was also a wonderful poet. During the first lesson, we were told that half of our grades would be earned through a journal we kept through the course and the other half would be earned from a paper. There was no direction for either one, though of course we could talk with him about our ideas.

At first, we were all trying to figure out what he wanted us to do. I was in a confused state of mind for at least three weeks. Fear led me. I tried to use prior knowledge to understand what I should write or what I should say in class when we were directly faced with a deep question, one which I now understand to be conceptual.

Then something happened. During the fourth week, we all just started answering whatever came to mind! We didn't allow long silences of searching for answers we thought he wanted to hear and to which he responded quizzically. We were freer, looser and class became fun. Professor Harper became animated. We had dialogues rather than just strange questions. We laughed; we had moments of silent reflection; we kept talking about ideas at the conclusion of each evening seminar as we walked across the snow-filled quad. We did the same in our journals, too. We let our investigations take us wherever we wanted them to go. We said what we thought. We examined paintings related to the poetry we read. We picked out our favourite parts of essays. We read suggested novels, like Ralph Ellison's *Invisible Man*, and extended our reading beyond the classroom.

At the end of the course, he sent each us a copy of his book, *Chant of Saints*, with a personalized message he wrote on his typewriter (this was 2002, so the typewritten text made an impression). This was mine:

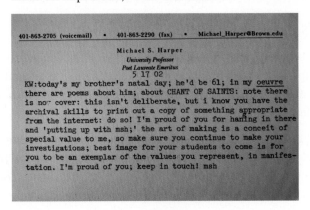

Poet Michael Harper, 1938–2016

None of the journals in our seminar with Professor Harper resembled the others in shape, length, scope or thought, and that was the beauty of them. They were unique and intentional representations of our thoughts over the semester.

Harper died in 2016, but I still find his voice a part of the way I approach reading, writing, teaching and *life*. I tell my students this story, not to liken myself to him, but to encourage them to take risks and find new ways of thinking once they leave my classroom, to use language and literature in their approach to the world around them.

I tell my students, 'Don't try to write what you think I want to read in these journals. Write what you *want* to write.' I tell them there will be time for more structure to their ideas as we work on writing formally. Those structures are important to tell the story, but it's still the story they want to tell. I will help them to make it so others can understand their ideas, their voices. It should be a free exploration (though I give more guidance and prompts than Harper allowed). They keep asking, 'Should I do this?' 'Can I add that?' To which I say, 'Do what you want!' It frustrates several of them at the beginning, but eventually they find their way.

■ What platform should we use for the journal?

We can get practical with a few things here. First of all: what platform should we use for the journal? Paper, digital? Within either option there are also many other options. This is about practically accessing and storing the work, but it is also about the learning process – handwriting vs. typing, methods of producing visual texts, physical vs. digital reading experiences and the effects on memory.

Well, the answer is simple to start with: use both. Why limit students? There is research to show the values of both handwritten and digital work. There are resources available online and through digital platforms that we do not have in a paper journal. There are also plenty of research studies that show the positive effect of handwriting on cognitive development, although typing is efficient and easily editable. Sometimes it allows a better flow of ideas when a student can type quickly, but we also lose the physical connection to the ideas this way. Further, exams are now in flux – DP exams are currently handwritten but will move to digital very soon. Universities are also in between. As such, both skills are important for now.

Some of your students may also have wonderful 'hand' note taking apps on their devices to allow them to 'write' on screen. However, the paper and pen add another element of the physical, the visceral. Look at the pros and cons together and ask students to try both approaches with you so they can at least experience what is best for their individual learning. I even ask students with learning support plans, allowing them to use computers for any assessment and note taking, to try some things out on paper. We first have to have trust together, of course, and we need respect among all students in the classroom, so they are not afraid of embarrassment. Unless the student literally has no physical capability to write, I have always found it a positive experience for them to try this out. Sometimes I suggest, 'Try to brainstorm or free write for five or ten minutes on paper, then you can choose to go to the computer'. Sometimes they continue on paper, other times they move right to the computer at ten minutes. It does not matter; they are still activating a different learning experience.

The simple answer, therefore, is make it both, or, if you do a lot of typed writing in class, make the homework all handwritten (and vice versa). I require at least half of the work on paper, but this is in part due to the way I see students using their computers at my current school. You will have to see what works best for your cohort. Regardless, you will find it practical to keep everything in one place. You can choose to have students scan/photograph written work into a Google folder or an online platform, or to print out digital work for a paper journal.

■ Should we assess journals or LP?

Again, the IB does not assess the LP or journal. I have created a rubric for journals (see below) that intentionally uses a lot of the language and setup of the TOK essay rubric. It has worked well for me and my students, providing a fair and meaningful way to not only assess but help students push their journals further in their individual learning experiences. I use it as one of the biggest marks each semester because it is a process piece that allows students to use skills and content toward conceptual understanding, draw on differentiated strengths and access extension materials as part of their learning process. However, you do not have to assess these at all. It may depend on your school philosophy and grading policy.

Regardless, you might choose to use this rubric, with or without the numbers. It can help students understand what a journal can be and how it can best be used for their individualized learning. I prefer not to keep them in the dark quite as much as Professor Harper did for us!

■ Journal and learning portfolio rubric

7	6	5	4	3	2	1
Demonstrates strong initiative and inquiry beyond the assigned tasks. Shows high-level critical thinking and creativity. Engages with the texts in a sophisticated way.	Demonstrates initiative and inquiry beyond the assigned tasks. Shows continued critical thinking and creativity. Engages with the texts in a critical way.	Demonstrates some initiative and inquiry beyond the assigned tasks. Shows critical thinking and creativity. Engages with the texts clearly.	Completes assignments. Shows moments of creativity and/or insight. Makes some use of and reference to the texts.	Some incomplete assignments. Lacks creativity or insight. Responds to the text without detail.	Incomplete assignments. Lacks creativity or insight. Strays from using and responding to the text.	Incomplete assignments. No references to the texts.
Sophisticated Creative	Articulate Inquisitive	Engaged Analytical	Basic Clear	Underdeveloped Vague	Incomplete Unclear	Minimum effort Unacceptable

■ Examples: assignments and student work

Scaffold by starting with a more structured questioning list and assignment tool then move toward more freedom. However, encourage freedom from the start. Eventually, students should be able to conduct a journal on a core text or conceptual focus without an assignment sheet. They take ownership of it and it becomes their creative space for thinking and playing with language.

I tend to write the journal assignments per text or group of non-literary texts rather than for a whole unit. This is to break down the content for students more; at times I use specific prompts to help them engage with comparisons or ideas that build on previous content.

Opposite is just one example of an assignment. Usually, I make the assignments into hypertexts, where related articles and collaborative classroom activities are linked directly to the original questions. However, this gives you an idea of the overview of the range of types of activities I ask students to complete. You will find the URLs to the hyperlinks, as well as sample student responses to these questions, on IB Extras: **www. hoddereducation.com/ibextras**

Text: *The Unbearable Lightness of Being* by Milan Kundera

<u>Audiobook</u>

<u>Film trailer</u>

Conceptual focus: Identity

Group inquiry topics – include notes in journals:
- Communism in Prague
  - ☐ Don't focus on Prague Spring; what is communism and how/why/when applied to Czech Republic (or what it was before)?
- Milan Kundera
  - ☐ <u>1968 Interview on *The Joke*</u>
  - ☐ <u>The Paris Review interview</u>, 1984 on this text
- 1968 Prague Spring
  - ☐ <u>Short explanation</u>
  - ☐ <u>History of Prague</u>
  - ☐ <u>Paris 1968</u>
- Nietzsche's Eternal Return (see below as well)
  - ☐ From <u>*Nietzsche Wept*</u>
  - ☐ <u>The School of Life</u>

In-class contextual investigation to start – read then respond with a free write.

Stanford Encyclopaedia of Philosophy:
- <u>Logic and Ontology</u>
- <u>Being and Becoming in Modern Physics</u>
- <u>Nietzsche</u>
- <u>Postmodernism</u> (see eternal return)
- <u>Deleuze</u> (see eternal return).

1 Make a chart of the dichotomies of positive and negative (see Part 1) and add your own associations. As you read, continue to add to the chart and write a response to one of the dichotomies. Does it deconstruct? How and why?

2 How can a suitcase contain a life (Part 1)? Is that a silly idea or not?

3 Make a drawing of the two main characters and the dog. Label them and add characteristics in any way you see fit.

4 Choose a paragraph to analyse in detail. Analyse the style and the language choice carefully.

5 Track the emotions that Tomas goes through in the text. To what extent are they reasonable or not? What does the conscious recalling of his emotions allow the reader to understand? (Maybe you can do this together as a visual.)

6 In what way(s) does this book fit into the dialogue of literature? What ideas or allusions make this a part of the literary dialogue?

7 Discuss a particular stylistic device Kundera uses, with at least three examples. What is the effect of the feature?

8 What ideas does the novel offer about human relationships? What does it say about love/marriage/sex/sleeping together/intimacy?

9 Give your ideas vs. Kundera's about Ontology (ways of being)/the meaning of life or how to live (this also might include visuals or research).

After reading, select one conceptual question related to 'Intertextuality: connecting texts' to come back to. Use references to other texts we have studied throughout the year.

Conceptual questions 3, 4 and 6:

3   In what ways can diverse texts share points of similarity? (What other texts have we looked at in this conceptual focus? What similarities do they have in looking at the idea of identity?)

4   How valid is the notion of a classic text? (Do you consider Kundera's novel a classic? Why or why not? How does it respond to classics?)

6   In what ways can comparison and interpretation be transformative? (What other texts clarify the point of this one? What do you better understand now after reading Kundera about a previous idea from a text we have studied?)

You can find some examples of student journal responses to this assignment on IB Extras: **www.hoddereducation.com/ibextras**

Foundational skill: the five-paragraph essay

Although we want to encourage students to play with language and structure, we need to give them basic structures that help make their writing clearer. They do this as they study text types and implicitly while they read, but a structure that I always come back to with students and in my own analytical writing – no matter how long the product – is the five-paragraph essay. I recount to students that even on my PhD dissertation, I came back to these basics to make sure my message was clear.

The five-paragraph essay grew to fame (or infamy) with the SAT version in the US. During my time as a student, this essay was meant to be written in 25 minutes. Yes, 25 minutes! It was largely a formula to follow: a simple structure, the best language skills you could muster at the time and the most you could let flow from your pen.

It is still a part of standardized testing and curriculum continuums and even provides the skeletal groundwork for the ideal IB essays or academic and professional analytical writing. However, the format moves from a basic understanding that must first be mastered, followed by more creative and advanced interpretations. The point is essentially clarity: allowing readers to understand (and be persuaded of) the message the writer intends.

■ Creativity in constraint

You can think of the nuts and bolts of the five-paragraph essay like learning your scales on an instrument. By practising this structure, other music is easier to play. By understanding the way notes work together in harmonies as well as the basic, structural rhythms of music, we can play more advanced pieces and also compose our own.

Jazz improvisation is a useful metaphor here. A jazz artist may sound as if they just pick up their saxophone and play whatever comes to their fingers, but it is the result of years of practising scales and structures, understanding the way notes and rhythms come together. As professionals, they do not even have to think about what comes out anymore; after so much practice, the musical experience is intuitive. In a similar way, the goal is to make persuasive writing intuitive.

Most of us use different kinds of graphic organizers as well as structures for other text types (sonnet form, news ledes (news leads), business letter templates), so we are familiar with the usefulness of these tools. We will look at some that can help with specific DP assessment in the next chapter. However, some teachers also think they are doing so at the *cost* of creativity. I disagree: you have to learn the mould to break it. Creativity comes from reinvention and prompts rather than empty space in a vacuum.

I went to a yoga workshop run by an interesting teacher named Raphan Kebe where we talked about movements in this way: whether experimental yoga or modern dance, each was rooted in the basics. Raphan helped us understand this model of work as the 'physical koan'. A koan is a Zen riddle without a clear answer. Instead of a language riddle, we had certain parameters to move our bodies to 'solve' the riddle, of which there were many solutions. Perhaps you will discuss koans if you are looking at certain types of Zen poetry or related literature (such as *Kafka on the Shore*).

I adapted the following exercise for the classroom and it takes just five minutes. You can use it to prompt discussion of the reason for learning essential essay structures that, to some students, feel constraining in a negative way.

I give students the following physical koan:

Stand at the wall anywhere in the room. Your goal is to move to the other side of the room with the following rules:

- You must keep one leg in the air at all times.

- You must conduct one 360-degree turn.

- You must not speak.

The last rule is only to allow students to think for themselves. Every single time I have used this exercise with different age groups, including other teachers, the participants hop on one leg to the other side of the room in the straightest line they can make and take a 360-degree turn on the same foot somewhere in the middle. They feel good about themselves; they have succeeded! However, is there a different way to solve the puzzle? They look perplexed, then someone usually gets it. They can switch legs as long as one is in the air. They can move in twists and turns around the room. The 360-degree turn can be an arm circle, a street dance-style bum spin or even a cartwheel. The list goes on. We then do it again, and everyone has a creative way to work within the constraints. That is when you can ask, 'Ok, why are we learning the structure of the five-paragraph essay?' or 'Why are we using a graphic organizer?' You should hear some pretty thoughtful reflections.

■ The 'nuts and bolts' of the five-paragraph essay

Now let's think about the nuts and bolts of the five-paragraph essay structure. Some of you are well-versed in this type of essay, so just skip this part and move on to why it is important for IB DP students. I will not go into much detail here because you can easily search online for many exemplars of the style and different types of graphic organizers to complete it.

Many people use a hamburger model to first teach the text type. I would say that to do so effectively, you really need a triple decker burger with sauces in between as the transitions between paragraphs. Of course, students will move beyond the five paragraphs, but this is what we use in late primary and early secondary school.

■ Paragraph 1: Introduction

The first paragraph introduces the topic, the argument. In this style essay, we break it down by suggesting a beginning **hook** that draws in the reader. It should not sound gimmicky; rather it is a thematic way to enter the essay and should make us want to

You can use the image of a triple-decker burger to illustrate all the components you need in a five-paragraph essay

read on. This is followed by a short **discussion** and/or **background information** needed to understand the way the student approaches the question or the topic. Then, we have a **thesis**, which should be clear, argumentative and concise. A **preview** of the three (or more) paragraph focus areas should either be a part of the thesis as simple keywords or should follow as a separate sentence or more. Ideally, the preview should list these keywords in the order that the paragraphs will follow.

■ Paragraph 2: First body paragraph

First, you will want a smooth **transition** into your next paragraph – call it the cheese if you like. Many teachers begin teaching PEE paragraphs at young ages and progress to PEELEELEELEEL, where the P is the **point** or topic sentence, the first E is the **evidence,** the second E is the **explanation** and the L is for **linking**. Alternatively, you can use an A for **analysis** instead of explanation, but this might also become interpretation or evaluation. I use explanation to keep it more generic and to allow students to move into these different levels of looking at evidence. It is important that students know each of these need not be a full sentence. The link is sometimes just a word or two, or even a method of embedding a flow of ideas through the paragraph. However, you can start with full sentences early on to make it clear, whether in younger grades or for students who are struggling with basic structure still in DP. This happens a lot and sometimes it is explained because of a regression caused by stress, a yearning to deviate from what has been learned or a background of language A study in a culture that does not value this style of writing.

■ Paragraph 3: Second body paragraph

The second body paragraph has the same set up with a topic that flows from the one before it. It is important to remind students that as the paragraphs go on, they should continue to link directly back to the main argument and keywords in the thesis. Ask them not to make the reader do too much work to find the connections. If they argue that it is boring that way, remind them that their examiners might be reading papers sometimes after a full day's work, on a computer screen, even perhaps with a glass of wine in hand. They are looking for clarity and do not want to dig around to find it themselves! Students should find that when done smoothly and effectively, these explicit links can still be creative and are much better ways to prove their points.

■ Paragraph 4: Third body paragraph

Again, we repeat the structure of the second paragraph. The student can have more than these three body paragraphs, which is one way to start advancing the text type as students master this original. Often, we teach that the best argument should be in the last body paragraph. This may be true, but also depends on the progression and development of the points. Ideally, we develop toward something spectacular, but likewise, an important element of the persuasion might need foregrounding. Tell students the 'rule' then allow them to break it.

■ Paragraph 5: Conclusion

Finally, the last paragraph (which may turn into paragraph 6, 7, 8 or 9 in the assessment) is, of course, the conclusion. It needs to be explicit. If a student is running out of time in an exam situation, they should jump and tack on a conclusion or they are sure to lose out on the organization part of the rubric. The conclusion should **restate the thesis** (ideally with new language to show development), **summarize the points** (ideally showing synergistic thinking of the development of the points' connections) and add **something fresh** at the end. This fresh aspect should link back to the hook and it should certainly not sound like something out of left field. There should be a direct flow to this sentence, whether a question or statement of fact or opinion. One way to think of it is as a link to a deeper conceptual understanding of global issues beyond the text(s). Make the purpose really clear: why should we bother to read this paper and how can we keep thinking about the topic when we are finished reading it?

■ From hamburger to DP essays … and beyond!

Earlier than DP, students should move beyond the simple hamburger and move beyond strictly five paragraphs. Even earlier, they move beyond an exact sentence count, some as early as Year 7. It depends on the student's literacy skills. You can easily differentiate your classroom in this way. You might have a very weak writer who needs to go back to the hamburger in their senior year. There is no shame in that.

Students should fully understand the basics so that they can break the mould. It will give them something to hold on to, especially as they enter timed exams. By that time, the basic structure should be so innate that they do not even have to think about it. A weak student might cling to its basic form, allowing them a decent grade if they have something meaningful to say. A stronger student will flow beyond this in creative ways but keep the skeleton so the reader can easily find the line of argument and accompanying evidence.

One way to make students aware of the way they are structuring (or not structuring) their writing is by asking them to colour code the above elements in their writing or planning. Often, they find the point comes at the end of the paragraph, which is a natural flow of thought as we understand what we want to say. However, it is also a confusing way for the reader to approach the evidence presented. Simple flipped movements will give the essay clarity or the student may find they are missing evidence or analysis. It is an easy way to self-check and become more aware of the choices they have in their work, rather than the teacher simply pointing out the faults.

Language skills and tools

Teaching 'grammar' is always a hot topic that divides people. Pedagogically, it has oscillated on the pendulum from diagramming sentences and knowing grammatical terms for any type of phrase that might exist to scrapping it completely for pleasure reading and intuition based on what students have read.

By the time we get to the DP level for language A, we should be looking at a very small amount of class instruction time, but the mini-lessons or differentiated feedback you give about language skills will still be effective. We have to make sure students do not stagnate or change their attitudes about the ways they use language in your classes and in exams.

■ How should we approach grammar?

Well, like most things, I would argue that the answer to this question lies in between. An article from Australian researchers Beverly Derewianka and Paula Jones sums up this argument articulately and concisely in 'From traditional grammar to functional grammar: bridging the divide' (2010). The article is concise and easy to understand even though it considers many decades and angles of research and ideas about teaching language. They conclude that we can use a bit of each side of the pendulum, calling their approach 'systemic functional grammar'.

A lot of the differences in pedagogy are also generational and based on how we learned best when we were at school. Well, on the whole, if we are all language A teachers, most of us probably did pretty well at languages and therefore think that whatever our teachers did is the best approach. That is not necessarily true for all students though, and perhaps our learning also came from our own unguided inquiry into languages. Further, we probably used transference from language B studies. Most of us did, and nearly all of our IB students will, learn at least one other language at school. You will have students coming from different academic language backgrounds with different language profiles (what is spoken at home or what languages have they been immersed in in the past) to add to the matrix of your pedagogical approach.

It is important for students (and adults) to be able to identify certain parts of speech so that they can both avoid mistakes and more creatively construct sentences. They can also grasp the meaning of difficult texts in this way. Likewise, research shows that types of functional grammar (this has a whole school of thought that you can learn about) or grammar in context can provide some of the best tools for students to improve their language and literacy skills. The reasons are in part tied to greater motivation and purpose to their learning, which sounds sneakily like the whole reasoning behind CBL.

■ Language skills in DP

Although the best way to improve language use is through reading, there also needs to be some structure and explicit instruction about choices students have, as well as addressing common mistakes or limitations. There is a danger that, like with inquiry learning, we could err on *just leaving it to the kids* without a way for them to actively gain knowledge and skills. If you can achieve a language-learning continuum at your school that allows your DP students to have a strong base, you will be in good shape.

At this level, students are considering language on a philosophical level in TOK: how and why is it used? What is the most effective sentence structure or word or register? Often, these simple prompts are all the students need to improve.

All of the above applies to vocabulary development as well. Is it best to learn long lists of difficult words? Sometimes these are SAT words or lists from vocabulary text books. Or, is it better to learn words as we read? Do we need to write them down? How can technology help us?

Some of the answers are quite simple. Both grammar and vocabulary development need some structure, but they also need a chance to play around. They need immersion and experimentation. The journals are a great place for this. Additionally, they need acknowledgment that there are often several ways of saying something. For example, IB examiners are explicitly told not to penalize students for explaining the analysis of a literary device without the actual terminology. Of course, the terminology can add to the detail of analysis, and this is why we still learn them in my classroom. It helps students to know what to look for. However, if a student talks about the repetition of an initial phrase with a certain effect rather than anaphora, the student should get the same credit on the mark scheme.

■ Make it dynamic

Quick lessons, embedded discussions or question prompts and methods of incorporating language focus in the editing process can go a long way. Do not think of language and grammar skills as a separate part of your curriculum. Just like analytical skills, they are essential in expressing the conceptual message. In fact, all teachers are meant to be teachers of language in the IB, so your colleagues are hopefully sharing the load. Try to reduce the approach in your classroom to an attitude toward using language that includes meaningful discussions when appropriate.

Essentially, I recommend you target the following in your DP classroom:

■ **LANGUAGE A COURSE CHECKLIST**

✔ Identify key grammar areas that need addressing (misplaced modifiers, parallel structure, particular verb forms, etc.).

✔ Include mini lessons or 'starters' for these areas. Better still, flip the classroom and ask students to make funny examples that need correcting, or even use YouTube video explanations (you can use Grammar Girl for examples).

✔ Create a list of literary terminology over the course that are both transferable and text-type specific.

✔ Discuss ways of varying sentence structure for effect. Note the way authors do that and look at how students can do so in their own writing.

✔ Encourage reading beyond your course texts, including texts written in a formal register.

✔ Value multilingualism as a dynamic force toward better writing and understanding.

✔ Cue students to use digital tools available to them, such as grammar and spellcheck, Grammarly, TransOver, OWL Purdue Writing Lab.

✔ Investigate language through articles that encourage debate, such as:

■ 'One space between each sentence, they said. Science just proved them wrong' (Avi Selk, 2018).

■ 'Further or Farther: A Theory' (Caleb Crain, 2015).

✔ Link discussions of language with TOK:

■ Sapir Whorf theory and language's connection with culture

■ language's connection with other subject areas

■ mathematics and grammar (Chomsky on 'generative grammar').

■ Reading for language skills

Reading is the best way to improve language and literacy skills. Students pick up vocabulary, grammar, variations of sentence structure, methods of forming paragraphs or verse and much more as they read. It happens implicitly over time, and this is proven by many research studies. However, we can enhance the effect even further by explicitly drawing out what can be learned in the reading. We do this in our language A classes all the time, and students can transfer the skill to their extension and pleasure reading.

A triangulation of student reading, language instruction in language A(s) and supported language development in language B(s) creates an effective dynamic toward student learning. As language and literature teachers, we all share a value of reading and have probably read research studies that show the incredible positive effect of reading on language skills as well as cognitive development and a continuous dexterity in the brain – through our whole lives. We can add onto these aspects a further development of international mindedness and perspective by reading widely from a variety of sources.

I ask students if they read the news. Of course, they all say yes. Then I ask them how many full articles they read per week. Most say zero. I ask the last time they read news they thought was a good piece of writing and again, most say they cannot remember one. So together, we try to find a way to navigate what is out there. I liken it to finding music. Do they just listen to 'The Global Top 50' on Spotify or do they find their own stuff? Do they seek out *good* music, whether old or new, and listen to it, learn from it, think about it? It is more embarrassing for them to admit a marriage to Top 50 hits than to Buzzfeed or to CNN, but the headline and alert stream on our smartphones mimic the several-second clip of each Top 40 hit in a radio montage more than the whole playlist.

I try to get my students on just a couple of good sources that curate news for you. Of course, this is already going through a filter, but one I find that does a good job of showing media from around the world (even in different languages) and from different perspectives is the *Quartz* 'Daily Brief'. Of course, *Quartz* is labelled as fairly liberal itself, originally started by editors from Boston-based *The Atlantic*. They share some of their own content in this daily feed as well, but for busy people overwhelmed by information coming from all directions and for students who just get the latest from Buzzfeed or their Facebook pages, this is a huge step in the right direction. The email comes at the time of your commute (you can change its settings by time zone) and gives a brief rundown of what's happening in the world with hyperlinks to many articles from around the world, sometimes even in different languages. It then also contains information and updates on economics, the arts and scientific or technological discoveries and debates. Another source I enjoy is the *New York Times* 'What We're Reading' update that comes once a week. This weekly update gives you long-read articles from around the globe curated by *New York Times* writers, who happen to be some of the best journalistic writers in the world.

There are other similar resources from around the world. Just remember, sometimes less is more. If you take on more than you can manage, you might not read any of it, or not read any of it well. We can be easily overwhelmed by the amount of content at our fingertips. I talk with students about reading well against reading too much. Their social media and news update feeds are likely to contain hundreds of links a day, but we talk about how it might be better to choose even just *one* full, well-written article than to scan a hundred in the same amount of time.

Likewise, teach students how to use Twitter (and other sites with hashtags) appropriately and effectively. Most students do not know that Twitter was first set up by journalists and many do not even know there is a purpose to a hashtag beyond humour. It might sound crazy, but poll your students to see if they really understand. Teaching students how to navigate Twitter is a way to give them access to resources around the world (in different languages) on a particular topic. Hashtags create an automatic curation of resources from professional news sources, off-the-record journalists and citizen journalists. Likewise, it gives students a platform to share their own voice on such issues.

Anyway, the point is to get students really reading and understanding why skimming the headlines is only a small piece of the picture. They also understand the difference between mediocre journalism and literary journalism, between unbiased reporting and labelled or un-labelled opinion pieces and among structures of writing that deliver different messages in a variety of effective levels. At the same time, they pick up vocabulary and cultural knowledge bases. If they read on a computer, they have the added benefit of features like the hyperlinks (as long as they return to the original article again) and online dictionaries and translators.

INTERNATIONAL MINDEDNESS

For online dictionaries and translators, you can help your students embed add-ons to make these hover features. TransOver, which works best on Chrome, is fantastic. Select the language you would like it to translate to, and as you hover your cursor/finger over a word, you see the translation and grammatical details pop up. I like to keep my French sharp by enabling this feature to French. You or your students can do it as you are learning a new language, or you can help students enable this feature to their mother tongue. This helps them both to keep up an academic and fluent level in their mother tongue (which most language teachers now understand is essential for cognitive development) and to perhaps understand better the language of instruction.

You may be aware that an enormous amount of publication on the world wide web is in English. One way to continue to help our students to live in the beneficial world of multilingualism is to install this add-on. Better than an enabled Google Translate that just translates the whole page immediately, this tool helps you to really learn both languages and make choices about the right language to use in translation, as it offers several translations when applicable. Of course, sometimes Google Translate is great! If you have no idea how to read Japanese, you really do not want to go word by word in an article about artificial intelligence. In fact, a great exercise is asking students to do a short translation so they can understand the nuances of how tricky this can be.

■ ATT & ATL

Curating reading material – differentiation, inquiry and research

- We are helping students with their literacy and perhaps with the ability to write analytically, through the vocabulary and structure they pick up, without realising it. For this reason, the commitment is useful for literature students as well. In fact, you can link your articles to the topics you study in the classroom or leave them completely free. I tend to do a combination, while sometimes asking for reflections or even printed or digitally tagged articles to be inserted in student journals. Another free online tool you can use to facilitate this is Scoop.it. This curatorial tool is easy to use and highly visual. You can pin articles or websites with searchable keywords (the same as hashtags on other sites). Then, on your curated site, you or your students can search back by keyword or simply look at your latest posts. I keep track of great finds related to inquiry and context around the topics we study. Often, we do not use these articles in class, but I share the page so that students can discover on their own. They can also make their own pages with the discoveries they make over the two years. They could make separate pages for different projects, like the HL essay or EE, or simply use those words as tags to separate them out later. If you choose to, you can all be connected and re-scoop from others' pages. You can follow public pages that have similar topics to your interests (you will see suggestions based on your posts).

- Alternatively, Diigo makes a great choice for organizing articles and making hypertexts of articles related to a topic. Diigo is less visually pleasing, and therefore less student friendly. However, there are added features that make it useful. You can make folders of study, create closed conversation groups for your classroom (for example, to respond to a particular article or to pin their own related evidence on a debated issue) and annotate live. With the Diigo add-on, you can start annotating with highlighters and comments on any webpage which you then save to your Diigo page, maybe within a group, a folder or an outliner on a particular topic. You can do it all directly on the other webpage without ever going to the Diigo site, making it fast and user friendly. In fact, you can also install this add-on for Scoop.it, so you scoop directly off the web as you browse, perhaps creating a 'read later' list.

- You can have an overwhelming amount of sources for your students this way. But this is why we go back to 'less is more'. Get an overview of what is out there, then carefully select a few interesting choices to read thoroughly. Helping your students through scaffolding the reading can help them to do it later on their own. Through your curating and perhaps comments or annotating, you provide a window in to a world that seemed un-navigable before.

The importance of purpose and global issues

Global issues, again, is a generic term for anything that is an important relatable takeaway from the content you study in your course. Of course, with wider reading, your students will have both a deeper vocabulary and knowledge base to talk about these issues.

The term sounds like it is more specific about something such as global climate change or world-wide approaches to nuclear weapons. However, the 'global' part of the term simply means relatable. Therefore, rather than have a global issue *about* class and caste in India, one might talk about the problem of class hierarchies or the rich–poor gap world-wide. The exploration from the student then might focus on India (and perhaps another place or two) but looks at it as a more universal issue. Likewise, the issue can be a human one, one that first seems very individual (isolation or overcoming mental illness), but in its individuality in the texts you study, it helps us understand something more relatable to humanity. For example, when we talk about Hamlet struggling with the meaning of life, we are not just talking about Hamlet but all of us.

You can probably see how the idea of cultivating a wide approach to reading is then important in helping students understand different perspectives more effectively. Hopefully, their TOK teachers are likewise encouraging this method through resources used in their classrooms.

Global issues are now an explicit part of the oral. Students were always meant to discuss themes in their oral and written work in the courses, but now the idea must go beyond the text and must have some relevance to relatable ideas. In fact, this is the heart of CBL. In MYP schools, units are each linked to one of the global contexts:

- personal and cultural expression
- globalization and sustainability
- orientation in time and space
- fairness and development
- identity and relationships
- scientific and technical innovation.

You can see how wide ranging they are. Come back to these if it helps your students understand the way they are meant to be used.

In this course, we are going beyond the text. Rather than scaring students, this makes them feel empowered. This is why they are studying the content of your course, after all! It is really not hard once students are trained to do it; even for really weak ones who are sometimes more 'street smart' and therefore able to get the relevancy outside the classroom. It is about *so what? Why does it matter? Why do we care?* I always say to students, 'If you don't know why you are doing or reading something, just ask. If I don't have an answer, you don't have to do it!'

Purpose is the hardest and easiest thing to teach. It is the thing that keeps kids from top scores, but it is also the thing that even a remedial class (if you have such a thing at your school) can do well. They are beings in the world, therefore they can understand purpose. So then, you have to connect analysis of the text to purpose. This is the root of CBL in the English classroom. How do you then find this evidence to express the ideas? How do you effectively and clearly express the ideas once you have them?

The purpose of a paper, I often tell my students, is like its spine. We are not always aware of our own spines or those of others. Instead we focus on external details as we 'read' another person or ourselves: fingerprints, the way we walk or the movement of our heads on our necks. It is the spine at the heart of any of these movements, or the place that binds appendages to a single person.

Sometimes I do an activity with students to demonstrate the metaphor of the spine as the purposeful centre. We stand up, close our eyes and I ask students to initiate movement in the spine only. They find it difficult, wanting to move other parts of the body. We then add on shoulder circles, then arm circles, then full body movements, all initiated in the spine.

I tell students the purpose of their papers – the global issue – is the same. They need it to initiate the movement and development of the points, evidence, and explanations. Although it may only be required of IB for the IO, it is something they should keep in mind for all of their written exams as well, and for other essays they may write in the future.

Creative writing

I would argue that *all* writing is creative writing. How we put language together to form meaning is unique and expresses our voices in creative ways. However, the limitations of the DP assessments for this course are in the form of analytical essays and an analytical oral. Students do not produce different text types or have the opportunity to perform a creative interpretation of a text as they once had in the course. That does not mean you cannot make creative text production a part of your course. It also does not mean creative text production will not help your students achieve high marks.

We will now briefly explore several methods of creative writing that can help your students in a variety of ways. Previously, we also looked at some oral work such as presentations, role plays and debates that can help your students achieve in this course.

These pieces of creative writing can be part of the journals and LP or they can be separate assessments, marked or not, to help students learn. They can be core requirements, extension work or differentiated assignments. If marked, you can use the journal rubrics, old written task rubrics or have students self-assess using the project-based learning 'Creativity and Innovation Rubric for PBL' designed by the Buck Institute for Education (see below). Here, students will play with CBL in their own way. They will play with language use (skills) and ideas/historical references (content).

■ **Creativity and Innovation Rubric for PBL (for grades 6–12)**

Creativity & Innovation Opportunity at Phases of a Project	Below Standard	Approaching Standard	At Standard	Above Standard ✔
Launching the Project **Define the Creative Challenge**	■ May just 'follow directions' without understanding the purpose for innovation or considering the needs and interests of the target audience	■ Understands the basic purpose for innovation but does not thoroughly consider the needs and interests of the target audience	■ Understands the purpose driving the process of innovation (Who needs this? Why?) ■ Develops insight about the particular needs and interests of the target audience	
Building Knowledge, Understanding, and Skills **Identify Sources of Information**	■ Uses only typical sources of information (website, book, article) ■ Does not offer new ideas during discussions	■ Finds one or two sources of information that are not typical ■ Offers new ideas during discussions, but stays within narrow perspectives	■ In addition to typical sources, finds unusual ways or places to get information (adult expert, community member, business or organization, literature) ■ Promotes divergent and creative perspectives during discussions	

Creativity & Innovation Opportunity at Phases of a Project	Below Standard	Approaching Standard	At Standard	Above Standard ✔
Developing and Revising Ideas and Products **Generate and Select Ideas**	■ Stays within existing frameworks; does not use idea-generating techniques to develop new ideas for product(s) ■ Selects one idea without evaluating the quality of ideas ■ Does not ask new questions or elaborate on the selected idea ■ Reproduces existing ideas; does not imagine new ones ■ Does not consider or use feedback and critique to revise product	■ Develops some original ideas for product(s), but could develop more with better use of idea-generating techniques ■ Evaluates ideas, but not thoroughly before selecting one ■ Asks a few new questions but may make only minor changes to the selected idea ■ Shows some imagination when shaping ideas into a product, but may stay within conventional boundaries ■ Considers and may use some feedback and critique to revise a product, but does not seek it out	■ Uses idea-generating techniques to develop several original ideas for product(s) ■ Carefully evaluates the quality of ideas and selects the best one to shape into a product ■ Asks new questions, takes different perspectives to elaborate and improve on the selected idea ■ Uses ingenuity and imagination, going outside conventional boundaries, when shaping ideas into a product ■ Seeks out and uses feedback and critique to revise product to better meet the needs of the intended audience	
Presenting Products and Answers to Driving Question **Present Work to Users/Target Audience**	■ Presents ideas and products in typical ways (text-heavy PowerPoint slides, recitation of notes, no interactive features)	■ Adds some interesting touches to presentation media ■ Attempts to include elements in presentation that make it more lively and engaging	■ Creates visually exciting presentation media ■ Includes elements in presentation that are especially fun, lively, engaging, or powerful to the particular audience	
Originality	■ Relies on existing models, ideas, or directions; it is not new or unique ■ Follows rules and conventions; uses materials and ideas in typical ways	■ Has some new ideas or improvements, but some ideas are predictable or conventional ■ May show a tentative attempt to step outside rules and conventions, or find new uses for common materials or ideas	■ Is new, unique, surprising; shows a personal touch ■ May successfully break rules and conventions, or use common materials or ideas in new, clever and surprising ways	
Value	■ Is not useful or valuable to the intended audience/user ■ Would not work in the real world; impractical or unfeasible	■ Is useful and valuable to some extent; it may not solve certain aspects of the defined problem or exactly meet the identified need ■ Unclear if product would be practical or feasible	■ Is seen as useful and valuable; it solves the defined problem or meets the identified need ■ Is practical, feasible	
Style	■ Is safe, ordinary, made in a conventional style ■ Has several elements that do not fit together; it is a mish-mash	■ Has some interesting touches, but lacks a distinct style ■ Has some elements that may be excessive or do not fit together well	■ Is well-crafted, striking, designed with a distinct style but still appropriate for the purpose ■ Combines different elements into a coherent whole	

Note: The term 'product' is used in this rubric as an umbrella term for the result of the process of innovation during a project. A product may be a constructed object, proposal, presentation, solution to a problem, service, system, work of art or piece of writing, an invention, event, an improvement to an existing product, etc.

Source: Buck Institute for Education

◼ Pastiche

Pastiche is a wonderful exercise for the DP language A CBL classroom. Many of you have probably used some form of pastiche to teach text type or genre before, including work toward the old written task for language and literature. It is a useful way for students to internalize the way writers use structure, voice or another element for meaning.

I love starting by looking at the etymology of the word *pastiche*. Looking at etymology at different times in your course is another way to bring multilingualism into the classroom and value students' different cultural and linguistic backgrounds. The Italians might be first to notice the connection to the words *pasta* or *paste*. This kind of medley stuck together to make pasta or a cake became the French word *pastiche,* first pulling on elements of other texts stuck together to make something new but with the connotation of a sort of homage to the original(s).

Creativity and creative thinking have become big focus areas for education, and are now one of the seven language A concepts, but we need to be careful that students are not just left to their own devices to explore. When we visit the two Picasso museums in Barcelona and Paris, we discover the journey that he went through in understanding both the skills and content of the artists who came before him. Diana Senechel argues in *Mind over Memes* (2018) that we need to more carefully understand this creative process; as Ephrat Livni puts it in *Quartz*: 'Senechel argues that no one can be creative without first learning about what came before. That involves a lot of study, thought, and practice—mastering the basics ahead of any dazzling innovations' ('The cult of creativity is making us less creative', 2018). Pastiche is one way to acknowledge this homage to the masters of the written word. Devoting time to their journals is where students can draw on what they are learning but also feel free to discover and innovate.

Using pastiche is a wonderful way to help students understand through mimicry. Have them create a political speech or poem that draws on the work of an author you are studying in class. To make it conceptual, however, you will want to go a step beyond and consider the relationship of the big ideas of the original and student-created texts.

One text I often use for pastiche is James Joyce's *Dubliners*. We create a class project as part of **writing the city** that ends up with a class printed or digital book of student pastiche. In Hong Kong, we created *HongKongers*, in Vienna it was *Vienners* … you get the idea. The students are able to write something localized about their experiences in their home city (whether from birth or just recently) and connect to themes from Joyce's text while utilizing elements of his style. I have a version of Joyce's short stories with old sketches that the students enjoy viewing after they have read the stories. I ask them to likewise include their own visual with their short stories: a sketch, photograph or painting.

Rather than mark these pastiches (although you could), I tend to have students engage in a sort of gallery feedback. The writer reads his or her piece aloud. The student to the left says something they like about it. The student two places to the left explains two connections to Joyce. The student to the right makes a suggestion to make it even better. Finally, the writer gets to explain if there were other stylistic or thematic connections to Joyce's stories.

The following is an example from a student in Vienna who plays with Joyce's thematic focuses on paralysis, repetition and work, as well as the symbols of the tram and the snow. This very short piece connects with several stories, including 'Clay', which takes us on and off a tram in Dublin. The movement through the city is both a symbol of modernity and of the grounded repetition many people go through each day, but the looking of Franz out the window also shows the possibility for reflection and self-assessment. As students write these ideas into their own creative work and discover them in each other's, they internalize the way authors use style and diction to create these purposes.

FIRST SNOWFALL

Franz gazed impatiently through the side window of the tram. The modern double tinted glazing projected the reflection of his face onto the venerable façade of the university. He watched as the light snow fell incessantly, with almost metronomic precision, only stopping to collect on the various gnarled decorative protrusions on the walls. He had three more shifts to go. Almost mechanically he ceased his engrossment and pressed the button to shut the doors. A series of loud blares was followed by the harmonized closing of the grey glass doors as they fused into a single flush surface. With a strained hum the tram rolled off. Three more hours and it would be his last month of civil service, and then he'd never have to drive a blasted tram again. Ernst finished the month before. He remembered how they celebrated and toasted to their bright futures. He hadn't seen him since that night, but apparently Gerold said that he'd got a job as a cashier in Hofer in the 22nd district.

The tram glid into the University station, completed the long turning circuit, stopped to collect passengers. Franz waited thirty seconds and pressed the button again.

■ Practicing text types

If you want to help students understand structure and purpose of shorter, non-literary text types, it may be more useful to take the artistic and thematic elements of the pastiche out of the activity.

Using your running list of text types and their definitions and conventional elements, have students recreate specific ones in relation to a topic you are studying in class or one that is currently in the news that you think students would benefit from writing about. You could even use this as a follow-up activity to a CAS trip week, if your school uses one, or a field trip or mindfulness activity your class has participated in. Making the text 'real' will help students understand the purpose.

This is an especially good activity for media sources. You can use the school newspaper as a real place of publication or create a classroom online publication. This might take different forms, such as: newspaper, travel blog or private YouTube advertising channel. If the text type work is made into an online publication, you can include student feedback in a different way that is also a teaching tool. Require students to make 'comments' on each other's works in a positive way. Here, you can continue to teach the added aspect of 'comments' at the end of online writing (sometimes included in IB materials) and discuss the impact of leaving comments on the writer.

■ Adaptation

You might be reading or viewing adaptations as part of your course material in forms such as graphic novels or films. Perhaps you are interested in the dialogue of literature or you are trying to understand something together about satire or an updated contemporary context. This is also an investigation of the IB concept **transformation**.

Whether you are or not, you can include students' own adaptations to re-interpret an original and learn what the original has to do with context and text type in this way. Students can practise another text type, engage with a text more deeply and make the text meaningful through a big idea that is the anchor of the new text.

Some examples of adaptations you might use are:

- film screenplays (or just a storyboard) for dramatic texts
- graphic novels for short stories
- a series of news articles for a novel
- a poem for a travel essay.

The possibilities are endless and can help your students both practise text types or genres and engage with the course content conceptually. They will implicitly understand better how to compare different text types for a single purpose.

■ Personal writing

Part of helping students find their voices is by letting them experiment with creative, personal writing. This type of writing will connect to your course content when you study elements of identity and relationships, philosophical views like existentialism or transcendentalism and through heavily personal genres or text types, like memoirs and often poetry.

Perhaps make the product into mixed genre or multimedia, to help students understand the dynamic nature of language and literature within the arts. Ask them to use visuals, or take them on a field trip to respond to visual prompts, either real meadows and city streets or galleries containing photographs or historic relics.

Use examples of professional writers who create through mixed media in this way. Eduardo Galeano's *The Book of Embraces* (1989) uses sketches with shorter reflective fictions or essays to engage with personal, philosophical ideas. Inua Ellams – poet, playwright, and more – uses elements of graphic novel, short story and dramatic dialogue in *Black T-Shirt Collection* (2012). Orhan Pamuk's memoir *Istanbul: Memories and the City* (2003) uses elements of the conventional genre along with a focus on place that could be considered travel writing. Additionally, he includes a great deal of photography of people and places, mostly from his friend, the photographer Ara Guler, and discusses what it felt like to select these photos for his memoir.

Images from Inua Ellams' *Black T-Shirt Collection*. Ellams mixes language and form to create meaning. What text type and genre would you apply to this text as a reader?

CORE CONNECTIONS

CAS

Allowing students the freedom to play with language in this way can help them cultivate a sense of understanding about our subject area. Beyond the classroom, you can encourage students to participate in writing clubs or contests and even create their own as part of the CAS programme. Students must reflect, either orally or in written form, on all their CAS activities, creating a kind of journal of experiences. Beyond this, they have the opportunity not only to join clubs like school newspapers or out-of-school classes on creative writing but also to create their CAS projects to reflect some use of writing in the community. Use Inua Ellams as an example; beyond writing, he performs his plays, has created and worked on poetry in the community (*The Rhythm and Poetry Party* and *SideStory*) and founded the Midnight Run: a 'nocturnal urban excursion'.

■ Journals and freewriting

Any of the above activities could be included as part of the journals, of course. Freewriting is something that you may also want to include, especially at the start of lessons. It might be the precursor to one of the creative writing assessments above, a way to play around with a conceptual question, or a method of entering conversation about a text read for homework.

By allowing students to write free of structure or text type, they are able to develop their voices uninhibited. Some students may need the suggestion of a structure to use to get started, whether a mind map or the beginning of a short story. Here we allow creativity unconstrained. Students process in different ways, so while the freewriting they accomplish to begin a task may lack structure and therefore clarity or purpose, it might be a necessary step for some students to complete before structuring their work and delivering it in a form that makes sense to others. By this point in their writing careers, they have also begun to internalize some elements of writing structure that can help them to get their voice down on paper in this way, whether it is by mimicking a known method or through deviating and responding to those structures used or read in the past. You can find examples of students' freewriting online at IB Extras: **www.hoddereducation.com/ibextras**

Approaching assessments

DP language A assessments

Throughout this book, we have looked at ways CBL connects to assessments in this course. You can refer back to the chart showing the 'required assessment for DP language A' in Chapter 2 (page 30) to give you an overview.

In this chapter, we shall look at methods of approaching the DP language A assessments, including developing topics, methods of structuring the work and attitudes toward exams. Largely, this chapter aims to help you understand how the assessments are integrated into a conceptually-taught framework. We consider the approach you might take to each assessment more fully. However, you will also want to refer to exemplars on My IB, as well as more detailed skills-based activities you can use with your students that you will find in the accompanying *Literary Analysis: Skills for Success* and *Textual Analysis: Skills for Success* books in this series.

Assessment objectives

Essentially, the IB understands the output in the assessments as a breakdown of three categories:

- knowledge and understanding
- analysis, interpretation and evaluation
- communication.

It lists assessment objectives more generally, rather than in connection to particular assessments. This also makes them transferable to other formative and summative assessments you will use in your classroom. The objectives are as follows:

1 Know and understand:
    - a range of texts, works and/or performances
    - elements of literary, linguistic and/or performance craft
    - features of particular genres or text types
    - the role of contexts in which texts are written and/or received.

2 Analyse, interpret and evaluate:
    - the ways in which the use of language creates meaning
    - the use and effect of literary, linguistic or theatrical techniques
    - the relationships among different texts
    - the ways texts offer perspectives on human concerns.

3 Communicate:
    - ideas in clear, logical, and persuasive ways.

Again, we see a combination of content and skills, where the first category is content, the second has elements of each and the third is skills focused and connected directly to one of the ATL skills. Three skill categories are essential for these assessments: communication, thinking and self-management. However, the other two – social and research – are used throughout the course in inquiry, collaborative work toward synergistic thinking and more, to enable your students to do the best they can on these assessments.

Besides the ATL skills, if you consider the approaches to the IB concepts through the methods of conceptual learning and valuing student voice, your students will already be prepared for the three or four (depending on level) assessments they need to complete. Here, we will simply make that preparation more explicit. Do this type of explicit prompting from day one in your course so students feel they are preparing all the time. Maybe it sounds like teaching to the test(s), but this is not a problem if the outcomes are transferable and related to understanding big ideas about themselves and the world around them.

Learner portfolios (LP)

Assessment	Description	SL: time + per cent of mark	HL: time + per cent of mark	Marking
Learner portfolio	The learner portfolio is a digital or paper-based (or mixed) portfolio of student work, which may include journaling and formative assessment as well as other types of classwork and homework. The LP is meant to keep a record of the learning process that the student can refer back to in preparation for the individual oral and HL essay.	Ongoing in class and at home 0%	Ongoing in class and at home 0%	Unmarked by IB (though teachers may use as assessment)

You should not feel like you are 'teaching to the test' but you should feel as though you are continuously preparing your students for the assessments. The paradox only works if you are explicit and transparent with students. You can help them understand why some of the more creative and inquiring activities you do together will still help them on assessment. However, not every day should end with: '… and that is where you will use it on the test …' or '… it will help you to score more points in …'. Doing this is counterproductive and overwhelming. Students need to feel that they are freely exploring a subject that will help them learn about themselves and the world around them as they find their voices. Through this greater meaning, you can reign it in to be meaningful for assessment.

The learning portfolio is therefore a great place to start. It leads to assessment but is not assessed itself. It is a requirement but one that is free and open. I suggest making the journal part of the portfolio, but also including any written work such as mock assessments, creative writing pieces, group projects, etc, as part of the portfolio. You can make the portfolio a combination of paper and digital (as discussed in the earlier section on journaling). If the digital portion is a Google folder, students can also keep collaborative work in there. Alternatively, if they set up another kind of blog or website of their work, they can link in other digital work in a single format and even take photos (or scans) of some or all of the paper journals.

■ ATT & ATL

Differentiation

- The IB guide asks teachers to allow student choice in format for the purposes of differentiation. I recommend you still encourage and even require some elements in different formats to help students develop different skills. A lot of research places enhanced learning and metacognitive skills with the use of handwriting, while typing and technology skills are of course also beneficial to student learning. Do not be afraid to seek the aid of your tech coaches (or any knowledgeable colleagues) to come and help students get set up with a digital tool. Beyond the format, there should be a great amount of differentiation in student choice of their responses to prompts or inquiry activities. See also page 159 for suggestions on this.

Students should complete something they can be proud of. It should be something that shows a progression of thought as well as skills development. There will be many rough and personal pieces but also polished writing that might even turn into something else in the future (an article, poem, blog entry or presentation perhaps).

Of course, these ideas are not limited to the classroom and our subject area. They can use the ideas and skills for TOK or a history course; they can use them when they run for student government at university; or perhaps they are developing a creative project of their own, for fun or publication, or both.

As discussed in the previous chapter, you can mark the journal part of the LP with the journal rubric (see Chapter 5, page 150). What is more important is that students have feedback on the work in the LP, though not necessarily on everything in it. Students will need to feel confident and validated as they move toward preparation for the IO.

Let them be proud of this work and it will not feel like work. They will never see their Paper 1 and Paper 2 exams with feedback. They can earn a 7 on these exams but they may never know why. The learner portfolio, though, is alive. It needs many forms of feedback to live – from you, from peers and from the student her/himself. Maybe some pieces are too personal to share with peers, but I encourage you to create an environment where the respect and trust in the classroom is such that all students are supporting and motivating each other. There should be a common understanding that students keep anything personal within the classroom and that sharing may be a difficult but necessary step toward improving. In essence: *we are in it together.*

Although you are the conductor, making yourself vulnerable at times by sharing your writing or independent thoughts might help students to share their own work. You can do this in a variety of ways. Sometimes we enter into poetry or a particular concept through song. I am a terrible singer, so I sing a chorus of a song I am referring to in order to embarrass myself. If we can laugh at ourselves with our students, we allow them to loosen up a bit as well.

Essentially, the learner portfolio is for your classroom experience and for your students. The IB will never see it, but the LP is needed for work toward the IO and the HL essay (HL students only). We will investigate the connection to the IO and then the HL essay in the next section.

The individual oral (IO)

Assessment	Description	SL: time + per cent of mark	HL: time + per cent of mark	Marking
Individual oral	Oral examination with the student and teacher, where the student has prepared a response to the prompt: 'Examine the ways in which the global issue of your choice is presented through the content and form of two of the texts that you have studied.' Literature: two literary texts, one in translation and one in original language A. Language and literature: one non-literary and one literary text (can be translated or originally in language A).	10 min + 5 min Q&A (before March of Y13; ideally end of Year 12) 30%	10 min + 5 min Q&A (before March of Y13; ideally end of Year 12) 20%	Internally assessed; externally moderated

■ Individual oral rubric

Individual oral	0	1–2	3–4	5–6	7–8	9–10
Criterion A: Knowledge, understanding and interpretation ■ How well does the candidate demonstrate knowledge and understanding of the extracts, and of the works/texts from which they were taken? ■ To what extent does the candidate make use of knowledge and understanding of the extracts and the works/texts to draw conclusions in relation to the global issue? ■ How well are ideas supported by references to the extracts, and to the works/texts?	The work does not reach a standard described by the other descriptors.	There is little knowledge and understanding of the extracts and the works/texts in relation to the global issue. References to the extracts and to the works/texts are infrequent or are rarely appropriate.	There is some knowledge and understanding of the extracts and the works/texts in relation to the global issue. References to the extracts and to the works/texts are at times appropriate.	There is satisfactory knowledge and understanding of the extracts and the works/texts and an interpretation of their implications in relation to the global issue. References to the extracts and to the works/texts are generally relevant and mostly support the candidate's ideas.	There is good knowledge and understanding of the extracts and the works/texts and a sustained interpretation of their implications in relation to the global issue. References to the extracts and to the works/texts are relevant and support the candidate's ideas.	There is excellent knowledge and understanding of the extracts and of the works/texts and a persuasive interpretation of their implications in relation to the global issue. References to the extracts and to the works/texts are well-chosen and effectively support the candidate's ideas.
Criterion B: Analysis and evaluation ■ How well does the candidate use his or her knowledge and understanding of each of the extracts and their associated works/texts to analyse and evaluate the ways in which authorial choices present the global issue?	The work does not reach a standard described by the other descriptors.	The oral is descriptive or contains no relevant analysis. Authorial choices are seldom identified and, if so, are poorly understood in relation to the presentation of the global issue.	The oral contains some relevant analysis, but it is reliant on description. Authorial choices are identified, but are vaguely treated and/or only partially understood in relation to the presentation of the global issue.	The oral is analytical in nature, and evaluation of the extracts and their works/texts is mostly relevant. Authorial choices are identified and reasonably understood in relation to the presentation of the global issue.	Analysis and evaluation of the extracts and their works/texts are relevant and at times insightful. There is a good understanding of how authorial choices are used to present the global issue.	Analysis and evaluation of the extracts and their works/texts are relevant and insightful. There is a thorough and nuanced understanding of how authorial choices are used to present the global issue.

Individual oral	0	1–2	3–4	5–6	7–8	9–10
Criterion C: Focus and organization ■ How well does the candidate deliver a structured, well-balanced and focused oral? ■ How well does the candidate connect ideas in a coherent manner?	The work does not reach a standard described by the other descriptors.	The oral rarely focuses on the task. There are few connections between ideas.	The oral only sometimes focuses on the task, and treatment of the extracts, and of the works/texts may be unbalanced. There are some connections between ideas, but these are not always coherent.	The oral maintains a focus on the task, despite some lapses; treatment of the extracts and works/texts is mostly balanced. The development of ideas is mostly logical; ideas are generally connected in a coherent manner.	The oral maintains a mostly clear and sustained focus on the task; treatment of the extracts and works/texts is balanced. The development of ideas is logical; ideas are coherently connected in an effective manner.	The oral maintains a clear and sustained focus on the task; treatment of the extracts and works/texts is well-balanced. The development of ideas is logical and convincing; ideas are connected in a cogent manner.
Criterion D: Language ■ How clear, accurate and effective is the language?	The work does not reach a standard described by the other descriptors.	The language is rarely clear or accurate; errors often hinder communication. Vocabulary and syntax are imprecise and frequently inaccurate. Elements of style (for example, register, tone and rhetorical devices) are inappropriate to the task and detract from the oral.	The language is generally clear; errors sometimes hinder communication. Vocabulary and syntax are often imprecise with inaccuracies. Elements of style (for example, register, tone and rhetorical devices) are often inappropriate to the task and detract from the oral.	The language is clear; errors do not hinder communication. Vocabulary and syntax are appropriate to the task but simple and repetitive. Elements of style (for example, register, tone and rhetorical devices) are appropriate to the task and neither enhance nor detract from the oral.	The language is clear and accurate; occasional errors do not hinder communication. Vocabulary and syntax are appropriate and varied. Elements of style (for example, register, tone and rhetorical devices) are appropriate to the task and somewhat enhance the oral.	The language is clear, accurate and varied; occasional errors do not hinder communication. Vocabulary and syntax are varied and create effect. Elements of style (for example, register, tone and rhetorical devices) are appropriate to the task and enhance the oral.

Total: ____ /40   IB mark: ____ /7

Commendations:

Areas for improvement or consideration:

Although the individual orals can be conducted at any time during the course, I recommend you conduct them at the end of the first year. You may have to juggle with other internal assessments as well as the extended essay in addition to rooming and proctors to ensure the timing that will work at your school.

If you are teaching the course for the first time or your school has just started with it, speak early to your DP coordinator about the timing and logistics. You will want a good plan for the schedule, the exam room (ideally sound proof), the waiting area and the method by which you will orally record the IO (I recommend Quicktime). The more you can do ahead, the less stress you and your students will feel about the whole experience.

You will want to make use of global issues from the early days of the course and by this time in the course there should be a variety of texts to choose from. Keep in mind that for literature, this means you should have several texts in your language A and in translation, while for language and literature you should be covering both literary and non-literary texts. Although you would do this by the end of the first year, you should also weave in some formative preparation that uses both types of texts early and do several mock assessment experiences – perhaps one with self-reflection, another with a peer and a third with you, the teacher. However, I would scaffold this work and begin with IO-style presentations in groups, where students can draw on each other's strengths, and feed back on examples related to course material (rather than just examples on My IB) can be freely discussed.

You can go back to use several CBL lessons to help students develop the global issue they have selected. The lexicons, big ideas charts and journal responses (see Chapter 3) are good places to start. Additionally, the literary theory charts and lessons (see Chapter 4) provide areas of comparison where students could easily choose an area of comparison that develops into a global issue. We have previously investigated the direction these could take. The only requirements are that the global issue has 'wide/large scale' significance, is 'transnational' and 'its impact is felt in everyday local contexts'. In other words, the global issue is conceptually relevant and transferable to any place or people. Political contexts, therefore, should focus on finding universal truths or big ideas that can help humanity find answers. The idea is similar to that of Cosmopolitanism theorists who work from a postnational world view.

The IB further proposes several categories in the guide, which are not prescriptive:

- Culture, identity and community
- Beliefs, values and education
- Politics, power and justice
- Art, creativity and imagination
- Science, technology and the natural world.

Make sure your students feel comfortable speaking with you about the course content, or the IO will feel like a scary experience. Although we keep a line between ourselves and our students, allowing them to talk and be heard, and including topics unrelated to your course, will be beneficial in a variety of ways for students learning in your classroom. In this way, although the IO is a formal assessment, the conversation during the Q&A should feel as natural and empowering as others you have had in the past

I recommend you use structures of delivering the content of the IO to help your students consider the required elements and work it clearly into the time. Ten minutes passes quickly, and part of the mark is on organization. In that time, they will be delivering a big idea while comparing the content and form of *two* texts. Without careful organization, it will remain on the surface, become lopsided to one text or they will neglect to make it purposeful or conceptual.

You can start by listening to examples together and breaking down what students have done structurally. Then, share a more universal graphic organizer like the one below. It is not a *must*, but it is a useful framework for students to consider in their planning. The IB will provide an outline template that students can bring into the exam room. Students might use this more scaffolded organizer before transferring it to the pared-back IB version. Students can also bring the two texts or excerpts into the exam room; they should be clean copies and should be approximately 40 lines: a full advertisement or shorter poem, for example. If you are unsure if your student's text choice is acceptable, write to IB Answers well before the exam. You must collect and keep the extracts and outlines after examination in case the IB should summon them for authenticity and your school's standards of practice.

■ Graphic organizer for IO

Time (approximate)	What to do	Details
0:00–0:15	Time start	Read the script your teacher provides for you with your personal code.
		At the beginning of the recording, the teacher says:
		'This is an individual oral assessment for [LEVEL, COURSE TITLE].'
		Student says:
		'My personal code is [CANDIDATE PERSONAL CODE].'
0:15–1:15	**Intro** *What is the point of telling us about this topic in relation to these texts?*	Try to draw listener in with a **hook**.
		Contextualize two texts: full title + author + genre/text type.
		Intro to the **global issue**.
		Thesis + preview.
1:15–2:45	**Point 1** *How do these texts demonstrate the global issue you have selected?*	State topic/point clearly, linked to **global issue**.
		Connect to each text and determine if it is similar or different for them and how.
		Discuss **content**, **form** or both.
		Use many quotes and **evidence** from the texts.
		Include researched evidence if necessary.
		Explain each example you use.
		Use **literary terms** whenever possible and refer to the **genre/text type**.
		Compare two texts throughout.
		Make some connections to other parts of the work/oeuvre/related texts throughout.
2:45–4:15	**Point 2** *How do these texts demonstrate the global issue you have selected?*	Same as above with **transition**.
4:15–5:45	**Point 3** *How do these texts demonstrate the global issue you have selected?*	Same as above.
5:45–7:15	**Point 4** *How do these texts demonstrate the global issue you have selected?*	Same as above.

Time (approximate)	What to do	Details
7:15–8:45	**Point 5** *How do these texts demonstrate the global issue you have selected?*	Optional/or make each point 15 seconds longer.
8:45–10:00	**Conclusion** *What is the point of what you have explained?*	Restate **thesis** and join together points. Explicitly link to **global issue** if not in the thesis. Explicitly mention both **content** and **form**. Connect to other texts that relate conceptually. Try to add something fresh, which relates to your hook.
10:00–15:00	**Q&A** *How well do you understand the texts in a conceptual framework?*	Your teacher will ask you questions designed to help improve your marks and to see how deeply you understand the texts' connection to the global issue. If you don't understand a question, ask for it to be restated. Anticipate what further questions there might be about your topic. Teacher will say: 'This concludes the IO. End of recording.'

Just like for the Paper 2 (which we will look at next), you can break down the comparative aspect differently. Students could start with one text, then follow to the other, as long as they continue to compare along the way. However, it is harder to do a good job of this and students will have time before the assessment to prepare these comparisons along the way. If each point is related to both texts, the points – or topic sentences – should be safeguarded as those connected to more easily and explicitly to the global issue or thesis. For this reason, though you may hear excellent examples that deviate from this structure, it is both a safer go-to for weak students as well as typically a stronger form for those who excel.

Note that for students to do well on the IO, they need a good understanding of content and strong use of analytical and organizational skills to develop the global issue, which is the conceptual understanding. This start at doing comparative work will help with the Paper 2, so as you begin to teach how to compare a new idea, an intertext or 'doughnut hole', you are doing double duty for assessments.

In the Q&A section that follows, you can help students to reach a deeper conceptual understanding. Let students know this section is meant to help them do better, not trick them. It also ensures students really know what they are talking about. Since they can prepare before, you will want to dig deeper to see how far their understanding goes, but you will also note if there is a gap that might need to be addressed. For example, if a student does not focus much on form, ask some specific related questions. If they do not do enough direct comparison, ask something of this manner. Students should not be aware of the questions you will ask before. However, you might have some ideas prepared to make it easier for yourself.

The higher level essay

Assessment	Description	SL: time + per cent of mark	HL: time + per cent of mark	Marking
HL essay	All HL students in each course will complete a thesis essay on a text studied in the course. The 1200–1500-word formal essay 'follow[s] a line of inquiry of their own choice.'	Not required	Sent to IB mid-March Y13 but suggest completion no later than November 20%	Coursework; externally assessed

■ Higher level essay rubric

HL essay	0	1	2	3	4	5
Criterion A: Knowledge, understanding and interpretation ■ How well does the candidate demonstrate knowledge and understanding of the work or text chosen? ■ To what extent does the candidate make use of knowledge and understanding of the work or text to draw conclusions in relation to the chosen topic? ■ How well are ideas supported by references to the work or text in relation to the chosen topic?	The work does not reach a standard described by the other descriptors.	There is little knowledge and understanding of the work or text shown through the essay in relation to the topic chosen. References to the work or text are infrequent or are rarely appropriate in relation to the chosen topic.	There is some knowledge and understanding of the work or text shown through the essay in relation to the topic chosen. References to the work or text are at times appropriate in relation to the chosen topic.	There is satisfactory knowledge and understanding of the work or text shown through the essay and an interpretation of its implications in relation to the topic chosen. References to the work or text are generally relevant and mostly support the candidate's ideas in relation to the chosen topic.	There is good knowledge and understanding of the work or text shown through the essay and a sustained interpretation of its implications in relation to the topic chosen. References to the work or text are relevant and support the candidate's ideas in relation to the chosen topic.	There is excellent knowledge and understanding of the work or text shown through the essay and a persuasive interpretation of their implications in relation to the chosen topic. References to the work or text are well-chosen and effectively support the candidate's ideas in relation to the chosen topic.
Criterion B: Analysis and evaluation ■ To what extent does the candidate analyse and evaluate how the choices of language, technique and style, and/or broader authorial choices shape meaning in relation to the chosen topic?	The work does not reach a standard described by the other descriptors.	The essay is descriptive and/or demonstrates little relevant analysis of textual features and/or the author's broader choices in relation to the chosen topic.	The essay demonstrates some appropriate analysis of textual features and the author's broader choices in relation to the chosen topic, but is reliant on description.	The essay demonstrates a generally appropriate analysis and evaluation of textual features and the author's broader choices in relation to the chosen topic.	The essay demonstrates an appropriate and at times insightful analysis and evaluation of textual features and the author's broader choices in relation to the chosen topic.	The essay demonstrates a consistently insightful and convincing analysis and evaluation of textual features and the author's broader choices in relation to the chosen topic.

HL essay	0	1	2	3	4	5
Criterion C: Focus, organization and development ■ How well organized, focused and developed is the presentation of ideas in the essay? ■ How well are examples integrated into the essay?	The work does not reach a standard described by the other descriptors.	Little organization is present. No discernible line of inquiry is apparent in the essay. Supporting examples are not integrated into the structure of the sentences and paragraphs.	Some organization is apparent. There is little development of a line of inquiry. Supporting examples are rarely integrated into the structure of the sentences and paragraphs.	The essay is adequately organized in a generally cohesive manner. There is some development of the line of inquiry. Supporting examples are sometimes integrated into the structure of the sentences and paragraphs.	The essay is well organized and mostly cohesive. The line of inquiry is adequately developed. Supporting examples are mostly well integrated into the structure of the sentences and paragraphs.	The essay is effectively organized and cohesive. The line of inquiry is well developed. Supporting examples are well integrated into the structure of the sentences and paragraphs.
Criterion D: Language ■ How clear, varied and accurate is the language? ■ How appropriate is the choice of register and style? ('Register' refers, in this context, to the candidate's use of elements such as vocabulary, tone, sentence structure and terminology appropriate to the HL essay)	The work does not reach a standard described by the other descriptors.	Language is rarely clear and appropriate; there are many errors in grammar, vocabulary and sentence construction and little sense of register and style.	Language is sometimes clear and carefully chosen; grammar, vocabulary and sentence construction are fairly accurate, although errors and inconsistencies are apparent; the register and style are to some extent appropriate to the task.	Language is clear and carefully chosen with an adequate degree of accuracy in grammar, vocabulary and sentence construction despite some lapses; register and style are mostly appropriate to the task.	Language is clear and carefully and carefully chosen, with a good degree of accuracy in grammar, vocabulary and sentence construction; register and style are consistently appropriate to the task.	Language is very clear, effective, carefully chosen and precise, with a high degree of accuracy in grammar, vocabulary and sentence construction; register and style are effective and appropriate to the task.

Total: ____ /20

IB mark: ____ /7

Commendations:

Areas for improvement or consideration:

This piece of assessed writing is a thesis essay. It is a lot like the old written assignment for the literature course. We all have approaches and tricks up our sleeves for teaching this text type; hopefully students are learning this type of writing earlier in MYP or whatever system they are in before reaching DP.

Although there is a lot you can do with this paper and there are many ways to approach it, I suggest you at least include these steps in the process:

■ Step 1: Selecting a text and topic for inquiry

Students have free reign of the texts they write on for this paper, but you could always limit the work to a conceptual unit or, for example, to the texts from the first year of the course. This will depend partly on the timing you select and coordinate at your school. The text, however, should be a core text, one studied as part of the course. Something very short considered on its own will not be a good choice unless it is framed within a series of texts together. For example, a single, short poem is not a good choice but may be considered with several in an oeuvre, even as the main focus. A single journalistic piece is also unlikely to be a good choice unless it is a pivotal and monumental piece, but even then, it may be considered in the context of others. This may seem like a subtle distinction, but it is essential in demonstrating student knowledge and making the inquiry element of the paper meaningful in a conceptual way.

Get students to use ideas they have begun to develop in the LP. Because students are meant to 'follow a line of inquiry', get them to make a series of questions they are interested in during a lesson. What areas have you worked on in class where they can dig deeper? The paper should not be a research paper but should have elements of investigation beyond the text. Some citation beyond core texts is possible but not necessary. Most of the inquiry is in the text itself, uncovering meaning through a closer analysis. However, some should also come from the framing – the historical context or philosophical references, the allusions or the publication and audience reception. These areas can and should be researched.

A lot of us language A teachers who likely studied literature, media, language or film at university probably felt an immense amount of freedom when we left high school and suddenly had the choice of course topics as well as the topics and text of our papers. The IB has allowed us to do this earlier, with more structures in place and more of a survey of literature and texts to help open students' minds.

When choosing a topic, I often tell students they are likely to chop it in half, then chop it in half again. The paper is not really that long once you get into textual analysis and include a proper introduction and conclusion. The same pertains to the EE which must include more research and background information. Keep the topics for both of these papers as focused as you can! The trick is that the student still has to consider the work as a whole or the oeuvre of poetry studied, etc. Therefore, very strong students will find it rewarding to look at an exceptionally detailed area that they can do an extremely thorough job of analysing and considering, while a student who struggles more with analysis and/or writing would find it easier to look at something a bit more broad but not unmanageable.

■ Step 2: Fine tuning the topic and making it matter

Students often have a fine idea about a text but have not put it in the greater conceptual realm. If a thesis is contained within a text – why a character behaves a certain way, how images create meaning on a blog – there is no real purpose. Do this simple exercise to help students understand the difference. Give them a mixed up set of 'good' (or conceptual) and 'bad' (or limiting) topics and get them to discuss if they would make good HL essay paper topics or not. This can be a 15-minute lesson starter and should help students to look at their own or a peer's topic.

Here are some 'bad' inquiry question examples – get students to explain why they are limited to the text (content):

- How does Sophocles portray lack of knowledge through irony in *Oedipus Rex*?

- In Yoshimoto's *Kitchen*, would it have been better if the characters stayed in a relationship together?

- In what way did *The New York Times* change journalistic text type with 'Snowfall'?

- To what extent can Helmer and Krogstad in *A Doll's House* be considered villains?

- What are the effects of heroism on characterization in Homer's *The Odyssey*?

- What visual and structural elements do Russian travel bloggers Murad and Natalia Osmann use to make people interested?

- Why did the gang need Ryuji to die in *The Sailor who Fell from Grace with the Sea*?

Here are some 'good' inquiry question examples – ask students to explain their conceptual focus:

- How does Rostand use Cyrano De Bergerac's individualism to critique the political structures of society?

- How do the urban and rural settings in Bao Ninh's *The Sorrow of War* show the transitions of war time?

- How do social media writers use historical elements of civil disobedience to make a point about gender in the #MeToo movement?

- In *Accidental Death of an Anarchist*, how does Fo use the farcical character of the Maniac to demonstrate the political ideas of the 1970s in Italy and warn us about the nature of authoritarianism?

- How does James Baldwin's essay 'If Black English Isn't a Language, Then Tell Me, What Is?' fit into the current discourse of Ebonics and what does it mean for Black identity?

- How does the motif of mountains in Li Bai's poetry expose the paradoxes of human nature?

- How and to what greater purpose does Garcia Lorca use colours in *Blood Wedding* to symbolize fate?

■ Step 3: Planning and structure

Once the topic is set, the planning begins. You can use any method of mind mapping and brainstorming, re-reading, inquiry and outlining you choose. In fact, you may want to offer students several methods to help them access knowledge through their own learning methods.

Because this is an inquiry paper, at some point you should include explicit instruction to use this method of questioning and seeking information through evidence from the text(s) and further research. Once the student has in some way gathered a lot of ideas in relation to the topic question, they are ready to start planning.

The plan right away should connect to structure, even if the structure changes later. Students can use different types of outlining. Draw on the skeletal structure of the five-paragraph or 'hamburger' essay (see Chapter 5) as a framework to ensure clarity in what your students are trying to say. You might want to use this simple graphic organizer to help, one that can be used again for Paper 1 and slightly modified for Paper 2.

■ Graphic organizer for HL essay

Paragraph 1:

Hook
Discussion (include author, title, text type, any key terms)
Thesis (big idea: argumentative, clear, meaningful)
Preview

Paragraph 2:

Point (connect to big idea)	
Evidence	Explanation
Evidence	Explanation
Evidence	Explanation

Paragraph 3:

Point (connect to big idea)	
Evidence	Explanation
Evidence	Explanation
Evidence	Explanation

Paragraph 4:

Point (connect to big idea)	
Evidence	Explanation
Evidence	Explanation
Evidence	Explanation

Paragraph 5 (optional, and can repeat for extra body paragraphs):

Point (connect to big idea)	
Evidence	Explanation
Evidence	Explanation
Evidence	Explanation

Paragraph 6:

Sum up points
Re-state thesis
Fresh idea (connect to hook)

Once the outline is done, have students talk through the proposal idea with you. This allows them to begin their synthesis and provides you with an opportunity to give oral feedback that should be both direct and encouraging (see the feedback overview in Chapter 5).

■ Step 4: Drafting

Then, students write. I usually give them some time to write in class, so they may ask immediate questions, but you may not have time for this, and the drafting can be done elsewhere. Students should try to use all the 1500 words, or close to it. If they go over, part of the next step can be to make things more concise.

Examiners want to see lots of quoting, and embedded quotes work best rather than long offset quotes that use up the word count and take away from the fluency of the argument. Examiners want to be able to read in flow and mark. They do not want to have to stop and think and wonder how the pieces of the paper fit together. They do not want to have to search for a thesis statement or topic sentence. Although this may sound rather formulaic, I would in fact argue that using this skeleton creates good analytical writing at any level. It certainly helped me to edit my 400-page dissertation! 'Where is the argument?' – my supervisor would ask this question in several paragraphs along the way. Every paragraph, no matter how long the paper, needs a point. It may be a subtle shift in a very long paper, but in a 1200–1500-word essay the points should continue to propel us forward clearly and articulately.

Once students have drafted, or while they draft, have them highlight the elements they should include as indicated below. It is an easy way for them to see what might be missing or misplaced.

1. Introduction
   a. Hook
   b. Discussion/terms defined/background
   c. Thesis
   d. Preview three points
2. Body paragraph 1
   a. Point
   b. Evidence
   c. Explanation
   d. Link
   e. (Repeat)
3. (Transition) Body paragraph 2 (as before)
4. (Transition) Body paragraph 3 (as before)
5. Conclusion
   a. Restate thesis and points
   b. Something fresh (connect to hook)

■ Step 5: Feedback

At this point, the student turns in the draft to you for feedback. You should not write directly on the draft (just like for the EE process). Instead, provide more general comment feedback and have a meeting with each student where you can discuss the paper. Use the rubric to show students where they currently stand and to use the language of the marking to help them improve their work. Demonstrate how, for example, simply changing some of the structure can also help make the ideas clearer, therefore improving both the organization and knowledge marks.

■ Step 6: Student final checklist

Once students have received your written and oral feedback, they are largely on their own. I provide a guided checklist to help them ensure their best work. You can modify the grammatical elements to fit your language and cohort of students, as well as the style of citation your school uses and the upload site (Managebac, Google Classroom, Turnitin.com, etc).

■ FINAL CHECKLIST FOR HL ESSAY IN SIX STEPS

1 Respond to and consider comments and feedback on your HL essay draft. Make sure there are:

- transitions
- clear points in each paragraph
- 'so what?' explanations
- sufficient details from the text with page numbers and a citation
- uses literary terms throughout
- uses form of present tense unless referring to something historical outside the text
- the author's FULL NAME and the FULL TITLE of the text in the intro.

2 Edit the grammar and use proper MLA Citation (or what your school uses).

- Pay extra attention to subject–verb agreement, caps, comma use, parallel structure, modifiers, pronoun use, run-ons and comma splices.
- See Purdue Owl or CiteBib for help with citations.
- MLA in-text:
  - ☐ if author is obvious, then just parentheticals (34)
  - ☐ if author not obvious, then, for example (Kafka 33)
  - ☐ No 'p.' or anything else.

3 Print the whole piece and read it out loud with no distractions. (You can also get your computer to read aloud to you.)

- Listen for problems with flow, grammar and argument.

- Is the point of your HL essay clear?
- Does the argument progress as you move down the page?
- Do you use specific language and avoid ambiguities?

4 Be sure you are within the 1200–1500-word count (try to use it all and indicate it on the page); anything you can cut that is redundant or superficial?

5 Make your edits on the computer and:

- take off your name and candidate number on all pages
- make a title page with:
  - i Course title
  - ii HL essay
  - iii Title (topic includes text)
  - iv Word count
  - v Person code
- Save file as LASTNAME_First name_Class_Assignment (WALLER_Kathleen_English A Lit HL_Essay).
- Make sure the format is a pdf or .docx or rtf (50 MB maximum).
- Then upload onto ManageBac (it will go through Turnitin.com and your teacher can show you the detailed report before we upload to IBIS).

6 Print a copy to give to your teacher and save the soft copy on your cloud/computer (just in case!).

Further, if there are specific questions or follow-up points from the oral conference, they can check in about it. However, at no point should you be marking another draft of work. This is unfair and goes against the nature of the assessment, where it should reflect the student's own work with some guidance from the teacher.

Once you get the clean copy, you will hold onto this until it is time to upload onto IBIS. Before this time, your school should store soft copies somewhere central, such as Managebac or Google folders. Depending on your school, it might be completed by the student, teacher or DP coordinator. The only thing I do with the final clean copy, besides checking the Turnitin.com report, is to give it a grade on the rubric. I do this for two reasons. Firstly, it gives students 'credit' in their marks for the course for the work they have done on this assessment. Secondly, it allows students a predicted indicator for their IB assessments, so they understand where they currently stand and have more information should they consider asking for a re-mark on the assessment after the IB marks come out.

Paper 1: Guided textual analysis

Assessment	Description	SL: time + per cent of mark	HL: time + per cent of mark	Marking
Paper 1	Written commentary on unseen text(s). SL = write on one of two texts, with response to question; HL = two of two texts. Literature: only literary texts (any form). Language and literature: only non-literary texts (any text type).	1h 15min 35%	2h 15min 35%	Timed exam; externally assessed

■ Paper 1: Guided textual analysis rubric

Paper 1	0	1	2	3	4	5
Criterion A: Knowledge, understanding and interpretation ■ How well does the candidate demonstrate an understanding of the text and draw reasoned conclusions from implications in it? ■ How well are ideas supported by references to the text?	The work does not reach a standard described by the other descriptors.	The response demonstrates little understanding of the literal meaning of the text. References to the text are infrequent or are rarely appropriate.	The response demonstrates some understanding of the literal meaning of the text. References to the text are at times appropriate.	The response demonstrates an understanding of the literal meaning of the text. There is a satisfactory interpretation of some implications of the text. References to the text are generally relevant and mostly support the candidate's ideas.	The response demonstrates a thorough understanding of the literal meaning of the text. There is a convincing interpretation of many implications of the text. References to the text are relevant and support the candidate's ideas.	The response demonstrates a thorough and perceptive understanding of the literal meaning of the text. There is a convincing and insightful interpretation of larger implications and subtleties of the text. References to the text are well chosen and effectively support the candidate's ideas.
Criterion B: Analysis and evaluation ■ To what extent does the candidate analyse and evaluate how textual features and/or authorial choices shape meaning?	The work does not reach a standard described by the other descriptors.	The response is descriptive and/or demonstrates little relevant analysis of textual features and/or authorial choices.	The response demonstrates some appropriate analysis of textual features and/or authorial choices, but is reliant on description.	The response demonstrates a generally appropriate analysis of textual features and/or authorial choices.	The response demonstrates an appropriate and at times insightful analysis of textual features and/or authorial choices. There is a good evaluation of how such features and/or choices shape meaning.	The response demonstrates an insightful and convincing analysis of textual features and/or authorial choices. There is a very good evaluation of how such features and/or choices shape meaning.
Criterion C: Focus and organization ■ How well organized, coherent and focused is the presentation of ideas?	The work does not reach a standard described by the other descriptors.	Little organization is apparent in the presentation of ideas. No discernible focus is apparent in the analysis.	Some organization is apparent in the presentation of ideas. There is little focus in the analysis.	The presentation of ideas is adequately organized in a generally coherent manner. There is some focus in the analysis.	The presentation of ideas is well organized and mostly coherent. The analysis is adequately focused.	The presentation of ideas is effectively organized and coherent. The analysis is well focused.

Paper 1	0	1	2	3	4	5
Criterion D: Language ▪ How clear, varied and accurate is the language? ▪ How appropriate is the choice of register and style? ('Register' refers, in this context, to the candidate's use of elements such as vocabulary, tone, sentence structure and terminology appropriate to the analysis.)	The work does not reach a standard described by the other descriptors.	Language is rarely clear and appropriate; there are many errors in grammar, vocabulary and sentence construction and little sense of register and style.	Language is sometimes clear and carefully chosen; grammar, vocabulary and sentence construction are fairly accurate, although errors and inconsistencies are apparent; the register and style are to some extent appropriate to the task.	Language is clear and carefully chosen with an adequate degree of accuracy in grammar, vocabulary and sentence construction despite some lapses; register and style are mostly appropriate to the task.	Language is clear and carefully chosen, with a good degree of accuracy in grammar, vocabulary and sentence construction; register and style are consistently appropriate to the task.	Language is very clear, effective, carefully chosen and precise, with a high degree of accuracy in grammar, vocabulary and sentence construction; register and style are effective and appropriate to the task.

Total: _____ /20

IB mark: _____ /7

Commendations:

Areas for improvement or consideration:

Paper 1 is a commentary of an unseen text – a close analysis of the language and text type or genre. However, it still needs a conceptual understanding! Just like with the HL essay, a thesis that stays within the text should elicit the response: *who cares?* You can use all the jargon of analytical tools just to say that 'a character is disappointed' or 'this travel blog is excellent at catching your attention', but it will be meaningless without a big idea that reaches beyond the text.

Students can achieve a pass by identifying enough textual features, but just barely. To do well and to find some meaning in this assessment, the entire essay should be rooted in a meaningful thesis that is carefully articulated. Each paragraph should progress through points that link analytical skills with the content of the text. It does not matter that the student has not studied this text or author. Instead, they should be able to understand aspects of the content through the skills they have developed and through their understanding of language and literature in general. The text type or genre will give them some information, as will aspects of the features they analyse. In this way, the unseen text can still be proof of a student's understanding of the way content and skills are used together to form conceptual knowledge.

Further, themes and topics discussed throughout the two years *will* pop up on the Paper 1. They will be more readily identifiable with the critical theory toolbox the student now possesses. The text is guaranteed to have something to do with one of the following topics, or link directly to one of the IB conceptual questions:

- Class struggle in society
- Family dynamics
- Humanity's relationship with nature or technology
- Inherent good and/or evil
- Gender conflict (either within or between individuals)
- Individual conflict against control from the government
- Aesthetic and intrinsic beauty
- Dealing with trauma.

These may look a lot like the discoveries we have found through the big ideas and literary theory chart. There are no surprises! Sure, there may be something new that a student can pick out, but students will be able to draw on conceptually-related themes already discussed through the course. A one-hour or two-hour exam is not the time to re-invent the wheel. By drawing on these themes they have discussed or written about, students can push through a CBL paper that fluidly connects the details to the purpose.

The Paper 1 is considered most important by IB, because, at least for HL, it is the component counting the most toward the overall grade. Why is this when it is unseen? It shows the importance of transferable skills development and the importance of students being able to understand *how* rather than remembering *what* was discussed in class. They must think about ideas on their own. At the same time, you can give them tools from day one to hold onto so that when they enter the exam, they are prepared.

Even though there is seemingly no content, only skills, for the Paper 1, it should be a part of your course from the very early stages. In fact, it makes a great diagnostic during the first week or two of your course to help students realize what is really at stake and where their writing really stands. Even if they understand the text you put in front of them, can they use the appropriate language and structure to articulate a purpose?

Though we shall look here at how you can scaffold students toward this assessment as part of the units and specific texts you study, perhaps giving a completely unseen commentary right away will show them where they need to get to. Although hopefully they have written commentaries during MYP or whatever system they were in, it might be their first unseen one and it will certainly be the first time they have really engaged with a DP rubric.

Some of the marks will be very low at this point, lower than students are used to, but it will be a wake-up call. It will help students to use the rubrics and understand their language. It will help them understand the expectations at the end of the course. If used as a learning tool with careful feedback, time for reflection and use in your first conceptual unit, the experience will be dynamic rather than traumatic.

You have to weave this paper through your whole course. A lot of formative work in class will be close analysis. Continue to remind your students that it is preparing them for Paper 1, otherwise they might tell you they have not done anything to get ready! They may not realize your sneaky ways, so make it explicit. Give them access to some mock exams early, but try to make the analysis and commentary a natural part of the classroom as well.

■ ATT & ATL

Building commentary skills into your course

- Surprise students with unseen text types to show a new perspective on a conceptual focus; ask them to transfer their analytical skills to understand the message and purpose.

- Use a graphic organizer, like the one for the HL essay (page 179), for groups to feed back their ideas about particular literary passages or short texts. They will have to start with a big idea and link details to points if they use it correctly. This might be a carousel activity, a short presentation or something along the lines of 'think-pair-share'.

- Use the formalist theory table on page 106 throughout the course when students are first introduced to a text.

A further consideration is in carefully understanding text types and genres throughout the course. We have discussed how to keep a running documentation of the text types you study. For this and for literary forms as well, you should also keep specific vocabulary related to analysis handy and use it throughout the course. Just giving students a sheet to memorize will be ineffective. As part of review, pairs could make visuals or even YouTube videos to focus on a particular text type or literary form. Though you will not be able to cover them *all*, talk with students again about the way they can transfer these skills.

Be as specific as possible with text types – this is a vagueness but is constantly a critique from examiner comments on the old written tasks or on Paper 1. Since HL students need to write on both, they really must know a wide range of specific text types. Let students know that even if they cannot name a text type specifically, the more they can say about audience, publication and purpose, as well as any adherence to, or deviation from convention will help them to accomplish this task.

INTERNATIONAL MINDEDNESS

Multilingual and multicultural Paper 1 practice

Get students to bring in their own texts or passages, from their cultural perspective, related to a conceptual focus you are working on. How they interpret their culture is up to them. These might be in their mother tongues, translated into the language you are working in. You can even encourage students to translate the works themselves, thereby focusing even more carefully on diction's effect on the reader. Either give students the floor right away to explain the significance of these texts or give them up to the other students for analysis and let the curator be the mediator of discussion. You can make activities like this into a tea/coffee circle so they don't even realize they are working hard.

Remind students that they're in it together! Exam preparation can be both an individual and communal experience. They are not fighting for marks from each other; rather, together, they can raise everyone up

Paper 2: Comparative essay

Assessment	Description	SL: time + per cent of mark	HL: time + per cent of mark	Marking
Paper 2	Comparative essay on two texts studied; students select from four questions. Students choose freely from course texts studied as long as they are 'literary' and have not been used for other assessment (oral/HL essay).	1h 15min 35%	2h 15min 25%	Timed exam; externally assessed

■ Paper 2: Comparative essay rubric

Paper 2	0	1–2	3–4	5–6	7–8	9–10
Criterion A: Knowledge, understanding and interpretation ■ How much knowledge and understanding does the candidate demonstrate of the works? ■ To what extent does the candidate make use of knowledge and understanding of the works to draw conclusions about their similarities and differences in relation to the question?	The work does not reach a standard described by the other descriptors.	There is little knowledge and understanding of the works in relation to the question answered. There is little meaningful comparison and contrast of the works used in relation to the question.	There is some knowledge and understanding of the works in relation to the question answered. There is a superficial attempt to compare and contrast the works used in relation to the question.	There is satisfactory knowledge and understanding of the works and an interpretation of their implications in relation to the question answered. The essay offers a satisfactory interpretation of the similarities and differences between the works used in relation to the question.	There is good knowledge and understanding of the works and a sustained interpretation of their implications in relation to the question answered. The essay offers a convincing interpretation of the similarities and differences between the works used in relation to the question.	There is perceptive knowledge and understanding of the works and a persuasive interpretation of their implications in relation to the question answered. The essay offers an insightful interpretation of the similarities and differences between the works used in relation to the question.
Criterion B: Analysis and evaluation ■ To what extent does the candidate analyse and evaluate how the choices of language, technique and style, and/or broader authorial choices, shape meaning? ■ How effectively does the candidate use analysis and evaluation skills to compare and contrast both works?	The work does not reach a standard described by the other descriptors.	The essay is descriptive and/or demonstrates little relevant analysis of textual features and/or the broader authorial choices.	The essay demonstrates some appropriate analysis of textual features and/or broader authorial choices, but is reliant on description. There is a superficial comparison and contrast of the authors' choices in the works selected.	The essay demonstrates a generally appropriate analysis of textual features and/or broader authorial choices. There is an adequate comparison and contrast of the authors' choices in the works selected.	The essay demonstrates an appropriate and at times insightful analysis of textual features and/or broader authorial choices. There is a good evaluation of how such features and/or choices shape meaning. There is a good comparison and contrast of the authors' choices in the works selected.	The essay demonstrates a consistently insightful and convincing analysis of textual features and/or broader authorial choices. There is a very good evaluation of how such features and/or choices contribute to meaning. There is a very good comparison and contrast of the authors' choices in the works selected.

Paper 2	0	1–2	3–4	5–6	7–8	9–10
Criterion C: Focus and organization ■ How well structured, balanced and focused is the presentation of ideas?	The work does not reach a standard described by the other descriptors.	The essay rarely focuses on the task. There are few connections between ideas.	The essay only sometimes focuses on the task, and treatment of the works may be unbalanced. There are some connections between ideas, but these are not always coherent.	The essay maintains a focus on the task, despite some lapses; treatment of the works is mostly balanced. The development of ideas is mostly logical; ideas are generally connected in a cohesive manner.	The essay maintains a mostly clear and sustained focus on the task; treatment of the works is balanced. The development of ideas is logical; ideas are cohesively connected.	The essay maintains a clear and sustained focus on the task; treatment of the works is well-balanced. The development of ideas is logical and convincing; ideas are connected in a cogent manner.
Criterion D: Language ■ How clear, varied and accurate is the language? ■ How appropriate is the choice of register and style? ('Register' refers, in this context, to the candidate's use of elements such as vocabulary, tone, sentence structure and terminology appropriate to the analysis).	The work does not reach a standard described by the other descriptors.	Language is rarely clear and appropriate; there are many errors in grammar, vocabulary and sentence construction and little sense of register and style.	Language is sometimes clear and carefully chosen; grammar, vocabulary and sentence construction are fairly accurate, although errors and inconsistencies are apparent; the register and style are to some extent appropriate to the task.	Language is clear and carefully chosen with an adequate degree of accuracy in grammar, vocabulary and sentence construction, despite some lapses; register and style are mostly appropriate to the task.	Language is clear and carefully chosen, with a good degree of accuracy in grammar, vocabulary and sentence construction; register and style are consistently appropriate to the task.	Language is very clear, effective, carefully chosen and precise, with a high degree of accuracy in grammar, vocabulary and sentence construction; register and style are effective and appropriate to the task.

Total: _____/30

IB mark: _____/7

Commendations:

Areas for improvement or consideration:

We continue with the *in it together* approach for Paper 2. Although you will also build to this exam assessment throughout the course, much of your final couple of months together will be devoted to this paper. At that point in the course, students are likely to need energy and motivation to keep going.

Again, like Paper 1 it is CBL! This paper should be proof that your students have achieved a conceptual understanding of literature, one that includes a variety of literary skills (writing, reading comprehension, analysis) and content-based knowledge (literary genres, movements and voices). Together, your students create the thematic approach that they will use to answer the Paper 2 questions.

We have discussed methods of direct conceptual comparison that comes back to evidence in the text: literary lens charts, big ideas charts, preparation for the HL IO, Socratic seminars, etc. You can continue to use these tools in collaborative and synthesized form, perhaps using digital tools like Google docs or Padlet to keep the information organized for students to both use and review. Use a particular colour for each literary text you plan to help students prepare for the Paper 2. This will help them review evidence and also do activities like the one I will discuss in a moment.

At this point, the skills you can focus on to support a clear presentation of this CBL understanding are: correctly selecting and unpacking questions and writing comparative essays effectively.

Relation to the question is a major part of the student's mark for the paper as part of criterion A, so they must understand what the question is really asking and define exactly how they are responding to it. After students unpack the question, they also need to be able to respond to it effectively, meaning, the thesis should contain a big idea that connects to both texts and directly addresses the question.

The structure of the essay should also contain the skeleton of the five-paragraph essay, but here include comparative elements. Students can draw on their work in the IO. All students will have used two texts to orally compare ideas about a global issue. Now, they are getting it down on paper.

Ideally, students will include both texts in each paragraph, connected to a point, but successful papers might also take a slightly different model. As long as the texts are compared and the essay is not lopsided toward one or the other, it is fine. However, I strongly advise you to dissuade your students from writing the first two or three body paragraphs about one text before moving on to the other. These nearly always turn into something that sounds like two separate essays or is at least lopsided.

Essentially the essays might look something like the approach shown in the table below, although the number of body paragraphs can be extended.

■ Suggested structure for the comparative essay

Paragraph	Outline A	Outline B	Outline C
1 – introduction	Text 1 + 2	Text 1 + 2	Text 1 + 2
2 – first point	Text 1 + 2	Text 1	Text 1
3 – second point	Text 1 + 2	Text 2 (some comparison to 1)	Text 2 (some comparison to 1)
4 – third point	Text 1 + 2	Text 1 (some comparison to 2)	Text 1 + 2
5 – fourth point	Text 1 + 2	Text 2 (some comparison to 1)	Text 1 + 2
6 – conclusion	Text 1 + 2	Text 1 + 2	Text 1 + 2

Here is an activity you can do that addresses all the areas of preparation. One of the key review aspects your students will need to do is to memorize some of the evidence from their literary texts for Paper 2. If you have designed a cohesive list together, you can play with these quotes and details in a review activity such as the one shown here:

■ Paper 2 review activity

You will need six stations (tables) with Paper 2 questions written on a large sheet of paper – each student sits with at least one other student at a station:

1 **Unpack the question** – keywords defined; what is the question really asking? Which texts would it work well with? Does it lend itself well to analysis of the texts? What are the challenges or tricks? Share briefly with the full group.

2 **Topics** – each student will then have coloured slips of paper with topics that connect the texts through specifics and/or quotes. These come directly from the review charts they created and are colour-coded the same for each book.

3 **Play music** as the students circulate through the room (like 'musical chairs'). As the music plays, they paste the cut-out topic on one question on the table that it could be used to answer.

4 **Thesis statements** – when the music stops, students sit at the nearest table. They look at the topics pasted on the big piece of paper and determine a suitable argumentative response to the question. They write their clear, concise, argumentative thesis on the poster. Add keywords of topics you might discuss if you have time.

5 Students **rotate** to another station and write a second thesis, different from the one on the poster.

6 Students rotate a second time and **evaluate** the two theses before them.

7 Finally, students choose a station to go to to work on a **Paper 2 outline** with a partner. They determine why one of the structural methods might work best for their ideas. Make sure they include at least three pieces of evidence per paragraph. They might choose to write the whole paper later and share it with you.

How are assessments examined?

■ School grades vs. IB marks

You can find the quarter, trimester, semester or year grades at your school any way you want. Most IB schools use the 1–7 DP grades for students to maintain consistency between the classroom assessments and those from IB, as well as making them all easier to understand for teachers, students and parents. Unlike some systems that may culminate in a single exam (the US Advanced Placement tests), the IB incorporates coursework and internal assessment, so the classroom grades really should be aligned with the course.

Additionally, you will have to provide a 'predicted grade' (PG) to universities at some point between May of Year 12 and October of Year 13. In order to avoid student confusion or parent arguments, it is best to keep the same 1–7 number system throughout, so you can share evidence of where the student currently sits in the course and how they might be progressing. The PG is meant to be a hopeful grade, one that a student would earn on a good day of exams and with a good year of preparation, but not an over-zealous mark. Those schools who constantly over-predict are noted at universities. Further, students find themselves in precarious or even seemingly tragic situations when they have not been able to achieve their PG and perhaps have no university placement (at least in the European system). The PG can be adjusted closer to the exam as you gather data for your school and IB, but this grade is not one that is sent to universities. Therefore, you have to also know your students well enough to try to predict the effort and motivation they will have going into the last seven months of the course.

■ Grade boundaries and rubrics

One reason to use the IB grading system at your school and in your course (if you have a choice) is to make it easier to use all the DP language A rubrics. There is a different rubric for each assessment, as there is for each component of each course the student is taking. We have discussed already the need for students to be familiar with the rubrics. Although you can adjust or scaffold for classroom assessments, the more you can use these the better and easier it is for you.

Even if you are going to make a *better* rubric, it will take more time and will likely confuse students and parents. One exception is the journal rubric you have seen here. However, it comes almost directly from the TOK essay rubric and can be applied to other types of creative writing you might use in your classroom.

Instead, you might choose to modify rubrics by adding assessment-specific indicators or using only one or two criteria strands. Both of these actions are encouraged in the MYP, so you might be familiar if you teach this within its framework. For example, perhaps you include partner presentation assessment to help students analyse orally and investigate a global context before completing their independent oral. It could be a very open assignment like the actual IB IO or it could specifically ask students to investigate a feature article of their choice on the topic of **civil disobedience** for a language and literature course. For a literature course, you might ask instead for an investigation of a single poem from the oeuvre you are studying in relation to a contextual element. The rubric could then be the IO directly, but you can add specific indicators for the task.

Alternatively, you can mark on fewer criteria than are necessary. This may depend on the needs of your students. When I moved to a particular school, I found that the students in my Year 13 classroom had wonderful ideas, analytical tools and language skills. However, the organization of their writing made it difficult to follow their lines of thought. I realized I was giving the same feedback to almost all of the students on their essay drafts: 'I can't find the thesis.' 'Is this your topic sentence there at the end of the paragraph?' 'Doesn't this evidence link with the idea in the previous paragraph more?' It was exhausting until I noted that it was a pattern, meaning something had not been taught. After querying the students, I found they had never used a graphic organizer, and had never been taught to outline. Instead, they were smart, able teens and their teachers had let them fly with their thoughts. This works for a minority of students. Perhaps students who are regularly reading shorter professional essays, for example, would, by osmosis, figure out the way to clearly organize their ideas. However, most people (and I include all ages here) need help to explicitly see the structures that work. As we looked at in the section on the five-paragraph essay (page 152), once you know the skeleton, you can be creative with it and papers will not look identical, but at the same time, I tell students that for an exam assessment, creativity only goes so far. Firstly, to help themselves, relying on the basic structure that works keeps them from having to think at all about structure during the exam. Secondly, it makes it easier for the examiner.

You or your students might be thinking: 'Who cares about the examiner? We are people, too!' But, ok, even if you do not care even a minuscule amount about the examiner's sanity, remember that *they* are people, too. This means that they're probably tired or in a time jam when they mark some of the papers. There are checks and balances for accuracy, which we look at next, but it is also important to think about this reality for students' organization. If I read a paper and can immediately identify the components I am looking for, I am already impressed. My eyes stay focused on the marking screen in front of me. I don't groan and look up at the ceiling, asking why I even decided to mark in the first place. I don't immediately pity the student for perhaps not being given the tools to organize the writing. No, instead I am impressed and I probably read with more alertness, taking in nuances or creativity the student may have included in the writing. So, instead of simply affecting the organization grade, organizing well affects *everything*.

As a result of this, we – my new class – did something. We first marked a round robin of five real Paper 1 exam papers only for criterion C – focus and organization. We highlighted some components such as thesis statements, topic sentences, evidence, explanation and conclusive points, each in a different colour. Then, we passed the papers round to each of five groups, giving students three minutes each to mark solely for criterion B. Of course, students have to do more than just note the colours, for example, 'Is there a development of a point as well?' 'Does the evidence connect to and advance the point?' However, although there were slight differences in marks among students, the consensus they came to agreed with the examiners *every single time*. Now, keep in mind this is exemplar material that has been put through the spinner: several examiners, and likely the chief examiner, have marked the paper. They are samples for a reason. Still, this understanding helped that class of students understand the value of organization.

We went a step further and, as I mentioned before, cut the rubric down to only criterion C. We did a Paper 1-style analysis of a page from a Borges short story we were studying. I gave the students just 45 minutes, since it was a seen text and a smaller mark for them. However, before conducting the exercise, we used graphic organizers, like the ones shown in this book, to help us understand the components of the papers we had analysed. Students were given the option to use the graphic organizer for the exam as well. Every student earned a 4 or 5 out of 5 mark – even the students who were probably a 1 in all the work I had seen from them. Then, they highlighted the parts of the structure they had used as shown on page 180. They were able to see what they had learned and why it was effective.

So, once you have established how each column of the rubric works, you need to help your students understand how the overall 1–7 grade is found. Grade boundaries can be a little confusing at first. They are the range of points needed in a particular assessment in a particular set of exams to earn the overall mark of 1–7. What does this mean? Well, the range changes year to year based on several factors but mainly a changing student population taking the exams and the difficulty level of the exams at a particular sitting. However, rather than using the boundaries for a particular year, I recommend always using the most recently published boundaries due to changing cohorts and marking instructions. This means that if you are giving a mock Paper 1 exam from three years ago, I think you will find most relevancy in using both the current rubric and most current grade boundary. This way, you can also have one set of published grade boundaries for students. They know where their grades are coming from. They also know how close they are to being one mark up or down, and you can share with them that on any given year, that shift might occur.

If you use fewer than all the criteria, you can calculate the mark by using ratios or percentages. If you only mark C as the example above, it is 25 per cent of the mark, so multiply each mark by 4 to use the grade boundary grid.

■ Examination

What happens when assessments are sent off to IB to be marked? For most students and some teachers, this is a mystery, but it need not be. The best way to be informed as a teacher is to start doing some examining yourself. After you have taken a cohort through the full language A course, you can apply to be an examiner through the IB website. You will need two recommendations, including that of your DP coordinator. If you are accepted, you will be asked to agree to a number of papers or orals to mark for a particular component. Usually the number is 200, but if you cannot finish the 200, it is also ok. Try not to let it overwhelm you and instead have a go to understand it from the inside out. However, if you are newer to the course or short of time, then you can understand by reading the explanation below and by asking others on your team or in the My IB network about their experiences.

Many examiners mark more than one component, but they only mark one at a time. This helps them focus and be more accurate. Examiners are not marking different subjects or levels (HL/SL) at the same time. We use an online system, even if the work is handwritten or oral. This has changed the nature of some of the examination. For example, examiners must now mark papers from all over and may not be prepared with the texts the students write or speak about. Some examiners will mark papers of texts they do not know! However, there are other checks and balances.

It may be useful for you and your students to hear that certain things are built into examiners' work during every year they prepare to examine. There is first a training round with new scripts and examiner notes, including a video from the chief examiners. This is then followed by a qualification round with feedback from the team leader, where examiners need to stay within certain marks. If they deviate too much, they need to go through a second round of five scripts. If they do not pass, they have to sit out that year's examining. Then, during the examination process, one in every ten scripts is a seed, where the examiner must mark closely enough to the established marks.

Finally, there is one last safety net. Students, usually in consultation with DP coordinators and teachers, can request a component or full course re-mark. Of course, this also means the grade can go down. However, if a teacher has provided accurate feedback along the way, the student should have a good idea if there is a strong deviation.

■ IB moderation of the IO

Though all other components are now externally assessed (as in the above process), the IO remains marked by teachers but with external *moderation*. Internally assessed, externally moderated: this means that you (and your team) send grades to IB for your students but you also send recordings of the IO assessment.

IB examiners then listen to a sample of your students' work, usually the highest and lowest, then several in between. They determine whether or not they agree with the marks and adjust as necessary. They might leave them all the same, bring them all up, bring them all down or change parts of the marking. For example, if they only think the top marks are too high, they will only bring down the highest ones (maybe the top 30 per cent go down by 1 point each) or if the spread is too large (high is too high and low is too low), they adjust lower at the top and higher at the bottom. This happens often when you have a small cohort because it is easy to want to use the full range of the rubric even if your students are rather similar in ability. The nice thing about moderation is that you also get some feedback on the method of your exam, the questioning and text choices. A good examiner will provide specific information that helps you and your team teach the task even better the next time around, or at least consider why you are doing what you are doing.

Remember, though, it is one opinion! Students can still ask for re-marks in this category and your team may be just as 'right' as the examiner. In the end, though, examiners are more aware of the constantly changing bell curve of grades and where your students sit on a global level. It is so difficult to take bias out of examining our own students or even any students where we teach. We compare internally rather than globally. This is why it is also important to continuously listen to any samples the IB provides, attend workshops (IB or otherwise) and perhaps engage in sharing of resources with other schools. The more dissimilar the schools when it comes to moderation, the better. You might have a colleague who worked at a school in another continent – great! Offer to trade a certain amount of high/low/middle IO with them. You will then have no idea how clever the student usually is in class or was in Year 8. You will have a different set of language and organizational issues, perhaps, if the more common mother tongue is, for example, Japanese instead of French.

Moderating in this way is fantastic professional development and you can do it with simple digital shares or with Skype. Be careful not to share any student information if you do share in this way, and only pass these orals online if they are mocks or past assessments rather than those of your current cohort. In this way, it becomes very dynamic live marking! Even if you do it for only three samples, the conversations should be valuable. Even better, take a trip across the world! Ok, maybe that would get a little expensive for your whole department, but, if there are just one or two of you (as there are in many small schools), take a chance to travel during your school holiday (maybe your school and the one you are visiting will share the cost for such a purpose) and visit one of these schools. Do some job-a-like things: visit classes, compare curricula, talk to students. Then, have a session of listening to orals together, some from each school. It is likely to help both of you for years to come. More than simply deciding on numbers, it will spark conversation of how you guide your students, what you look for in a great IO and what types of questions you use in the follow-up section.

Using moderation with colleagues and students

We sometimes get lost in those 20 or 100 students we have in our DP classes. There may be reasons they are collectively different from the average DP language A student. Maybe they all have the same mother tongue; they all have learned the same language B; they have had different MYP or GCSE training; or the school culture focuses on something in particular.

We forget that we are in a bit of a vacuum, so we need to moderate to make our own grades and predicted grades, as well as advice to students wanting re-marks, accurate. Even better if you have examiners on staff who are constantly looking at assessment from all over the world as they usually mark from a different continent. This is true beyond the IO explained above. Although you will not be sending any other marks to IB, it is important to understand the rubrics in practice, and moderation is an excellent way to do this. However, do not limit this practice to you and your colleagues. Allow students to take part in moderation of sample papers online, past assessments from your students or even with their own and each other's work, if done in a caring and positive framework.

It is so important to be transparent with students. They deserve to know where their IB marks and course grades come from. By engaging in moderation together, they will see that grades are not as random as they once thought. They will also feel empowered to understand better where they stand on the rubrics and what they need to do to improve. Sometimes small shifts like paying attention to organizational structures can move a student from a 5 to a 6 and give them a chance to attend a different university.

To understand the whole process, students should also be allowed an opportunity to mark papers. By doing such, in guided live marking of samples, students find they are remarkably accurate. If they can see what the right grade should be, they also see the fairness in marks from IB (and yourself) as well as hopefully understanding better what they need to do to improve their own marks.

Marking papers together sounds like a boring, tedious lesson. However, it can create dynamic conversations about writing style and the purpose of the tasks. It can allow students to see where they may have questions or see gaps they previously were unaware of. Finally, it can be used for guided self-reflection and self-assessment.

■ ATT & ATL

Moderating assessments – collaboration

Here are a few easy ways to use moderation marking with students or fellow colleagues:

- *Colour-code components:* assign a part of the rubric and a colour to each group around the room. With a sample paper at each table, highlight what fits with that part of the rubric and give the paper a mark. Alternatively, have the whole class or teacher group focus on just one rubric section.

- *Live marking:* ease pressure on getting the 'right' mark by discussing the good, bad and the ugly of a sample paper together. Move toward rubric criteria and through discussion related to the rubric's language, come up with a mark together.

- *Puzzle pieces:* cut up exemplar papers to be pasted together again. Rather than just looking at structure here, students or teachers will look at the development of an idea and use literary language to determine the order. Score the paper at the end and compare to that of another group.

- *Annotate a rubric:* make a massive, living rubric for one of the components that gives you and your students more information about the marks. Either use large sheets of paper with markers and post-it notes or a digital version that can carry many direct comments. As you look at 'real marks' on sample papers in small groups, try to understand what language like 'poor', 'good', 'sufficient' and 'excellent' mean on the rubric. Add details and examples to the rubric.

During Paper 1 and Paper 2, students will only have a couple of hours to prove all they have learned. For that reason, it is essential that they are given practice in many forms to be familiar with the task. It is also essential that students improve their learning with each set of practice. Doing papers over and over without understanding them from the inside out does nothing for student learning and/or student achievement.

In Chapter 7, we will attempt to understand how the course your students go through with you can be about much more than exam grades, while still including these as important and meaningful parts of the course as well.

Beyond the classroom

Developing lifelong learners

Some of the most recent discussion points have been on how to get the best marks. Sometimes this is a separate conversation from learning, but I do not think it ever has to be, at least in a CBL course like the IB. Even if you are helping students 'beat the test', there are still skills they are learning that go beyond those couple of hours in the exam. Talk with students about this! Otherwise, they may shut off or they may limit the application of the learning experience in your classroom.

This concluding chapter aims to make the purpose of the course clear, not only for assessment grades and university applications, but also for relevance in the real world. It will discuss how the course develops transferable skills and prepares students to be lifelong learners.

A focus on such in your classroom can also be motivation for you. Without purpose beyond the exam, we become a skills and content factory. It is in the realization of conceptual understanding (or at least questioning) that we go beyond the classroom walls and numerical data points. If your biggest concern year to year is the average grade of your students, you are likely to burn out quickly, or at least get frustrated and stressed. If you can instead focus beyond the numbers on the purpose, you will likely also have the side benefit of positive numerical results. There needs to be some balance and you need to do your job, but part of the design of the far-reaching course is the purposeful nature for all.

We are lucky to have this course for its scope and range of texts, cultures and concepts as well as for its flexibility in allowing teachers to teach their passions and those of their students. Likewise, it is important that there are well-moderated assessment tasks that measure aspects of student learning, though it is essential to recognize that there is more learning than what is measured here.

Let us look at how you can make the wide and grand nature of the course into something manageable and meaningful for you and your students. Then, let us investigate what your students can actually learn here, beyond that final 1–7 mark and beyond their university placement or decisions about the future.

■ Listening

Our classes are in large part about listening. There are no conclusions, only questions – students come up with the conceptual understandings. They are not spoon-fed information. Of course, there are some things that are right and wrong, some skills to discover and facts that are important, but once these are set, the big ideas and the way we get there are always changing.

Students want to try out their own ideas but they also want a confident teacher. They want some advice and some discoveries to come from you as well. Do this sparingly though and show them you are really listening. Show them through feedback and through space and time to allow them to speak. Tell them they can talk with you after class. Our course is about communication of the human condition and our relationship with ourselves and the world; if we cut off dialogue, then we are failing.

Attitude is everything. Students want to know they are in good hands and can ask for advice even though most of what you will do is cultivate their own self-reflection and thinking skills. You will help them find who they are – to speak and write their own voice.

■ Personal meaning

There is a lot of opportunity for the voice you help cultivate in your students to go beyond the classroom walls. The pastiche example in the place you live, writing about experiences, travelling to other places on field trips, learning about cultures and learning about how humans get along!

Try to include at least one core text that shows a really explicit exploration of an individual through writing. This might be a memoir, the existentialists' consideration of the meaning of life or a poet's abstract yet meaningful personal experiences.

Prague

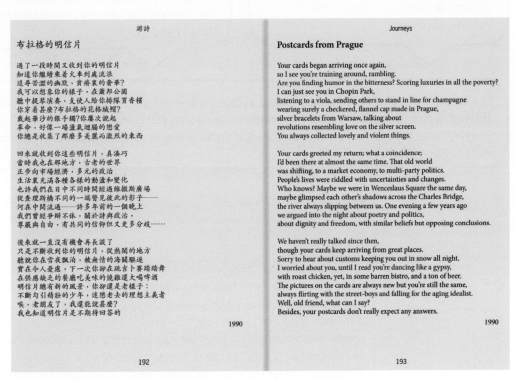

Yesi's 'Postcards from Prague', *City at the End of Time* (2012)

Multilingual, multicultural, multispatial ... but still universal ideas about humanity. Take a poet's reflections on his personal experiences in a world that is often difficult to navigate and let students explore their own ideas. Allow and encourage students to engage with these ideas in a personal way in their journals. As students form big ideas, they will become very personal. They are conclusions students are making about the world around them through the content of your classroom. The conclusions are not fixed, but they allow for further reflection and *aha!* moments.

■ Skills and knowledge for the future

Some of the transference to the real world may happen after your students graduate, sometimes even a decade in the future. This is ok! However, you can prime them by bringing in examples, even real people, who use writing, podcasting, reporting, speeches, etc, in their professions and in their philanthropy. What would the world be like if we stopped reading and producing literature as an art? What if everything we read was reduced to simplistic information like we see on a newsfeed? How would we process the world around us? And how would we understand ourselves? You can also make it slightly more immediate by asking alumni students to discuss their experiences at university: which skills from your course have they used to help them succeed or find meaning in their first year(s) away from secondary school?

These questions can be a central part of your classroom. Though you need to do a lot of close analysis and skills preparation, try to always come back to the bigger reason that we communicate with language. Instead of cheap exit tickets, make the end of your class into a quick but deep discussion that will keep students thinking (and talking, or maybe even writing) beyond the classroom walls.

> Ok, we've just finished analysing another Paper 1 practice, this time on a letter. How do you think letter writing vs. email vs. message applications changes the nature of human communication? Let's have a five-minute discussion.

> That was a really strong close analysis we have now finished of Monseigneur in *A Tale of Two Cities*. I think you understand all the symbols and motifs of the chapter. Who do you think would be a 'Monseigneur' in our current (local) society? Should anything be done to change this or does this figure create more jobs or capital for others? How can you use Marxist theory to also analyse the city you live in?

> In *Kafka on the Shore,* we've just looked at fate vs. free will in an interesting way. Do we have to go through a difficult path to find the answer? Are allegories still relevant to our lives today? Is Kafka's journey culturally specific to Japan or does it transfer elsewhere? What types of views about fate and free will have you discussed in TOK?

CORE CONNECTIONS

CAS

Students can begin to develop or at least play around with these ideas of using skills from your course outside of the classroom through the CAS programme. They can join a club offered at your school, take a class outside of school or start a CAS project of their own. These activities might be school newspapers or magazines, writing clubs, media internships, writing competitions, literacy development with young children or refugees who want to speak the language of your classroom, book clubs – the list goes on. Not only will it count for the CAS portfolio, but it will also give students agency in using what they have learned in the real world.

Transference and interdisciplinary relevance

■ Drawing on skills and knowledge

The idea behind the explicit integration of ATL skills in the DP as an extension of PYP and MYP is about the ability to transfer skills freely between subjects. The added benefit is that these skills should enable students to access them more freely when they need them. A student has individual needs and learning styles; they can cue themselves to use a skill if they understand its purpose. These cues might be during lessons or assessments, and they might be in the future – at university or in the workplace, or in dealing with an interpersonal relationship. Students who understand their own metacognitive functioning might not necessarily have, for example, the best critical thinking or organizational skills, but they can determine when and how they need to use them or if they need to seek help to complete or understand something.

In your language A course, you are developing skills that students can take to their other subjects: the writing process, creative and critical thinking, discussion strategies, self-management of long-term work and more. You can remind them of this, allowing them to feel less overwhelmed by the amount of learning they are meant to accomplish in the 18 months of DP.

Likewise, you can draw on skills from other subjects. Remind students that they may have learned research skills for inquiry (used for the HL essay or EE in your subject) in history or biology, for example. As you tackle visual texts – graphic novels, advertising, blogs, etc – draw on their skills and terminology from visual arts and film studies courses. In understanding the design and purpose of *new textualities*, specifically web-based texts, draw on student work from design and technology (DT) or information technology in a global system (ITGS). If you cue students to do this several times, they will start to do it themselves and offer to you and the class when the connections are being made in further, unanticipated areas.

CORE CONNECTIONS

EE

The EE should be an extension of the skills and content learned in the DP programme rather than a new add-on. Yes, it is a longer research paper than they write in any course, but it works within the same parameters of choosing a line of inquiry, conducting research, engaging in the research process and more. The difference is that though there is a supervisor, students are left in large part on their own to finish the writing. However, if they know which skills they can draw on, they are likely to do better and have more confidence.

Language A is the second most popular EE subject after history. Therefore, you are likely to have students who would like you to be the supervisor. If you have not done this before, I encourage you to read the material from IB on the EE and speak with your EE coordinator to move toward this role. Even when EEs do not turn out as beautifully as we would like, the process is a meaningful learning engagement for the students and rewarding for you as their supervisor.

■ Joint projects

Of course, in addition to transferring skills, content or knowledge from other subject areas can be transferred, showing even more deeply the conceptual nature of students' understanding. Learning should not stop and start between different classrooms. As other subjects slowly transition to conceptual courses in DP (depending on when the course is up for review), other teachers and students will be more aware of these connections.

Why not work on a connection through some kind of team teaching or a field trip or project together? Logistics will shape some of this possibility. If you are at a small school, it may be very easy to collaborate with the history and geography teachers and even shape your curricula together. The units where you can focus on place and identity, in relation to literary movements and the culture of texts, would be good places to start. We have seen examples such as, Japan, India and **writing the city** but you could extend to the Harlem renaissance or Russian futurism.

Alternatively, if you are at a large school, you might be able to select students in particular courses for collaboration. For example, if you want to work with the ITGS teacher on a concept about ethics and the media, you might be able to create a single language A class of all the ITGS students. Perhaps you develop a project together where students are both investigating and producing media in relation to a certain topic before presenting it back to the class. The project would be enhanced through the use of specific ethical lenses the students will learn in TOK.

CORE CONNECTIONS

TOK

TOK should relate to all DP subjects and we have already looked at some integration of TOK in your course. You could go a step further and do a joint class with a TOK teacher (or bring the classes together yourself if you teach the subject).

We have looked at how many of the ways of knowing (WOK) (see Chapter 2, page 38) relate to language A, especially language and memory, but also any of the others. If you are struggling with time, simply prompt students during the lesson to ask them what WOK they are investigating and how it relates to your course. Or, as you look at a particular text or passage, assign a different WOK to each student to investigate in relation to the text.

There might also be particular topics or areas of knowledge (AOK) of relevance to your conceptual focus areas as well. Through work in TOK, students should be able to articulate literature's place in the arts and consider what personal and shared knowledge come from this AOK. If you want to look at how authors create parallel universes, even metaphorically, look at it from a physics lens as well. Many texts will address fate and free will, another popular topic of TOK courses. Ethical lenses should be taught explicitly in TOK and can be drawn on to determine together the ethical actions of a character or the ethical considerations of a media topic. The list goes on. If you do not teach TOK yourself, try to connect with one of the teachers or ask your students what topics are being studied. There are bound to be connections that you can draw on.

The world around you

■ Local and global

The IB asks us to focus on both the local and the global. In the IB document: *What is an IB education?* the first focus is on international mindedness:

> International mindedness is a multi-faceted and complex concept that captures a way of thinking, being and acting that is characterized by an openness to the world and a recognition of our deep interconnectedness to others.

To be open to the world, we need to understand it. IB programmes therefore provide students with opportunities for sustained inquiry into a range of local and global issues and ideas. This willingness to see beyond immediate situations and boundaries is essential as globalization and emerging technologies continue to blur traditional distinctions between the local, national and international. (Page 2)

Further, the IB mentions the 'local and global significance' of being 'knowledgeable' (one of the learner profiles) (page 3) and explicitly states that ATT should be 'developed in local and global contexts' (page 6).

What do they mean by these references? For the global, we have a lot of connection to international mindedness through our study of perspectives, culture and translation throughout the course. Our students may engage in international trips for our courses or CAS, or they may simply explore the world through inquiry that takes them beyond the classroom walls.

The local is sometimes more difficult to pinpoint or integrate, depending on where your school is located, how well you know the local culture and language and where your students come from. What is essential is that we understand boundaries and differences so that we may navigate the differences.

Cricket players in Mumbai, India (2016). What does this cricket match have to do with the local, national and global? Where does it fit into Mumbai's, India's and the world's cultural and literary histories?

One of the reasons the local is so important in an international education is to ensure that a certain perspective does not dominate or attempt to erase culture. Most IB schools function in English no matter where they are located. If the teachers also happen to be mainly British or American, for example, the danger is that no matter what the attempt to include global perspectives might be, the result is a largely 'westernized' and 'anglicized' view of the world.

Therefore, we need to work harder on the local. We can look for literature or media text types from the local culture and ask local students or teachers for help if we are unsure. We can immerse ourselves in the local places and spaces, its language and its history; we can do it in our own explorative time or with our students.

We can also localize global issues. When discussing topics like translation, immigration or censorship, what does the topic look like in the local context? Investigate both contemporary and historical discourse. Bring in experts from local libraries or schools. People are usually excited to share their knowledge with others.

Likewise, an anglophone IB school in the US with little funds for international travel might feel that their local is insignificant in adding to a rich global cultural study. However, any local place has value and importance. Even if the language is English, local literature and media can be rich resources. The voice of the local is important – how is it the same and different from the national voice? How have other cultures shaped the local culture? You can also draw on individual students' experiences here.

■ Trips

Get out of the classroom! Go, go, go!

Yes, planning field trips sometimes feels like a nightmare of legal paperwork and permissions, but the benefits are great. Some schools have easier protocols for senior students, and you can additionally send students off on (safe) explorations of their own.

Your classroom will become much more dynamic if you can include experiences outside of it. The room itself might be contained, and this is not a bad thing – it is where you all feel automatically comfortable with each other. In the classroom you can build something together (even on the walls) and you might all feel freer to share your philosophies there.

However, getting out is also great. Some schools have built in CAS trips, where you can add in elements related to your course. Some schools have the possibility for you to head to Prague when you study Kafka or to Tokyo when you study Yoshimoto.

Essential elements of a Japanese tea ceremony: sensory experiences can help you build deeper conceptual understanding of your curriculum

Even on the local stage, you can find experiences. Pay attention to the arts events where you are – the stage, museum shows, poetry readings. Even if you are not in London, New York or Paris, there is bound to be something of interest and possibly even related to your conceptual focus. Other places you can visit are local libraries, media centres or advertising agencies. Still further, explore through food or other experiences related to your texts and topics of study. One of the experiences I remember most at university is when our late great Art of Zen professor, Cliff Olds, recreated a Japanese tea ceremony for us. Go for sushi and ramen when you read *Kitchen*. When you study Pamuk, eat Turkish food at a restaurant or even make it yourselves in the school kitchen. This will help you and your students to find meaningful and unique experiences together, but will also allow them to understand the relevance beyond the text.

Some international students travel all the time and even move to many countries, but other IB students may not have a passport and live in a small, suburban town where the school has taken on the DP curriculum. You can still bring these experiences to the local place through transferable spaces and experiences. You can instill a curiosity beyond their home that allows them to see multiple perspectives and consider their world views in new ways.

A New England landscape

If you are studying transcendentalism, or more generally nature writing, take students into nature to be observant and reflective. If you are studying texts about the urban experience, (see page 41, city as text), go right to the heart of the city together. You can simply talk about the experience, take photographs and create a blog project or assign personal journal writing as a result. Make the learning real in this way.

■ Reading and writing the world

We want our students to find their voices and to do this we can show them models of people in the community who share their voices in a variety of ways.

Your school might have good connections and the money available to bring in known authors; perhaps you already work with the librarian or other language teachers on bringing these people in. As you seek new visitors, try to find authors who can directly relate to students and who write in a variety of ways. There is no reason the invited authors cannot be bloggers, journalists or advertising designers. Try to validate different types of writing and different experiences. People who write as a profession might have different attitudes than those who do it as a hobby or extension of their work. Just think of some of the famous doctor-poets such as William Carlos Williams and Glenn Colquhoun. Try to find multilingual authors or those who had a learning disability in school, too. Benjamin Zephaniah might not be the easiest to bring in due to his fame (though he does do school visits!), but he talks and writes about his experience with dyslexia in a wonderfully empowering way. Many immigrant writers, especially, embrace multilingualism in their writing and talk with students about how their many languages can be an advantage.

If your school lacks resources (or even if it does not), local professionals in the community can be your go-to. You should be able to find local media people, at least, who would be willing to either come to your school or allow students to visit their place of work. If you cannot find published authors, take writers who are *unpublished* but who still have something to say about the place of writing in their lives. Alternatively, go the opposite direction and bring in publishers or editors who can talk more about the industry and its future and purpose.

You can also forgo the live visits and do video calls. I have been getting my brother, a journalist and editor at Boston.com, to do this for years, no matter the time zone! I have him speak about his experience at university, transitioning from paper to online media and generally the nature of the industry first. Then, he works on a particular article or articles with students related to our conceptual focus. This is a great way to 'bring in' different guests.

Show students the power of language beyond the classroom in whatever format is available to you. In addition to the focus of outcomes you place on the dialogue, the result will have real-world relevance and unknown outcomes for both students and teachers.

Taking care of yourself and your students

We are all learning in the classroom. Show your students you are comfortable learning as well. You have a deeper content knowledge and you understand how the skills they need work, but you can all move toward deeper understandings together. You can all discover nuances of language. You can all bring different texts to the discussion.

Sometimes students and teachers feel stress, anxiety or a sense of being overwhelmed by the DP curriculum. Our course promises a big delivery of outcomes and conceptual understandings, but if we take our time, structure the course well and draw both on what we know and what students bring to the discussion, we will be sure to go far and make exciting discoveries along the way together.

Ultimately, we are helping students find their voices. We are helping them read the world with an understanding of its signs and layers. We are giving them the tools to learn and to share their learning with others. We are helping them succeed in assessment to get to whatever next step they have selected. We are enabling them to make those next steps meaningful for themselves and the rest of the world.

■ Challenging yourself

We have talked about challenging our students in the course, but it is equally important to challenge ourselves. Without it, we are burnt out, bored and even overwhelmed.

We may be stressed by all the pulls of being a teacher, but some of this small detail does not feel cumbersome when we are engaged and excited by the dynamic experience of teaching and learning. Of course, if you are in your first couple of years, these details may take up more of your time and attention, and I do not mean to say they are not important for anyone. However, if you intentionally focus on learning and expanding, you will be rewarded through a conceptual knowledge you develop yourself.

Here are a few ways you can expand your practice and take on interesting challenges:

- Become an EE supervisor or TOK teacher.

- Apply to be an IB examiner or exam writer (after you have taken through a cohort – two years – you are eligible to apply).

- Discover local texts and language to include in your curriculum.
- Offer one-off workshops at your school to share best practice or new content (not just with language A teachers).
- Engage in other activities or classes that might become a part of your classroom, such as another language, yoga, first aid, graphic design, etc.
- Observe other teachers and let them observe you, or even co-teach.

Of course, you can also take graduate courses or work toward another degree. You can engage in writing of your own. Many language A teachers do these things; they might do them for themselves and then discover that they become a part of the classroom experience.

Perhaps the most important, and most simple, advice is *to keep reading*. A lot of us feel we are busy, too busy, to read during the school year, but even a little bit can go a long way. Language A teachers who keep reading literature from now and other time periods can share these discoveries with each other and their students. Even the shorter texts – the essays in the *London Review of Books*, pop culture articles in a magazine or ethical angles in *Quartz* – can offer fantastic conceptual focus points for your classroom.

■ Modelling balance

Take these challenges and embrace stress and anxiety for what they are. A small amount is proven to help us and make us happier, if we know how to channel it and use it as a cue toward our own success. Live the way you want your students to and share with them. Of course, we keep our boundaries and sharing personal information can back fire, but sharing the way you go about your own learning and understanding of the world can be a rich experience for all of you.

You are also a model for your students. You are only as good as you feel, so if you can find this balance, students will feel the energy in the classroom and be unafraid to take risks. They will come up with better, deeper ideas and they will be willing to try, sometimes failing, to move toward a better result.

■ Less is more

The DP language A course, we have determined, is *endless*. We have also determined that this is a benefit when structured and curated rather than becoming an overwhelming circle. I hope that in using this book as a guide, you are now able to spend more time carefully designing a conceptual curriculum that will unfold on its own.

Choose core texts carefully and engage with them dynamically; take your time. Consider it a taster of other literature out there that your students will surely discover and now have the tools to understand on their own. Likewise, choose assessments and written work to provide feedback on carefully. Less assessment and more learning is the method pedagogical research has shown works best.

This book has offered many ways to go about a meaningful CBL classroom. It has attempted to streamline the approach so that you can both condense your focus for the course and offer a great variety of extension considerations that take the curriculum beyond the classroom spatially and beyond graduation or exams chronologically.

■ Love what you do

We are language A teachers because we love the world of literature of different kinds. If we limit ourselves from it due to time constraints, we are harming ourselves and our students. Sometimes reading a book or setting the layout correctly on our websites instead of offering more detailed feedback for students can do a lot more for this whole learning place. Sometimes dropping the unnecessary details can allow you to engage in a freer dialogue with your students. Sometimes not looking at email or marking once you leave the work place, but going on a walk or scribbling down a poem about your feelings that day, will help *you* and will also help your students. We are also teachers because we care about our students, but we are no good to them if we do not take care of ourselves first.

If you act from a place of love instead of fear, you cannot fail. Love for the subject, the students, the learning and for yourself. In this way, your course will become a space of individual and shared discovery of yourselves and the world. In this world you engage in with your students, languages and texts allow you to communicate your ideas, hopes and philosophies. Communication on any level is an art, and we must not forget what this art can accomplish. It is more than a tool; it is a way for us to be human.

Appendices

ABBREVIATIONS

AOK – Area of knowledge in the TOK course

ATL – Approaches to learning; skills broken into five areas: thinking, communications, social, self-management and research

CAS – Creativity, activity, service: a required part of the IB Diploma, considered part of the IB core

CBL – Concept-based learning

DP – Diploma (years 12–13)

EE – Extended essay, a required component of the IB Diploma: a 4000-word research essay, considered part of the IB core

FC – Free choice: texts considered the free choice of the teacher, though they should have literary value and help to achieve the other requirements of the syllabus

HL – Higher level

IA – Internal assessment (that is assessed by the teacher/school, but moderated by the IB)

IB – International Baccalaureate

IO – Individual oral, a required assessment for all language A students

LP – Learner portfolio, a digital or paper-based compilation of student work and reflections; it is not assessed by the IB

MYP – Middle Years Programme (years 7–11)

NL – Non-literary texts, those not in the four classical genres or considered to be without artistic value (see definition in Chapter 2)

P1 – Paper 1, commentary exam

P2 – Paper 2, comparative essay exam

PD – Professional development

PRLa – Prescribed reading list, found online at My IB; a = only those works published by the author in your language A

PRLt – Prescribed reading list, found online at My IB; t = only those works in translation from your language A

PYP – Primary Years Programme (early learning–year 6)

SL – Standard level

TOK – Theory of knowledge, a course required for the IB Diploma, considered part of the IB core

WOK – Way of knowing in the TOK course

Year 12 (UK) = grade 11/junior year (USA) = DP 1 = premiere (France) …

Year 13 (UK) = grade 12/senior year (USA) = DP 2 = terminale (France) …

BIBLIOGRAPHY
Sources cited

The following are referred to or quoted as reference/research throughout the book.

Abbas, A. (1997) *Hong Kong: Culture of the Politics of Disappearance*, Hong Kong University Press

Amrani, I., 27 Feb 2018, 'I have a spotlight now. People listen to me.', *The Guardian*

Appleman, D. (2009) *Critical Encounters in High School English*, Teachers' College Press

Bachelard, G. (1958) *The Poetics of Space*, M. Jolas (trans.) Beacon Press

Barthes, R. (1967) 'Death of the Author', Aspen, No. 5–6

Barthes, R. (1971) 'From Work to Text', S. Heath (trans. 1977), http://faculty.georgetown.edu/irvinem/theory/Barthes-FromWorktoText.html

Bassnett, S. (1993) *Comparative Literature: A Critical Introduction*, Blackwell

Baudrillard, J. (1990) *Fatal Strategies*, New York: Semiotext(e)

Benjamin, W. (1999) 'The Work of Art in the Age of Mechanical Reproduction', *Literary Theory: An Anthology*, J. Rivkin and M. Ryan (eds.), Blackwell

Bissinger, B. (2015) 'Caitlyn Jenner: The Full Story: Bruce Jenner's journey from Olympic icon to transgender woman', *Vanity Fair*

Bourdieu, P. (1993) *The Field of Cultural Production*, Randal Johnson

Braganza, C., 7 Oct 2016, 'Why we decided to capitalize Black, Aboriginal and Indigenous', *tvo: Never Stop Learning*

Brooks, G. (1994) 'To Those of My Sisters Who Kept Their Naturals', *Blacks*, Third World Press

Butler, J. (1991) 'Imitation and Gender Insubordination', reprinted in *The Judith Butler Reader*, S. Silah (ed.), Routledge

Butler, J. (1991) 'Imitation and Gender Insubordination' in *Inside/out: lesbian theories, gay theories*, D. Fuss (ed.), Routledge

Butler, J. (1997) *Excitable Speech: A Politics of the Performative*, Routledge

Coscarelli, J., 16 Apr 2018, 'Kendrick Lamar wins Pulitzer in "Big Moment for Hip-Hop"', *The New York Times*

Coughlin, D. (2006) 'Paul Auster's City of Glass: The Graphic Novel', *MFS Modern Fiction Studies*, Volume 52, Number 4, Winter 2006

Crain, C., 23 Oct 2015, 'Further or Farther: A Theory', *The New Yorker*

Crisp, R., July 1987, 'Persuasive Advertising, Autonomy, and the Creation of Desire', *The Journal of Business Ethics*, Vol. 6, No. 5, pp. 413-418

Damour, L., 19 Sep 2018, 'How to help teenagers embrace stress', *The New York Times*

de Beauvoir, S. (1949) *The Second Sex*, www.marxists.org

Deleuze, G. and F. Guattari. (1996) *What is Philosophy?*, H. Tomlinson and G. Burchell (trans.), Columbia University Press

Deleuze, G. and F. Guattari. (2009) *Anti-Oedipus: Capitalism and Schizophrenia*, R. Hurley (trans.), Penguin Classics

Derewianka, B. and Jones, P. (2010) 'From traditional grammar to functional grammar: bridging the divide', *NALDIC Quarterly*, 8 (1), 6–17

Derrida, J. (1967) *Of Grammatology*, G. Spivak (trans.), Johns Hopkins University Press

Derrida, J. (2018) *Before the Law: The Complete Text of Préjugés (Univocal)*, S. van Reenen and J. de Ville (trans.), University of Minnesota Press

Ellams, I. *www.inuaellams.com*

Eagleton, T. (2002) *Marxism and Literary Criticism*, Routledge

Eng, David L. et al. (2005) 'What's Queer about Queer studies now?', *Social Text*, Vol 23

Erickson, H.L. (2006) *Concept-based Curriculum and Instruction for the Thinking Classroom*, Corwin

Erickson, L. (2011) 'Synergistic Thinking and Conceptual Understanding in the IB Programmes', www.IBO.org

Flood, S., 6 Aug 2015, 'Sexism in Publishing: my novel wasn't the problem, it was me, Catherine', *The Guardian*

Foucault, M. (1980), *Language, Counter-memory, Practice*, Cornell University Press

Foucault, M. (1980) *The History of Sexuality: 1*, R. Hurley (trans.), Penguin Books

Freud, L. (1999) *Interpretation of Dreams*, J. Crick (trans.), Oxford Classics

Freud, S. (1919) 'The Uncanny', First published in *Imago, Bd. V.*, 1919; reprinted in *Sammlung, Fünfte Folge*, A. Strachey (trans.): www.MIT.edu

Freud, S. (2010) *Interpretation of Dreams*, J. Strachey (trans.), Basic Books

Gandhi, M. 'The Practice of Satyagraha,' *Mahatma Ghandi's writings, philosophy, audio, video and photographs*: mkgandhi.org

'Genderqueer Bodybuilder Siufung Law Is Both He and She (and Could Still Kick Your Ass)', 19 Oct 2016, *South China Morning Post*

Gladwell, M. (2007) 'Seven Seconds in the Bronx', *Blink*, Back Bay Books

Green, J., 15 Nov 2012, 'How and why we read: Crash Course English Literature #1', *CrashCourse* Youtube.com channel

Greenblatt, S. (1998) 'Invisible Bullets', *Literary Theory: An Anthology*, J. Rivkin and M. Ryan (eds.), Blackwell

Greenblatt, S. ed. (2018) *The Norton Anthology of English Literature*, W.W. Norton & Company

Guattari, F. and Deleuze, G. (1986) *Kafka: Toward a Minor Literature*, University of Minnesota Press

Gunckel, K.L. and F.M. Moore (2005) 'Including Students and Teachers in the Co-design of the Enacted Curriculum', *NARST 2005 Annual Meeting*, Dallas, Texas

Hagener, M. and T. Elsaesser (2010) *Film Theory: An Introduction Through the Senses*, Routledge

Hattie, J. 'Feedback: The First Secret John Hattie Revealed', www.evidencebasedteaching.org.au

Hattie, J. (2009) *Visible Learning: A Synthesis of 800 Meta-Analyses Relating to Achievement*, Routledge

Jackson, P.A. (2000) 'An Explosion of Thai Identities: Global Queering and Re-Imagining Queer Theory', *Culture, Health & Sexuality*, Vol. 2, No. 4, Oct–Dec 2000

Jameson, F. (1974) *Marxism and Form: 20th Century Dialectical Theories of Literature*, Princeton University Press

Jameson, F. (2002) *The Political Unconscious: Narrative as a Socially Symbolic Act*, Routledge

Kristeva, J. (2002) '"Nous Deux" or a (His)tory of Intertextuality', *The Romanic Review,* Vol. 93, No. 1–2

Kristeva, J. (Autumn, 1981) 'Women's Time', A. Jardine (trans.), *Signs*, Vol. 7, No. 1

Lacan, J. (1998) *The Seminar of Jacques Lacan: Four Fundamental Concepts of Psycho-Analysis*, A. Sheridon (trans.), W.W. Norton and Company

Lanning, L. (2012) *Designing a Concept Based Curriculum for English Language Arts*, Corwin

Lanser, S. (1986) 'Toward a Feminist Narratology', *Style*, Vol. 20, No. 3

Livingston, J. (dir.) (1990) *Paris is Burning* (film)

Livni, E., 7 November 2018, 'The cult of creativity is making us less creative', *Quartz*

Mäkelä, T., 2018, 'A Design Framework and Principles for Co-designing Learning Environments Fostering Learning and Wellbeing', *Jyväskylä Studies in Education, Psychology and Social Research*, Vol 603

McWhorter, J., 19 January 2016, 'What's a Language, Anyway?', *The Atlantic*

Mishra, P. and D. Mendelsohn, 18 March 2014, 'How would a Book like Harold Bloom's Western Canon be received today?', *The New York Times*

Montrose, L., 1998, 'Professing the Renaissance: The Poetics and Politics of Culture', *Literary Theory: An Anthology*, J. Rivkin and M. Ryan (eds.), Blackwell

Murdoch, K., 28 Nov 2015, 'What does it mean to be an inquiry teacher?', www.Youtube.com

Nietzsche, F. (2001) 'Eternal Return', *The Gay Science*, Cambridge University Press

Perlman, M., 23 Jun 2018, 'Black and White: Why Capitalization Matters,' *Columbia Journalism Review*

Riffaterre, J. (1984) *Semiotics of Poetry*, Indiana University Press

Robinson, M., 19 Nov 2015, 'President Obama and Marilynne Robinson – A Conversation II', *The New York Review of Books*

Rubin, G. (1998) 'Sexual Transformations', *Literary Theory: An Anthology*, Blackwell

Rushdie, S. (1990) *Is Nothing Sacred: Herbert Reid Memorial Lecture – 6 February 1990*, Granta

Schuggart, A., 2017, 'The best in interactive multimedia journalism 2017: pushing the limits of storytelling', *Medium*

Selk, A., 4 May 2018, 'One space between each sentence, they said. Science just proved them wrong.', *Washington Post*

Senechel, D. (2018) *Mind Over Memes*, Rowman & Littlefield Publishers

Stam, R. (2000) 'Beyond Fidelity: The Dialogics of Adaptation', *Film Adaptation*, J. Naremore (ed.), Rutgers University Press

Tharps, L.L., 18 Nov 2014, 'The Case for Black with a Capital B', *The New York Times*

Van den Bosch, J., *EAL-Time website,* https://eal-time.com/

Wargo, E. (2011) 'Beauty is in the Mind of the Beholder', *Psychological Science*

Wollestonecraft, M. (1792) *A Vindication on the Rights of Women*, www.gutenberg.org

Zephaniah, B., 2 October 2015, 'Young and dyslexic? You've got it going on', *The Guardian*

Teaching texts

The following are used or at least mentioned in this book.

@amyschumer Instagram feed (and stand-up comedy)

@whitneyzombie Instagram feed (post of Aphrodite sculpture juxtaposed with Amy Schumer)

Achebe, C. (1959) *Things Fall Apart*

Aciman, A. (2011) *Essays on Elsewhere*

Ackerman, D. (1990) *A Natural History of the Senses*

Adichie, C.N. (2017) *Half of a Yellow Sun*

Adiga, A. (2008) *The White Tiger*

Akhtar, F. (dir.) (2005) *Bride and Prejudice*

Angelou, M. (1969) *I Know Why the Caged Bird Sings*

Atwood, M. (1985) *The Handmaid's Tale*

Austen, J. (1803) *Northanger Abbey*

Austen, J. (1818) *Pride and Prejudice*

Auster, P. (1985) City of Glass (*The New York Trilogy),* Penguin

Auster, P. (25 Dec 1990) 'Dec. 25, 1990: A Brooklyn Story', *New York Times*

Auster, P. (2009) *Invisible*

Auster, P. (2017) *4321*

Baldwin, J. (1956) *Giovanni's Room*

Baldwin, J., 17 November 1962, 'Letter from a region in my mind', *The New Yorker*

Baldwin, J. (1979) 'If Black English Isn't a Language, Then Tell Me, What Is?'

Barendson, S. (b. 1976) Poetry

Basho (1644–1694) Poetry

Beastie Boys (1986) 'Girls' (song)

Beatty, P. (2015) *The Sellout*

Bolaño, R. (1998*) The Savage Detective*

Borges, J.L. (1941) *Fictions*

Branch, J., 19 Feb 2012, 'Snowfall: The Avalanche at Tunnel Creek', *The New York Times*

Brontë, C. (1847) *Jane Eyre*

Brooks, G. (1994) *Blacks*

Butler, J. (1997) *Excitable Speech*

Calvino, I. (1972) *Invisible Cities*

Calvino, I. (2009) *Why Read the Classics?*

Campion, J. (dir.) (2009) *Bright Star* (film)

Camus, A. (1942) *The Stranger* or *The Outsider*

Capote, T. (1966) *In Cold Blood*

Chance the Rapper (2013) 'Paranoia' (song)

Chang Rae-Lee (1995) *Native Speaker*

Chang, E. (1943) *Love in a Fallen City*

Chang, E. (1979) *Lust, Caution*

Charlie Hebdo: https://charliehebdo.fr/en/

Chomsky, N. (2003) *On Language*

Clooney, G. (dir.) (2005) *Good Night, and Good Luck* (film)

Cole, J. (2011) 'Lost Ones' (song)

Colin, H., 8 November 2018,'The Acosta Video Debate is the Future of Fake News', *Medium*

Conrad, J. (1899) *Heart of Darkness*

Coppola, S. (dir.) (2003) *Lost in Translation* (film)

Crain, C., 23 Oct 2015, 'Further or Farther: A Theory', *The New Yorker*

Dai Sijie (2000) *Balzac and the Little Chinese Seamstress*

Dai Sijie (dir.) (2002) *Balzac and the Little Chinese Seamstress* (film)

Darwish, M. (1941–2008) Poetry

Darwish, M. (1995) *Memory for Forgetfulness: August, Beirut, 1982*

DeLillo, D. (1985) *White Noise*

Demick, B. (2009) *Nothing to Envy*

Demme, J. (dir.) (1993) *Philadelphia* (film)

Deperdieu, G. et al. (dir.) (2006) *Paris Je t'aime* (film)

Dickens, C. (1859) *A Tale of Two Cities*

Dillard, A. (1974) *Pilgrim on Tinker Creek*

Dorfman, A. (1991) *Death and the Maiden*

Dostoyevsky, F. (1866) *Crime and Punishment*

Du Fu (712–770) Poetry

Duffy, C.A. (b. 1955) Poetry

Duffy, C.A. (2016) 'After Orlando: Gay Love', *The Guardian*

Durant, A. and Lambrou, M. (2009) *Language and Media: a resource book for students*

Egan, J. (2010) *A Visit from the Goon Squad*

Ellams, I. (2012) *Black T-Shirt Collection*

Ellis, B.E. (1991) *American Psycho*

Ellison, R. (1952) *Invisible Man*

Esquivel, L. (1989) *Like Water for Chocolate*

Eugenides, J. (2002) *Middlesex*

Faulkner, W. (1930) *As I Lay Dying*

Fitzgerald, F.S. (1925) *The Great Gatsby*

Flaubert, G. (1856) *Madame Bovary*

Foer, J.S. (2003) *Everything is Illuminated*

Foer, J.S. (2005), *Extremely Loud and Incredibly Close*

Frost, R. (1874–1963) 'An Old Man's Winter Night' (1916)

Galeano, E. (1989) *The Book of Embraces*

Gaylord, G. (2012) *I Do*

Ghosh, A. (2008) *Sea of Poppies*

Grande, A. (2018) 'God is a Woman' (song)

Guevera, C. (1954) *The Motorcycle Diaries*

Ha Jin. (2008) *The Writer as Migrant*

Hamid, M. (2017) *Exit West*

Han Kang, (2007) *The Vegetarian*

Harper, M. (1979) *Chant of Saints*

Heller, J. (1961) *Catch 22*

Hemingway, E. (1932) *Death in the Afternoon*

Hitchcock, A. (dir.) (1954) *Rear Window* (film)

Holland, M. (ed.) (2003) *Irish Peacock and Scarlet Marquess: The Real Trial of Oscar Wilde*

Hughes, K. (dir.) (1960) *The Trials of Oscar Wilde* (film)

Hui, A. (dir.) (1984) *Love in a Fallen City* (film)

Huxley, A. (1932) *Brave New World*

Ibsen, H. (1879) *A Doll's House*

Iman, A. et al., 27 February 2018, 'I have a spotlight now. People listen to me.', *The Guardian*

Irwin, A. (2011) 'Language and the Media' in: *Language, Society and Power: An Introduction*

Jackson, S. (1948) 'The Lottery', *The New Yorker*

Joost, H. and A. Schulman (dir.) (2010) *Catfish* (film)

Journeywoman: http://journeywoman.com/

Joyce, J. (1914) *Dubliners*

Kadare, I. (1978) *Broken April*

Kafka, F. (1883–1924) Short stories

Kafka, F. (1915) *Metamorphosis*

Kafka, F. (1919) 'In the Penal Colony'

Karasik, P. and D. Mazzucchelli (2004) *City of Glass* graphic novel, adapted from P. Auster

Keats, J. (1918) 'Ode on a Grecian Urn'

Kesey, K. (1962) *One Flew Over the Cuckoo's Nest*

Kessel, A. (2016) *Eat Sweat Play: How Sport Can Change Our Lives*

Keys, A. (2007) 'Superwoman' (song)

King, M.L. Jr. (1963) 'Letter from Birmingham Jail'

Kundera, M. (1984) *The Unbearable Lightness of Being*

Kundera, M. (2013) *The Festival of Insignificance*

Lang, F. (dir.) (1927) *Metropolis* (film)

Lee, A. (dir.) (2007) *Lust, Caution* (film)

Lee, H. (1960) *To Kill a Mockingbird*

Leitch, V.B. (2018) *The Norton Anthology of Theory and Criticism*

Lessing, D. (2008) *Alfred and Emily*

Leung, P.K. [also known as Yesi] (1949–2013) Poetry

Leung, P.K., Leung E.M.K. and Osing, G. (2012) *City at the End of Time: Poems by Leung Ping-Kwan*

Lorca, F.G. (1898–1936) Poetry

Lu Xun (1918) 'A Madman's Diary'

Lugn, K. (1993) Idlaflickorna ('The Idla Girls'), Dramatens Förlag

Lungulov, D. (dir.) (2009) *Here and There* (film)

Machiavelli, M. (1513) *The Prince*

Mahfouz, N. (1961) *The Thief and the Dogs*

Márquez, G.G. (1981) *Chronicle of a Death Foretold*

Melting Butter: www.meltingbutter.com

McCarthy, C. (1985) *Blood Meridian*

McCarthy, M. (1959) *The Stones of Florence*

Melville, H. (1853) 'Bartleby, the Scrivener'

Melville, H. (1855) *Benito Cereno*

Melville, H. (1924) *Billy Budd, Sailor*

Mikhail, D. (b. 1965) Poetry

Miller, A. (1953) *The Crucible*

Milton, J. (2003) *Paradise Lost*

Mishima, Y. (1963) *The Sailor Who Fell from Grace with the Sea*

Moore, A. and D. Lloyd (1989) *V for Vendetta*

Morrison, T. (1970) *The Bluest Eye*

Muller, H. (1994) *The Land of Green Plums*

Murakami H. (2002) *Kafka on the Shore*

Murakami, H. (1997) *The Tokyo Gas Attack and the Japanese Psyche*

Murakami, H. (2007) *What I Talk about when I Talk about Running*

Murdoch, I. (1973) *The Black Prince*

Myers, W.D. (1999) *Monster*, Harper Collins

Nafisi, A. (2003) *Reading Lolita in Tehran*

Nelson, T.B. (dir.) (2001) *O* (film)

O'Brien, T. (1990) *The Things They Carried*

Okri, B. (b. 1959) Poetry

Onion, The: www.theonion.com

Osmann, M. and N. *Osmann*: https://followmeto.travel/

Owen, W. (1893–1918) Poetry

Palahniuk, C. (1996) *Fight Club*

Pamuk, O. (2002) *Snow*

Pamuk, O. (2003) *Istanbul: Memories and the City*

Pichler, P. and Preece, S. (2011) 'Language and Gender', *Language, Society and Power: An Introduction*

Plath, S. (1963) *The Bell Jar*

Puchner, M. ed. (2018) *The Norton Anthology of World Literature*

Reitman, I. (dir.) (1984) *Ghostbusters* (film)

Rinsch, C., (dir.) (2013) *47Ronin* (film)

Rodgriguez, R. (dir.) (1996) *From Dusk Till Dawn* (film)

Roy, A. (1997) *The God of Small Things*

Salinger, J.D. (1951) *The Catcher in the Rye*

Salles, W. (dir.) (2004) *The Motorcycle Diaries* (film)

Satrapi, M. (2000) *Persepolis*

Scorsese, M. (dir.) (1976) *Taxi Driver* (film)

Scott, R. (dir.) (1982) *Bladerunner* (film)

Selbourne, R. (2009) *Beauty* by

Selk, A., 4 May 2018, 'One space between each sentence, they said. Science just proved them wrong.', *Washington Post*

Sexton, J., 29 Nov 2018, 'I don't want to shoot you, brother', *ProPublica*

Shakespeare, W. (1602) *Hamlet*

Shakespeare, W. (1604) *Othello*

Shakespeare, W. (1606) *King Lear*

Shakespeare, W. (1606) *Macbeth*

Shelley, M. (1823) *Frankenstein*

Shteyngart, G. (2010) *Super Sad True Love Story*

Smith, Z. (2000) *White Teeth*

Smith, Z. (2005) *On Beauty*

Smith, Z. (2008) 'EM Forster, Middle Manager', *The New York Review of Books*

Smith, Z. (2009) 'Middlemarch and Everybody', *Changing My Mind: Occasional Essays*

Smith, Z. (2012) *NW*

Soderbergh, S. (dir.) (2011) *Contagion* (film)

Sophocles. (429 BC) *Oedipus Rex*

Sophocles. (442 BC) *Antigone*

Soseki, N. (1914) *Kokoro*

Steers, B. (dir.) (2016) *Pride and Prejudice and Zombies* (film)

Stevenson, R.L. (1886) *Strange Case of Dr Jekyll and Mr Hyde*

Stone, O. (dir.) (1987) *Wall Street* (film)

Stoppard, T. (1966) *Rosencrantz and Guildenstern are Dead*

Tamura, R. (1923–1998) Poetry

Tempest, K. (b. 1985) Poetry

Thoreau, H.D. (1849) 'Civil Disobedience'

Thoreau, H.D. (1854) *Walden*

Thoreau, H.D. (1864) 'The Maine Woods'

Twain, M. (1884) *Huckleberry Finn*

Twain, M. (1865) 'The Celebrated Jumping Frog of Calaveras County'

Updike, J. (2000) *Gertrude and Claudius*

Village People, (1978) 'Macho Man' (song)

Wallace, D.F. (2006) 'Authority and American Usage', *Consider the Lobster and Other Essays*

Wallace, D.F. (2005) 'This is Water' graduation speech at Kenyon College

Wallace, D.F. (2006) 'Roger Federer as Religious Experience', *New York Times*

Wang, W. (dir.) (1995) *Smoke* (film)

Wilde, O. (1890) *The Picture of Dorian Gray*

Williams, T. (1947) *A Streetcar Named Desire*

Wong Kar-wai (dir.) (1994) *Chungking Express* (film)

Woolf, V. (1927) *To the Lighthouse*

Woolf, V. (1928) *Orlando: A Biography*

Woolf, V. (1929) 'A Room of One's Own'

Wright, R. (1945) *Black Boy*

Xu Xi. ed. (2003) *City Voices: Hong Kong Writing in English, 1945 to the present*

Yoshimoto, B. (1988) *Kitchen*

Yoshioka, M. (1919–1990) Poetry

Index

Acknowledgements

The Publishers would like to thank the following for permission to reproduce copyright material.

Photo credits:

p.3 © Kathleen Clare Waller; **p.13** © International Baccalaureate Organization; **p.18** © Murad and Nataly Osmann; **p.29** © Syda Productions/stock.adobe.com; **p.35** © Victor Habbick Visions/Science Photo Library/Alamy Stock Photo; **p.36** © Enea Kelo/Shutterstock.com; **p.42** © Kathleen Clare Waller; **p.56** © MysticaLink/stock.adobe.com; **p.57** © Christian Bertrand/Alamy Stock Photo; **p.58** © Jstone/Shutterstock.com; **p.59** © Vkara/stock.adobe.com; **p.72** © Kathleen Clare Waller; **p.75** © Alizada Studios/Shutterstock.com; **p.80** © Amplion/stock.adobe.com; **p.83** © Raisondtre/stock.adobe.com; **p.103** © Minoli/Shutterstock.com; **p.120** © Samanthainalaohlsen/Shutterstock.com; **p.127** © FineArt/Alamy Stock Photo; **p.128** *both* © Kathleen Clare Waller; **p.140** © Everett Collection Inc/Alamy Stock Photo; **p.143** © Akira Kaelyn/Shutterstock.com; **p.147** *right* © Sergey Nivens/stock.adobe.com, *left* © Bruce Bisping/Minneapolis Star Tribune/Zuma Press/PA Images; **p.148** © Kathleen Clare Waller; **p.149** © Dorothy Alexander/Alamy Stock Photo; **p.153** © Family Business/stock.adobe.com; **p.164** © Alper/stock.adobe.com; **p.166** *both* Black T-Shirt Collection © Inua Ellams, 2012, by kind permission of Oberon Books Ltd.; **p.172** © Rms164/stock.adobe.com; **p.186** © WavebreakmediaMicro/stock.adobe.com; **p.197** *middle* © Kathleen Clare Waller; **p.201** © Snehal Pailkar/123RF; **p.202** © Snehal Jeevan Pailkar/Shutterstock.com; **p.202** © Grafvision/stock.adobe.com; **p.203** © ARENA Creative/Shutterstock.com

Text credits:

p.59 preface from *The Picture of Dorian Gray* by Oscar Wilde (1890) Penguin Classics (2003 edn); **p.61** from Poem 'To Those of My Sisters Who Kept Their Naturals — never to look a hot comb in the teeth' in Blacks by Gwendolyn Brooks (1994) Third World Press. Reprinted By Consent of Brooks Permissions.; **p.63** extract from Irish Peacock and Scarlet Marquess: The Real Trial of Oscar Wilde, compiled by Merlyn Holland (2003). Reprinted by permission of HarperCollins Publishers Ltd © Merlyn Holland 2003; **p.65** from 'Authority and American Usage' in *Consider the Lobster and Other Essays* by David Foster Wallace (2005, pages 69–71) Back Bay Books (Hachette). Reprinted by permission of Little, Brown & Company, an imprint of Hachette Book Group, Inc.; **p.77** extract from *City at the End of Time: Poems by Leung Ping-Kwan* by PK Leung, EMK Leung and G Osing (2012), Hong Kong University Press. Reproduced with permission.; **p.84** extract from *Orlando* by Virginia Woolf (1928, pages 229–30), Vintage Classics (2016 edn); **p.84** extract from The Unbearable Lightness of Being by Milan Kundera (1984, pages 4–5) Faber & Faber (2000 edn). Reproduced with the permission of Faber & Faber Ltd.; **p.85** extract from Hamlet by William Shakespeare (V, ii, 194–8); **p.85** extract from 'How Would a Book Like Harold Bloom's *Western Canon* be received today?' by Pankaj Mishra and Daniel Mendelsohn, The New York Times (18 March 2014); **pp.86–7** extract from Why Read the Classics by I. Calvino (2009, pages 3–9), M. McLaughlin (trans.) Penguin. Used by permission of Penguin Random House LLC. All rights reserved.; **p.104** extract from *Pilgrim at Tinker Creek* © Annie Dillard, 1974, 2011. Published by Canterbury Press. Used by permission. rights@hymnsam.co.uk; **pp.104–5** 'Funes, el memorioso' by Jorge Luis Borges. Copyright © 1995, María Kodama, used by permission of The Wylie Agency (UK) Limited (worldwide digital rights). "Funes, His Memory" from COLLECTED FICTIONS: VOLUME 3 by Jorge Luis forges. translated by Andrew Hurley, copyright © 1998 by Maria Kodama. translation copyright © 1998 by Penguin Random House LLC. Used by permission of Viking Books, an imprint of Penguin Publishing Group, a division of Penguin Random House LLC. All rights reserved (print).; **p.121** extract from Milan Kundera's *The Unbearable Lightness of Being* (1984, pages 58–59), Faber & Faber (2000 edn). Reproduced with the permission of Faber & Faber Ltd.; **pp.121–2** extract from the novella *Kitchen* by B. Yoshimoto (1988), Faber & Faber (2018 edn). Reproduced with the permission of Faber & Faber Ltd.; **p.122** 'After Orlando: Gay Love' by Carol Ann Duffy. Published by Guardian 2016. Copyright © Carol Ann Duffy. Reproduced with the permission of the author c/o Rogers, Coleridge & White Ltd., 20 Powis Mews, London W11 1JN.; **pp.124–5** extract from *The Things They Carried* by Tim O'Brien (1990). Reprinted by permission of HarperCollins Publishers Ltd.; **p.130** extract from 'Diary of a Madman' by Lu Xun (translated by Yang Hsien-Yi), (1918, Part III), Foreign Language Press. Reproduced with permission.; **pp.130–1** extract from *Things Fall Apart* by Chinua Achebe (1959), Penguin Red Classics, 2006, Chapter 21, Penguin Red Classics. Used by permission of Penguin Publishing Group, a division of Penguin Random House LLC. All rights reserved.; **p.131** extract from *Madame Bovary* by Gustave Flaubert (1856, Chapter 12), Oxford World's Classics, OUP; **pp.133–4** extract from 'A Room of One's Own' by Virginia Woolf (1929), Penguin Classics; **p.134** 'An Old Man's Winter Night' by Robert Frost (1916); **p.135** extract from 'Letter from a region in my mind' by James Baldwin, published in *The New Yorker* (17 November 1962). Reproduced with the permission.; **pp.161–2** Creative and Innovation Rubric for PBL produced by PBL Works, Buck Institute for Education. Reproduced with the permission of Buck Institute for Education.; **p.197** Poem by Leung Ping Kwan, 'Postcards from Prague', from City at the End of Time (2012). Reproduced with the permission from Hong Kong University Press.